There from the Beginning

Women in the US Air Force

MARISSA KESTER

CAPTAIN, USAFR

HISTORIAN

Air University Press

Maxwell Air Force Base, Alabama

On the cover: Elizabeth L. Remba Gardner of Rockford, Illinois, WASP (Women's Airforce Service Pilots), Class 43-W-6, at Harlingen Army Airfield, Texas, 1943. (Source: NARA)

Published by Air University Press in August 2021
600 Chennault Circle, Building 1405
Maxwell AFB, AL 36112-6010

Donna Budjenska, *Project Editor*   Megan N. Hoehn, *Print Specialist*
Tim Thomas, *Illustrator*   Tameka Kibble, *Distribution*

AIR UNIVERSITY PRESS

https://www.airuniversity.af.edu/AUPress/   https://www.facebook.com/AirUnivPress
                                                   https://twitter.com/aupress

Library of Congress Cataloging-in-Publication Data

Names: Kester, Marissa N., author. | Air University (U.S.). Press, issuing body.

Title: There from the beginning : women in the US Air Force / Marissa N. Kester.

Other titles: Women in the US Air Force

Description: Maxwell AFB, AL : Air University Press, [2021] | Includes bibliographical references. | Summary: "Women have served in the United States Air Force since its inception, the first US military branch to rightfully claim that distinction. This monograph explores that history through research in archives, other published sources, and oral interviews"-- Provided by publisher.

Identifiers: LCCN 2021027376 (print) | LCCN 2021027377 (ebook) | ISBN 9781585663101 (paperback) | ISBN 9781585663101 (Adobe pdf)

Subjects: LCSH: United States. Air Force--Women--History. | Women soldiers--United States--History.

Classification: LCC UB418.W65 (print) | LCC UB418.W65 (ebook) | DDC 355.00820973--dc23 | SUDOC D 301.26/6:W 84

LC record available at https://lccn.loc.gov/2021027376

LC ebook record available at https://lccn.loc.gov/2021027377

This book is dedicated to all the women who have served to protect their nation, communities, and families, and to the men who have supported them.

The difficulty lies not in new ideas, but in escaping from the old ones.

—John Maynard Keynes

Contents

List of Illustrations   *ix*

Foreword   *xi*

About the Author   *xiii*

Preface   *xv*

Acknowledgments   *xix*

Abbreviations   *xxi*

1   Pioneers: Inception–1947   1

2   Beginnings: 1948–1953   17

3   Survival: The 1950s and 1960s   37

4   Revolution Stirring: Public Law 90-130 and Vietnam   61

5   Turning Points: The 1970s   73

6   Having It All?: The 1980s and 1990s   97

7   A New World: 2000–2020   117

8   Conclusions and Observations: 2021 and Beyond   155

Appendix A: Women in the Air Force (WAF) Directors   171

Appendix B: Women's Armed Services Integration Act of 1948, Title III: Air Force   173

Appendix C: Recommendations for Further Reading   181

Chronology   183

Bibliography   191

Index   205

List of Illustrations

Figures

1	Pioneer American aviator Jacqueline "Jackie" Cochran	8
2	Four WASPs leave their B-17 Flying Fortress	9
3	Barbara Erickson receiving an Air Medal	11
4	Eight WASPs at the Army Air Force's advanced single engine pilot school, 1943	12
5	Col Geraldine Pratt May	20
6	The first Air Force uniforms, early 1950s	25
7	Excerpt from 1957 WAF handbook offering makeup application routines	40
8	Members of the Officer's Training School, 1960	43
9	Esther Blake McGowin, the first woman to enlist in the Air Force, 1948	46
10	Col Jeanne M. Holm with other directors of US women's forces	62
11	Air Force nurse 1st Lt Linda V. Bowser, 1974	68
12	US Air Force Academy yearbook highlighting first female graduates, 1980	81
13	The first 10 Air Force women to graduate from Undergraduate Pilot Training, 1977	83
14	Aircraft mechanic A1C Janet E. Wuco, 1974	84
15	WAF air traffic controller assigned to the 2021st Communication Squadron, 1974	87
16	Airman 1st Class Scott during Exercise Bold Eagle, 1982	100
17	TSgt Tony Tesori briefs aircrews during Operation Desert Storm	104

18 General McPeak introduces the Air Force's first female combat pilots, 1993   110

19 Amn Anne Moor, 24th Security Police Squadron, 1996   111

20 SSgt Melishia Francis prepares her breast pump, 2018   133

21 Lt Col Christine Mau, first female to fly the F-35   137

22 39th Security Forces Squadron Airmen in new body armor, 2021   139

23 Maj Christina "Thumper" Hopper   141

24 The first all-female C-130 combat mission, 2005   142

Table

1 Women in Regular and Reserve Components of Air Force   117

Foreword

This book documents the many significant and diverse contributions made by women in the United States Air Force. Capt Marissa Kester has captured their legacy in this concise volume by tracing this important history from its inception. The contributions made by this group of Citizen Airmen parallel the history of the broader Air Force narrative, and this book provides the reader with insight into how women, over time, have served in all Air Force missions.

The contributions of women have expanded to include all aspects of Air Force operations as they overcame challenges and pursued their goals with a relentless determination. Moreover, their history includes their rise to the highest and most sensitive leadership positions and executing the most dangerous of missions. This volume documents those achievements by telling many of the stories of valiant women war fighters serving their country while working in their communities and supporting their families. This narrative also illuminates the story of how, in the face of doubt and criticism, women have met many challenges in quiet fashion and proved themselves to be highly capable professionals.

These contributions and notable achievements provided over many decades add an important and significant depth to the broader Air Force history narrative. In 2002, Rebecca Grant referred to women Airmen as "quiet pioneers."[1] Since then, they have emerged as a loud voice by way of their accomplishments and leadership. This book captures that voice for the reader.

I want to thank Captain Kester for her tireless effort in the pursuit of her research. The results are obvious in the following pages. It is my hope that her book will not only provide a recording of the past but will also light the path for the future of women in the Air Force.

DONALD C. BOYD, PHD
Director, History & Heritage
Air Force Reserve Command

---

1. Rebecca Grant, "The Quiet Pioneers," *Air Force Magazine*, 1 December 2002, https://www.airforcemag.com.

About the Author

Marissa Kester is a captain in the US Air Force Reserve currently serving as a senior historian and individual mobilization augmentee to the Air Force Reserve Command history and heritage office. She graduated with a bachelor's degree in history from the College of Charleston in 2010 and earned a master's degree from American Military University in 2013; she served for five years on active duty before transitioning to the Reserve in 2016. Captain Kester has served as an intelligence analyst and instructor and is widely published on both classified and unclassified domains. Her current research involves women and leadership through history.

Preface

Until the lions have their own historians, tales of the hunt shall always glorify the hunter.

—Nigerian proverb

In December 2015 Secretary of Defense Ashton Carter announced that as of 1 January 2016 women could enter any military career field and serve in any military unit for which they met the standard.

This moment was a culmination of all moments prior.

Since the Women's Armed Forces Integration Act of 1948 first allowed women a permanent position in the regular and reserve forces, there have been doubts surrounding their inclusion in the military. Even after policy decisions were put in place, questions lingered. Was this the right choice? Should women be allowed in the services? To what extent? What should they be allowed to do? What are they capable of? Is it worth the trouble of accommodating women in a "masculine" institution, both logistically and culturally? What are the appropriately "feminine" parameters of their inclusion?

The history we collectively hold and share is primarily documented through the eyes and voices of men. The story of the United States Air Force is no different. This book is an attempt to understand the Air Force narrative from a different point of view. Not from the standard, inherently male, outside-looking-in-on women perspective, but from that of an Air Force woman looking around. Though all members of the Air Force, past and present, collectively refer to and think of themselves as Airmen, the experiences, available opportunities, and perceptions of all Airmen have not been the same. The point is not to sit in judgment or cast blame but instead to understand so we can move forward from this present moment with more awareness and understanding. Dealing intelligently with force-management issues requires that policy makers and those who vote them into power understand how we got to where we are today. Why do we have the current policies, constraints, and reoccurring issues pertaining to women in the Air Force that we do?

This book is an attempt to begin to answer—or at least identify—those questions as well as establish a foundation for future study. It is not intended to recount in detail everything that happened but instead offer a big-picture, broad-brush history that identifies major players, key events, and crucial decisions affecting women and their integration into the Air Force from 1948 to 2020. The scope of this work is defined by and limited to the study of women in the Air Force as defined by biological sex. While the further breakdown of women by race, sexual orientation, or other qualifiers certainly warrants further study, as those experiences were very likely different from the generic female experience in the Air Force, it is beyond of the scope of this book to do so.

Although it is known that women have served in and with the United States armed forces since the beginning of the nation's history, documenting the exact nature and extent of their participation remains difficult due to the physical loss and selective preservation of many applicable early records. Likewise, for the first two decades of their official service, women in the military were largely viewed as a reserve-type force, perhaps even a temporary experiment. Government records specific to Air Force women are sparse, and those related to Air Force Reserve women are even more difficult to find, particularly as women and reservists became more integrated into the total force during the 1980s and beyond. While interviews and memoirs prove to be incredibly helpful in recounting the experiences of women in the Air Force, this study has been written with the conscious exclusion of tens of thousands of women's stories—all of which deserve to be told.

A final disclaimer and inescapable aspect of this topic is that the history of women in any context is often a story of absence, which can make it difficult to write about. Additionally, presenting an established historical narrative from a new or different perspective might imply a reader's beliefs or assumptions are wrong or outdated, which can make it hard to read about. Throughout its 73-year history, the Air Force has often led the way in terms of allowing equal opportunity within the service. Unlike the other US military branches, the Air Force has never known an existence without women in the ranks. This fact has helped shape the status, integration, opportunities, perceptions, and ultimately utilization of female Airmen throughout the decades. However, at any point in history the Air Force is still a product of its time and associated political, economic, and social constructs. Curiosity and morality do not mix well, and as such it is not my intention to politicize or assign judgment on any aspect of women or gender integration in the Air Force.

The 2015 decision to open all career fields to women seemed to put an end to most of those questions that had followed women in the military since 1948. For the first time, women reached a status of full legal inclusion in the Air Force, something their female predecessors likely never dreamed was possible. Though this was a major milestone and step for not only women in the Air Force but women in America, the full value of women in the military still has yet to be realized. As the push for greater diversity of thought, experience, and skill within the force has become a strategic defense imperative, gender integration becomes arguably even more important as we look to the force of the future—one that we cannot risk handling in superficial and temporary ways. Looking back to understand the path and experience of women in the Air Force provides immeasurable context when deciding where we want to go.

Acknowledgments

First and foremost, my sincerest thank you to Dr. Donald Boyd (director, Office of History and Heritage, Air Force Reserve Command) and Dr. Paul Larson (senior historian, Office of History and Heritage, Air Force Reserve Command) for not only trusting me with the idea for this project but also assuring me that it was one worth pursuing. I am forever grateful for the guidance, time, support, and man days you gave me so that I could research, write, and publish this book. Without those very necessary things this idea would likely have never left the ground. Many additional thanks to all of my colleagues in the Air Force Reserve Command History and Heritage Office who somehow always had a point of contact, reference document, or next lead whenever I got stuck. To my mentor Lt Col Laura Cox, thank you for sharing your time, patience, and hard-won wisdom with me over the years as I have navigated the learning curve of being an individual mobilization augmentee and historian in the Air Force Reserve.

Thank you to all the personnel at the Air Force Historical Research Agency, as well as to those involved with the Betty H. Carter Women Veterans Historical Project at the University of North Carolina at Greensboro and the Women in Military Service for America Memorial Foundation. Likewise, thank you to all the scholars before me who have researched, taught, and written about women in the military. Without your dedication and effort so much of this history would be lost and forgotten to time.

A big thank you to everyone at Air University Press who put so much time and energy into not only ensuring this book was up to AU press standards, but also turning out an even better product than I ever expected. In particular, I am indebted to my editor, Donna Budjenska, whose patience, kindness and superb editing skills cannot be overstated.

On a more personal note:

To my dad, thank you for being the biggest supporter of my writing, my thought process, my interests, and my goals—both personal and professional. For being my frontline editor, sanity checker, and showing me how to navigate the book writing and military officer world with humor and resolve. For always encouraging me to think critically, question assumptions, keep an open mind, and eventually . . . somehow . . . manage to get that mess into words on paper. Thank you mom for being my no. 1 fan, no matter what. For raising me to know that strength, wisdom, and power come from being a woman, not in spite of it.

To my husband, this book in print is a testament to your legendary stubbornness to get the job done, even when it's not your own. Thank you for not letting me quit when things got tough or tedious. Thank you for showing me and our boys how to stand firm in our convictions, regardless of outside pressure or opinion. And thank you most of all for your support, sacrifices, love, and willingness to listen to me talk about this topic for years on end.

To my sons, thank you for keeping me humble, curious, and ready (or not) to embrace every day with an open heart. It turns out writing a book and having young children are similar in that both like to keep you up night, so thanks for the many multitasking opportunities. Like most parents, I want nothing more than to help create a better world for you now, and to raise you both to be kind, wise, and conscious leaders of the world that follows. When in doubt in life, look to the women—here you will find the strength, perspective, and compassion you are seeking.

To all my other dearest friends and family, I am beyond grateful for your support, love, and presence in my life. I love you all.

And finally, I offer my deepest gratitude to all the men and women who have ever served in the US military. As a writer, I value nothing more than the freedom to question narratives and speak truth as I see it. As a citizen, I feel there is nothing more important to defend. Thank you for all you do and have done, for your countless unseen, and often forgotten, sacrifices to allow this freedom and many others.

To all the Air Force women who have come before me, who I serve with currently, and all who follow: Every single one of you matters. Thank you, and unapologetically keep going.

What started out as genuine obliviousness quickly turned into a research project, turned into an essay, turned into a special study, and then turned book . . . and somewhere along the way also turned into a labor of love. While there is so much credit to be shared, any errors or omissions are entirely my own.

Abbreviations

AAF	Army Air Forces
AFBAWG	Air Force Barrier Analysis Working Group
AFIT	Air Force Institute of Technology
AFMC	Air Force Materiel Command
AFQT	Air Force Qualification Test
AFR	Air Force Reserve
AFRC	Air Force Reserve Command
AFROTC	Air Force Reserve Officer Training Corps
AFSC	Air Force Specialty Codes
AFWST	Air Force Women's Selection Test
ATA	Air Transport Auxiliary
ATC	Air Transport Command
AVF	all-volunteer force
AWACS	Airborne Warning and Control System
BAQ	basic allowance for quarters
BOQ	bachelor officer quarters
CIP	Career Intermission Program
CSO	Combat Systems Officer
DACOWITS	Defense Advisory Committee on Women in the Services
DGCDAR	Direct Ground Combat Definition and Assignment Rule
DOPMA	Defense Officer Personnel Management Act
EMMA	Equality for Military Mothers Amendment
EO	executive order
ICBM	intercontinental ballistic missile
IRR	Individual Ready Reserve
JAG	judge advocate general
JCS	Joint Chiefs of Staff
JWLS	Joint Women's Leadership Symposium

MAJCOM	major command
MATS	Military Air Transport Services
MLDC	Military Leadership Diversity Commission
MOMS	Mothers of Military Service
MST	military sexual trauma
NDAA	National Defense Authorization Act
NOW	National Organization for Women
OCO	overseas contingency operation
OCS	Officer Candidate School
OEF	Operation Enduring Freedom
OIF	Operation Iraqi Freedom
OMB	Office of Management and Budget
OSD	Office of the Secretary of Defense
OTS	Officer Training School
PL	public law
PME	professional military education
POW	prisoner of war
PTSD	posttraumatic stress disorder
RQS	rescue squadron
SAC	Strategic Air Command
SAPR	sexual assault prevention and response
SAPRO	Sexual Assault Prevention and Response Office
SARC	sexual assault response coordinators
Scud	surface-to-surface missile system
SEA	Southeast Asia
SFS	security forces squadron
SIOP	single integrated operational plan
UPT	undergraduate pilot training
USAFA	US Air Force Academy
USAFR	US Air Force Reserve
VA	Department of Veterans Affairs
WAAC	Women's Army Auxiliary Corps

WAC	Women's Army Corps
WAF	Women's Airforce Service
WAFS	Women's Auxiliary Ferrying Squadron
WASP	Women Airforce Service Pilots
WAVES	Women Accepted for Volunteer Emergency Service
WFTD	Women's Flying Training Detachment
WIT	Women's Initiatives Team

Chapter 1

Pioneers

Inception–1947

Long before they were legally considered citizens or held the right to vote, women volunteered to join ranks with men in defense of the United States. For most of our nation's history they did so with no recognition, protection, benefit, or support. While some women pretended to be men to get to the frontlines, most served as laundresses, nurses, cooks, or even spies.[1] The first women hired to work with the military as contractors were nurses. During the War of 1812, the Navy hired two civilian nurses to serve aboard the USS *United States*, and during the Spanish-American War (1898), 1,500 civilian nurses worked in Army hospitals.[2]

The early American women who chose to serve their country risked everything by defying both cultural expectations and laws regarding what women were allowed (and mostly not allowed) to do. In the early history of the United States, women were not considered citizens or persons in the eyes of the law, and therefore almost all educational and employment opportunities, as well as outlets for political involvement, were denied.[3] During the eighteenth and nineteenth centuries it was understood that women were the possessions of men, typically their husbands and fathers.[4] The assigned roles of dutiful daughter, nurturing mother, and "helpmate" wife created the cultural expectations and structure in which a woman existed and was reflected back to her in the values of American government, laws, and social institutions.[5]

During the twentieth century the revolutionary notion that women were also American citizens started to challenge women's long held roles and expectations. By the end of the nineteenth century, American women embodied a very different image than they did at the start. Owing primarily to industrialization and its offshoots (mass education, urbanization, and the growing use of recently developed technologies such as the typewriter and telephone), women started stepping away from the home and into the community in a different manner than before. By the first decade of the twentieth century many American businesses were hiring women as clerks, typists, telephone operators, and factory workers. Preparations for war allowed women to enter the skilled, industrial labor force, working in shipyards, mills, and factories manufacturing aircraft and weapons. What used to be high-paying "man's jobs" became lower-paying jobs that "could also, apparently, be done by a woman."[6]

This same wave of social change also produced the first military servicewomen. Through history, the most common way women have served with and in the US military has been as part of the medical services, typically as nurses. These first female nurses worked almost exclusively in combat zones and were immune from protection or benefits related to their actions since they served strictly in a civilian capacity.[7] However, as has been illustrated time and again, legal status does not protect one from the hardships and horrors of war, which was something nurses often dealt with firsthand. Following their service in the Spanish-American War, the Army established the Nurse Corps in 1901 (under the Army Reorganization Act) as an auxiliary within the Army Medical Department; the Navy followed suit in 1908. While these first "official" servicewomen wore military uniforms, they only served in a quasi-military status, not receiving rank and insignia until 1920, a retirement pension until 1926, and eligibility for a disability pension if injured in the line of duty until 1926.[8]

Though at the time American culture generally dictated the proper place for women was at home,[9] as was—and will continue—to be the case for women in the military, wartime personnel needs soon tipped the scales, overriding cultural values. A few weeks before President Woodrow Wilson asked Congress to declare war on Germany, the US Navy became the first service to place women in full military status. When Secretary of the Navy Josephus Daniels asked his legal advisor if there was any law specifying Navy enlisted clerks must be men and was told that due to vague wording technically there was not, he began enlisting women in the Naval Reserve as Yeomen (F), stating that by enlisting women "we will have the best clerical assistance the country can provide."[10] On 19 March 1917 the Navy Department authorized the enrollment of women into the Naval Reserve, and when the US entered World War I on 6 April, the Navy was in a good position to immediately begin employing those women. A year later, the Marine Corps also started enlisting women into its reserve. During World War I, approximately 13,000 women served as "Yeomanettes" and "Marinettes" in primarily clerical positions. While they received pay and benefits equal to those of their male counterparts, when the war ended so too did their authorization in the Navy and Marines.[11]

Despite the Navy and Marine Corps's example and the urgings of Army commanders, women were still not allowed to serve in the Army during World War I. However, aiming to improve communications on the Western front between the Allied Forces, Gen John J. Pershing hired 450 civilian female switchboard operators, known as "hello girls," to work overseas for the Army. Formally known as the Signal Corps Female Telephone Operators Unit, these women were sworn into the US Army Signal Corps, wore US Army uniforms, and were subject to Army regulations; however, they were still considered civilians employed by the military because those Army regulations specified members must be male.[12]

Interwar Years

The nearly two decades between world wars is where the story of women in military aviation, and the precursors to the first female airmen, begins. By the end of World War I, military aviation had gone from an almost exclusively reconnaissance mission to one that embraced rapid technological improvements to perform multiple specialized roles. By the end of the war, American airmen were convinced that air superiority and strategic bombing were vital to winning any future wars. For many, airplanes seemed to answer the question of how to never again repeat the horror, destruction, and bloodshed of trench warfare during World War I. Air leaders such as Gen Billy Mitchell believed aircraft—specifically strategic bombers—would make future conflicts shorter and less deadly. However, many military and political leaders still viewed airpower as an auxiliary weapon available to commanders when necessary.

Entrenched in postwar fatigue and its accompanying antiwar sentiments, the American public was not interested in the militarization of aircraft so much as the glamorization of it. Due to the rapid development and mass production of aircraft during World War I, by the early 1920s not only were airplanes much more reliable and capable than previous iterations, but there was also an abundance of them as wartime aircraft were auctioned off to the public at low prices. Suddenly, planes were everywhere with aircraft manufacturers releasing newer, bigger, and better models every year. Daring aviators of both sexes capitalized on this period of abundance and popularity, setting their sights on establishing and breaking aviation speed and distance records. These barnstormers and air racers captured the imagination of an American public enamored with the newest and best flying machines. Notable female aviatrixes such as Amelia Earhart, Louise Thaden, and Jacqueline Cochran were pop-culture icons, actively proving women were just as capable as men when it came to piloting aircraft. By 1939 "women were no longer oddities in any area of aviation,"[13] serving as pilots, stewardesses, engineers, mechanics, and specialists who demonstrated and sold airplanes.

However, despite female presence in the skies, piloting an airplane was still by and large culturally perceived as a masculine endeavor. The use of aviation during World War I, particularly the creation of the "ace," assigned courage in aerial combat as a distinctly male trait.[14] This combined with the American cultural taboos against women in combat, such that the possibility that women would be able to become military pilots was never seriously contemplated prior to 1942.

The early interwar years featured attempts to democratize aviation with New Deal programs such as "An Airplane for Everyman" and the Civilian Pilot Training Program, both of which were designed to stimulate the private flying business by offering affordable aircraft to Americans.[15] However, as the roaring twenties gave way to the Great Depression, flying was still a somewhat exclusive activity, or in the words of Smithsonian scholar and author Deborah Douglas: "a wealthy, white man's sport."[16] Racial minorities and women were routinely disenfranchised from aviation due to segregation laws, economic restrictions, and other prejudices that were inextricably woven into the socioeconomic fabric of America at the time. Those women, such as Cochran and Earhart, who dominated the skies during the golden years of aviation were primarily able to do so because they were of financial means. Nonetheless, their many successes and participation in the world of civilian aviation set the stage for women to be used as military pilots during World War II.

Women Airforce Service Pilots (WAFS/WASP)

As the United States watched Hitler's Germany invade Austria, Czechoslovakia, and finally Poland in September 1939, Cochran wrote to Eleanor Roosevelt proposing a women's flying division in the Army Air Forces (AAF).[17] She made clear her opinion that qualified female pilots could do all of the domestic, noncombat aviation jobs that might soon become necessary in order to release more male pilots for combat. In her letter, Cochran asserted that "the real bottleneck in the long run is likely to be trained pilots," something she believed women could help with. A few weeks later she made the same pitch to the Ninety-Nines, a premier international women pilots association, but the idea did not gain any traction for another year and a half.

In March 1941 Cochran served on the committee for the Collier Trophy, an annual aviation award presented by the National Aeronautic Association. After the presentation at the White House, she went to lunch with Gen Henry H. "Hap" Arnold, commanding general of the Army Air Forces and chief of the Air Corps, and Clayton Knight, the acting head of an American recruiting committee for the British Ferry Command. While at lunch, Cochran reiterated her idea that female pilots could be used in the newly formed Air Corps Ferrying Command but was again told there was no need to use women at that time.[18] Instead, Arnold promised Cochran the director position if ever such a group was to be formed. Knight, however, was interested in using Cochran's skills and offered her an opportunity to augment the British Air Transport Auxiliary (ATA) as a ferrying pilot. After passing the required flight tests and arriving in the United Kingdom, Cochran met Pauline Gower, one of England's premier women pilots, who asked if it were possible for her to recruit additional American women pilots to augment the group.[19]

Immediately upon her return to the United States in July 1941 Cochran set to doing just that. After a long lunch with President Roosevelt and Eleanor Roosevelt, Cochran was put in touch with Robert A. Lovett, assistant secretary of war for air, who arranged for Cochran to be appointed to work (without pay) with General Arnold and Gen Robert Olds.[20] After working with Nancy Harkness Love a year earlier, Olds had been very interested in hiring highly qualified female pilots to ease his shortage in the Air Ferrying Command. Cochran worked furiously to put together a proposal package for a women's pilot division that would be organized and commissioned in the Air Corps Specialist Reserve. As much as Arnold and Olds liked the idea, ultimately neither was willing to recommend the creation of a significant new military subgroup—particularly one composed of women. At this point, during the summer of 1941, there were more pilots than aircraft in the Air Corps, and leadership was not convinced they had to go to such an extent as to hire women to fulfill military roles.[21] Pushed off once again, Cochran returned to New York and began to recruit a team of women pilots to serve with Britain's ATA. In March 1942 Cochran took 24 trained American female pilots with her back to Britain to form the

ATA's American contingent. She saw this as a way to demonstrate the validity of her proposal to the American military and stay at the forefront of the aviation industry.[22]

Despite the continual resistance met by Cochran, Nancy Harkness Love was able to successfully create a way for the AAF to use women pilots. An excellent pilot in her own right, she and her husband, Maj Robert Love, a Reserve officer in the Army Air Corps, started a successful aircraft sales company, for which she piloted flights ferrying American aircraft to the Canadian border. These flights brought her into contact with the Army Air Corp's Air Ferrying Command (known as of March 1942 as the Ferrying Division of the Air Transport Command, or ATC), a connection that was reinforced when her husband was recalled to duty in Washington, DC, as the deputy chief of staff of the ATC.[23] There Love obtained a civilian position with the ATC Ferrying Division operations office in Baltimore.

One day Major Love happened to mention to Col William Tunner, commander of the Ferrying Division in ATC headquarters and in the neighboring office to Love, that his wife was commuting 80 miles daily by airplane from Washington to Baltimore for her job. Tunner quickly arranged a meeting with Nancy Harkness Love and shared his need for pilots to deliver aircraft to airfields around the country; she shared her conviction that women could do that job. Tunner and Love submitted a proposal to Gen Harold George, ATC commander, and after a few discussions Love received the go-ahead to send telegrams to potential candidates.[24] On 10 September 1942 the Women's Auxiliary Ferrying Squadron (WAFS) was established. As civil service personnel attached to the Army Air Force's 2nd Ferrying Group at New Castle Army Air Base in Wilmington, Delaware, the 28 women who showed up to in-process the unit were nicknamed "the Originals" and became the first to fly for the US military. The WAFS completed their first delivery on 22 October 1942 when six female pilots took L-4Bs from Lockhaven, Pennsylvania, to Mitchel Field on Long Island, New York.[25]

Meanwhile, while Cochran was abroad with the ATA, the US military was making progress in regard to women's corps across the services. The WAFS (later WASP), Women's Army Corps (WAC), and the Navy's Women Accepted for Volunteer Emergency Service (WAVES) were all developed simultaneously, as advocates for using women in the military used progress in one service to push for progress in another. The legislative starting point was 28 May 1941 when

Representative Edith Nourse Rogers introduced H.R. 4906 to establish a Women's Army Auxiliary Corps (WAAC) as a group that would not be in the Army but with the Army.[26] As proponents carefully lobbied Congress during the summer of 1941, even General Marshall became a supporter, believing women could be used to counter future military labor shortages. In December 1941 the Army Air Forces began to exhibit considerable interest in creating an Air Force section within the proposed WAAC. The bill was finally passed on 15 May 1942, and the next day Oveta Culp Hobby was sworn in as director of newly minted WAAC.

Following the WAAC's initial success, in the spring of 1943 the Army asked Congress to integrate the corps into the regular Army so as to provide benefits and services not available to the WAAC as auxiliaries. In July 1943 the WAC was established, and all the women who had served as WAACs were offered a position in the WAC but had no legal obligation to enlist.[27] All WAC appointments were temporary (neither regular nor Reserve) and were valid only until the end of postwar demobilization. Throughout WWII, as many as one-third of WACs served overseas at any given time, but all were barred from combat assignments.

The Army Air Forces was the first service component to take the lead in using female troops, developing plans early on to employ them in "nonstandard" roles such as aircraft mechanics and radio operators. The WAACs assigned to the AAF were referred to as Air WAACs (later Air WACs), and were the first US female airmen. At its peak in 1945, the Air WACs boasted over 32,000 women, with approximately 40 percent of all WACs serving in the AAF. More than 200 enlisted and 60 officer occupational specialties were available to women, and by January 1945 only about 50 percent of Air WACs worked in the assignments traditionally seen as appropriate for women, such as stenography, typing, and filing. As early as November 1942 it was suggested Air WAACs be employed as Link trainer instructors; however, the first significant assignment for many of the women was to operate listening posts for the Aircraft Warning Service, which monitored US borders for possible enemy attack. Many Air WAACs/WACs served as weather observers, cryptographers, radio operators, aerial photograph analyzers, control tower operators, parachute riggers, maintenance specialists, and sheet metal workers.

Fig. 1. Pioneer American aviator Jacqueline "Jackie" Cochran in the cockpit of a Curtiss P-40 Warhawk fighter plane

Upon Cochran's return from England in September 1942, she was shocked to learn another women's pilot corps—the WAFS headed by Love—had been established in her absence. Cochran had been promised the director position by President Roosevelt and General Arnold in 1941; Arnold quickly rectified the situation, and five days after the WAFS were established the Army Air Forces announced Jacqueline Cochran would form and command the Women's Flying Training Detachment (WFTD). Designed to train women pilots in the traditions, regulations, and flying methods of the Army Air Forces, the purpose of the WFTD was to "create a pool of trained women pilots from which will be drawn, as needed, personnel for non-combat flying purposes, to release as many men pilots as possible for combat and other important duties."[28] According to a War Department press release of 14 September 1942, "under Miss Cochran, women will be trained in cross-country flying, using all navigational aids, to qualify as operating personnel for Mrs. Love's and other such units as may require it."[29] The press release also confirmed Cochran would be director of this organization and serve in civil service status.

Shortly after the WAFS began their missions, WFTD pilot-training classes began at Howard Hughes Field, Houston Municipal Airport, in November 1942. Cochran's pilot training consisted of a six-month course paralleling male pilot trainees, but without gunnery and other specific combat training.[30] However, classes soon grew too large, and just six months later (April 1943) they moved to Avenger Field in Sweetwater, Texas. Although 25,000 women applied to the program, only 1,800 were selected for training, and of those only about 1,000 received their pilot wings. According to a September 1943 article written by Cochran for the *Australian Women's Weekly*,[31] the female trainees lived in barracks at the training field or officer quarters on the base and were subject to strict discipline, despite their civil service status.[32] The first class of WFTD pilots graduated 24 April 1943.[33]

Fig. 2. Four WASPs leave their B-17 Flying Fortress at Lockbourne Army Air Base in Columbus, Ohio.

Continued pilot shortages and impressive performance by both the WAFS and WFTD convinced General Arnold to train more female pilots. In mid-1943 Arnold ordered both groups be combined, with Cochran as director in charge of all the women pilots flying for the Army and Love as executive for women pilots of the Ferrying Division, still answering to now-General Tunner.[34] On 5 August 1943, after being appointed director of the Office of Special Assistant for Women Pilots in June,[35] Cochran changed the collective women pilots' name to the Women Airforce Service Pilots (WASP). While most women ferried planes to bases and other flight schools, some were instructors and test pilots. Others flight-tested aircraft that had only recently been repaired before the male pilots were allowed to fly them again. Other women towed targets for artillery gunners or transported equipment and personnel.[36] However, delivery of pursuit aircraft to other airfields within the country remained the WASP's primary mission.[37]

Despite their successes, the women also received their share of backlash. Some women reported finding grass or sugar in their gas tanks and acid in their parachutes, had flight controls become loose after takeoff or their aircraft tires slashed.[38] Camp Davis, on the southeast coast of North Carolina, had the most of these reports; at least 11 female pilots had to make forced landings.[39] Despite this, none of the allegations were ever proven and often went unreported by the women due to fear of losing their opportunity to fly. Many years later in an interview, former WASP Lorraine Zillner assessed that these incidents happened because of men "who didn't really feel that women had any business in a cockpit."[40]

Demobilization

After the WAAC was converted to the WAC in July 1943, many believed the incorporation of the WASPs into the regular Army would be next. However, General Arnold's efforts to militarize the pilots (which would have resulted in full military status and benefits) were denied. Shortly after D-day, on 21 June 1944, the WASP militarization bill was defeated, and six months later, on 20 December 1944, the WASPs were deactivated. Throughout the 28-month duration of the program, 1,102 WASPs conducted a wide variety of flying jobs at 120 US military bases, flying over 60 million collective miles in every type of military aircraft. Of these women, 134 qualified as pursuit pilots and 38 died in service, primarily due to plane mechanical failures. However, almost immediately after the war ended these women were largely forgotten. Even during the time of their service, the

WASPs received very little publicity or recognition. It took 32 years for former WASPs to receive militarized status (in 1977) and 33 more years to be recognized and awarded a Congressional Gold Medal for their service (in 2010).[41]

Fig. 3. Barbara Erickson became the first WASP to receive the Air Medal for meritorious achievement as a pilot. Erickson received her medal for completing four 2,000-mile deliveries of three different types of aircraft in slightly more than five days of actual flying. (Source: NARA)

By the end of the war, on 2 September 1945 (V-J Day), the WAC had 90,779 members.[42] As Edith Disler points out, "as many women served in uniform during World War II as there are people—men *and* women—in the entire US Air Force of 2010. And, of course, that total doesn't include women in the Office of Strategic Services . . .; women working with the Manhattan project; women building ships, tanks, and aircraft; and thousands if not hundreds of thousands of women who contributed directly or indirectly to that war effort."[43]

Fig. 4. Original caption: "Swinging down along the ramp at the AAF's Training Command's advanced single engine pilot school at Foster Field, Victoria, Texas, are eight feminine pilots, members of the AF WASP. Left to right: Pauline S. Cutler of Cleveland, Ohio; Dorothy Ehrhardt, Bridgewater, Mass.; Jennie M. Hill of Harvey, Ill.; Etta Mae Hollinger, Paola, Kans.; Lucille R. Cary, Joliet, Ill.; Jane B. Shirley, Brownfield Tex.; Dorothy H. Beard, Sacramento, Calif.; and Kathryn L. Boyd, Weatherford, Texas." Circa 1943. (Source: NARA)

Some Army officers, such as Lt Gen Ira C. Eaker, then the deputy commander of the Army Air Forces, recommended WAC retention in the regular Army based on their good performance during the conflict. Other Army officers and public figures feared that retaining women in the military would weaken the nation's moral fiber.[44] Additionally, many wartime heroines now found themselves standing in the way of returning Soldiers who wanted their jobs back. Since the creation of the WAC was predicated on combat necessity, there was no peacetime component available to women. For these reasons many, including Hobby, favored disbanding the WAC as soon as the war ended. In the end, both men and women were rapidly demobilized, leaving WAC strength on 31 December 1946 at less than 10,000.[45]

Over the course of World War II, 29,323 women served in the Army Air Forces.[46] Though most were discharged after the war, about 2,000 enlisted personnel and 177 officers continued to work in Air Corps units. Many of these pioneers, the first generation of female Airmen, transitioned to the new Air Force and some even remained in the service through the Vietnam War.

Notes

(All notes appear in shortened form. For full details, see the appropriate entry in the bibliography.)

1. Monahan and Neidel-Greenlee, *A Few Good Women*, xvi.
2. "America's Women Veterans," 1.
3. Devilbiss, *Women and Military Service*, 38.
4. "Could and Should," 10–11.
5. Dicker, *A History of U.S. Feminism*, 21–24.
6. Holm, *Women in the Military*, 11–12.
7. Holm, 9.
8. Holm, 17.
9. Monahan and Neidel-Greenlee, *A Few Good Women*, 5.
10. The 1916 US Naval Reserve Act permitted the enlistment of qualified "persons" for service in the Navy. Holm, *Women in the Military*, 9–10.
11. The Naval Appropriations Act of 1919 placed all of the women on inactive duty status, though did not formally discharge them until 1920. Patch, "Female Yeoman."
12. USA Signal Center, "Hello Girls."
13. Douglas, *United States Women in Aviation*, 8.
14. The concept of a fighter pilot "ace" emerged during World War I at the same time as aerial dogfighting; pilots who had five "kills" to their credit were aces. By 1916 governments began to recognize aviators as having nationalistic and propagandistic value, providing the home front with a hero during what was otherwise a long war of attrition. Maksell, "What Does It Take."
15. Douglas, *Women in Aviation*, 3–4.
16. Douglas, vi.
17. Eleanor Roosevelt was very interested in women in aviation. As a good friend of Amelia Earhart and later a relentless advocate for using women pilots during WWII, Mrs. Roosevelt's own desire to learn to fly was precluded by the secret service, who feared sabotage. Douglas, *Women in Aviation*, 27–28.
18. In early 1941 Gen George C. Marshall expressed the official military position towards women, setting the tone of a potentially permissive envi-

ronment: "While the United States is not faced with an acute shortage of manpower such as has forced England to make extensive use of women, it is realized that we must plan for every possible contingency, and certainly must provide some outlet for the patriotic desires of women." Douglas, *Women in Aviation*, 8.

19. Douglas, *Women in Aviation*, 29.

20. Early in 1940, then–Lieutenant Colonel Olds, as part of Plans Division of the Air Staff, worked with Nancy Harkness Love to compile a list all the women pilots in the United States holding commercial ratings. Douglas, *Women in Aviation*, 30.

21. Douglas, *Women in Aviation*.

22. Douglas, 31.

23. Douglas, 29.

24. Texas Woman's University, "The Leaders."

25. Rickmann, "So, Who Are the WASP Anyway?," 1.

26. Holm, *Women in the Military*, 21–22.

27. Holm, 58.

28. War Department, "Cochran Named Director."

29. War Department.

30. Cochran, "American Women Pilots."

31. Cochran.

32. According to Ann Carl, an experimental test pilot with the Air Force and the first woman to fly a military jet aircraft, Jackie Cochran organized the Women's Airforce Service Pilots (WASP) training program to model exactly the Army Air Force cadet program of primary, basic, and advanced flight training and ground school. In their memoirs, former WASPs often half-jokingly refer to the unit as "Cochran's convent," due to the strict nature of her high expectations. Carl, *A WASP Among Eagles*, 36–37.

33. Rickmann, "So, Who Are the WASP Anyway?," 2.

34. Nancy Love managed the extensive administrative duties first for her 25 WAFS and then for the expanded group of WASPs assigned to the Air Transport Command. Through her impressive performance, Love gained Tunner's implied approval to fly any military airplane. On 27 February 1943 Love became the first woman to fly the P-51, the Army's fastest pursuit aircraft at the time. Her other female piloting firsts included flying the C-47, B-25, B-17, and P-38. Rickmann, "So, Who Are the WASP Anyway?," 2.

35. Arnold, "Office of Special Assistant."

36. Known as Battery X, WASP pilots towed targets to help to train the Women's Army Auxiliary Corps (WAAC) for domestic antiaircraft artillery duty; 55 officers and 973 enlisted women participated in this secret training operation. Rickmann, "So, Who Are the WASP Anyway?," 4.

37. Rickmann, "So, Who Are the WASP Anyway?," 4.

38. Jacqueline Cochran personally discovered sugar in the gas tank of a plane that had crashed, killing her colleague Betty Davis. Waxman, "Hidden Risk."

39. Waxman, "Hidden Risk."

40. Waxman. What started as light humor and resentment of military men towards military women, primarily WAAC/WAC, eventually turned into full scale slander by 1943. The most common accusation was that military women were little more than uniformed prostitutes. In fact, the accusations were so widespread and vicious that the War Department (under the assumption it was an enemy effort to undermine morale), asked the Federal Bureau of Investigation (FBI) to investigate the claims. The FBI found that enlisted men were the culprits. Partially fueled by the antifraternization policy that prohibited relationships between officer and enlisted personnel and lax enforcement of that policy on male officers, the false belief emerged that that women made themselves available to male officers to get special treatment. The likely primary heartache was with men resenting women taking noncombat jobs to free them for combat duty—as was so widely advertised. This was such a problem that the Army had to drop any reference of the idea from their women's recruiting materials. Holm, *Women in the Military*, 51–54.

41. Carl, *A WASP Among Eagles*, 111.

42. Wackerfuss, "Women's Army Auxiliary Corps."

43. Disler, "The Feminine as a Force Multiplier," in Parco and Levy, *Attitudes Aren't Free,* 366.

44. Wackerfuss, "Women's Army Auxiliary Corps."

45. Wackerfuss.

46. More than 7,000 Air WACs served overseas in every theater of operations, and three WACs received the Air Medal. Wackerfuss, "Women's Army Auxiliary Corps."

Chapter 2

Beginnings
1948–1953

The end of World War II marked the beginning of a new era for the United States. Somewhat suddenly left standing as a major world power, the nation could no longer shrink back into a defense policy based in noninvolvement or get by with only a small standing military that required wartime mobilization and a heavy reliance on maritime power. Though the Navy had long been America's first line of military defense, the creation and use of nuclear weapons "stripped the shield of time and space" from the illusion of national security.[1] This new world required the US to adopt a deterrence-based national security strategy, of which airpower was a key part. Meanwhile, a widening domestic consensus to challenge growing Soviet aggression enabled President Truman to restructure the nation's military force. Two years (1945–1947) of political battling ended with a compromise: the National Security Act of 1947. The act created a new national military establishment under a civilian secretary of national defense, a Joint Chiefs of Staff, and four separate, coequal services, one of these being the brand-new Air Force.

The path to a separate Air Force was not an easy or obvious one. While airpower was new and flashy, appealing to the nation's love of technology and a strong post–world war desire to avoid mass casualties, many believed it was best to keep it part of the Army. Crucial to the battle for a separate Air Force was the influence of Jacqueline Cochran.[2] Working closely with Hap Arnold, she employed her signature network of political connections, sales skills, and substantial personal financial resources to lobby for an independent Air Force. On 18 September 1947 that dream came to fruition. Seven months later, on 14 April 1948, the Air Force Reserve was created, and all reserve personnel and units previously attached to the Army Air Force reserve program were transferred to the Air Force Continental Air Command.[3] To quickly build a robust standing and reserve military force, Truman elected to reinstate the draft, requiring men 18–26 years old to serve 21 months on active duty and five years in the Reserve, effectively creating a "ready to serve," standing reserve force. This law, which was to remain in effect until June 1950, also allowed the president to mobilize reserve forces for 21 months without declaring a national emergency or war.

The Women's Armed Services Integration Act

While the postwar United States military scrambled to reorganize under mounting tension with the USSR, the glaring gap between current military capability and public deterrence rhetoric helped justify two culturally radical manpower reforms: Public Law (PL) 625 and Executive Order (EO) 9981. Not entirely altruistic or morally progressive, the need for sheer manpower, tinged with political expediency towards gaining the female and African-American vote, were enough to push the reforms through the system.[4] Of additional concern was the inevitable shortage of available manpower if a national emergency occurred within the next decade. Because of the low birth rate during the Great Depression in the 1930s, the number of young, healthy men projected to be available for military service during the 1950s and 1960s was small, especially when compared to the numbers available for World War II.[5]

The success of the WASPs during World War II helped promote the belief that women could play a valid support role in the military, and though the WAC faced termination after demobilization, the Army Air Force worked to prevent that from happening. By April 1946 the Air Staff had drawn up a plan for a women's contingent numbering around 2,600 in an independent Air Force. The Air Board approved the idea, and in October 1946, 250 regular billets were set aside for female officers. While the Air Force wanted women in both regular and reserve components, Congress was intent on authorizing only Reserve status. Gradually, with the help of Senator Margaret Chase Smith (R-Maine), a member of the Senate Armed Services Committee, Congressional attitudes shifted, and women were allocated regular billets as well.

On 12 June 1948, after a year of bitter congressional and public debate, President Harry Truman signed PL 625, known as the Women's Armed Services Integration Act. This act established, for the first time, a permanent place for women in the regular and reserve Army, Navy, Air Force, and Marine Corps as commissioned officers, warrant officers, and enlisted members.[6] One month later, EO 9981 established the equality of treatment and opportunity in the armed forces (based on race, not gender), paving the way for racial desegregation of all services, including the newly created Air Force.

The point of the Integration Act was to create a means for mobilizing "womanpower" in the event of sudden or large-scale war. As a carryover from most of World War II, the newest female service members were still largely thought of as an auxiliary force with the purpose of "freeing a man to fight." This mindset translated into numerous restrictions on female service members' careers that proved difficult to challenge legally and culturally within the coming decades. These restrictions included the following.[7]

- Women could constitute no more than 2 percent of regular force strength.[8]
- The number of female officers could total no more than 10 percent of the 2 percent.
- No more than 10 percent of female officers could hold the rank of lieutenant colonel (regular force). The grade of O-5 was the highest permanent rank a woman could obtain.[9]
- Promotion lists were separated by gender for each grade.[10]
- The minimum enlistment age was 18, with parental consent required for those under 21. (For men, the minimum enlistment age was 17 with parental consent required for those 18 and under.)
- Each service was limited to one female regular, line O-6/colonel, and only on a temporary basis. This rank was held by the "Women's Corps Director" of each service. She could retain the rank if she retired directly from the position, but if she wanted to continue serving, she was only allowed to do so as an O-5.
- Women were barred from serving aboard Navy vessels and from duty in combat aircraft engaged in combat missions.
- Women were denied spousal benefits for their husbands unless the men depended on their wives for over 50 percent of their support.
- Women were not allowed to serve if they had any dependents or children under 18 years of age, regardless of custody arrangements.[11] Female members could be married but required a waiver.[12]

- The service secretaries were authorized to terminate the regular commission or enlistment of any female member at any time, for any unspecified reason.[13]
- Each service secretary was authorized to specifically prescribe how much authority women might exercise and the kind of military duty to which they were assigned.
- Women were precluded from having any command authority over men.

Inherent in much of the Integration Act was the responsibility of each service to interpret and apply the rules concerning their female members as they saw fit. Because the military application of airpower was still a new concept, civilians were the most experienced aviators during World War II. As these civilian aviators joined and bolstered the Army Air Forces, their civilian nature carried over to the service's structure and general attitude towards women. In direct opposition to the traditional Army abhorrence of the idea of women in war, the AAF enthusiastically employed women during WWII; there were few jobs Air WACs were not allowed to do. The principal complaint was that they were not fully integrated into the AAF—a mistake the new Air Force was intent on fixing.

Fig. 5. Col Geraldine Pratt May, first director of Women in the Air Force, 1948

In an effort to break from the parent Army Air Corps mindset and establish its own traditions, the Air Force specifically avoided creating any separate corps within its service, to include a separate women's corps, even though this was done in all the other services.[14] Aiming to be as integrated as possible from the start, the Air Force maintained single promotion lists for all officers, a coed officer training school, and separate but similarly structured basic training.[15] As is often the case when applying social change to an institution, theory and intention did not always match practical application. Inherited Army traditions and service culture templates often proved difficult to break, and indeed women in the service were often referred to as the "WAF corps" or "Women's Air Force" when in reality no such separate women's corps or service existed. However, because the policies that governed male and female Airmen were different, "WAF" (standing for Women in the Air Force) soon became the accepted term when referring to female Air Force personnel, either collectively or individually.

Though the law did not require one, the Air Force chose to quickly establish a female director position. Geraldine Pratt May was selected as the first female Air Force colonel and director of the WAF on 16 June 1948; she served in that role until 1951.[16] According to Air Force Regulation 35-20, the director and her small staff were meant to function as a directorate under the deputy chief of staff of personnel.[17] Officially, May was responsible for advising the chief of staff and Air Staff on policies and plans regarding women in the Air Force as well as commanders in the field on the utilization, training, administration, and well-being of women in their units. However, by design the director had no authority over anyone or anything outside her small staff and in practice was relegated to the periphery of the chain of command for any decision making. She was hired to give advice, but no one was required to follow it, quickly making coordination with the WAF director simply a matter of courtesy.[18] Retired Air Force Maj Gen Jeanne Holm, WAF director, 1965–1972, noted in an interview that the director

> had no direct authority per se. We were advisors to the Chiefs of the services and their staffs and to the Secretaries. We were advisors to the Congress when they asked for our opinions. We had more imagined authority than real. In other words, people thought we had far more authority than we had because of our positions and our access to the power structure of our services. But in truth, we had to request changes. We had to convince the people in power of

changes that were needed. Sometimes it was difficult to impossible to influence the people in power to get things done.[19]

Using the generous power of interpretation written into the Integration Act, the Air Force elected to enforce additional restrictions upon the WAF. One of the first moves was to restrict women from any military flying, not just combat associated duty as was stated in the Integration Act. This meant that despite their recent training, military qualification, and performance as WAFS, WFTD, and WASPs, women were not allowed to be pilots. All previously qualified pilots, such as Jacqueline Cochran, were diverted to the Air Force Reserve or put into federal civilian status if they wanted to fly.

Recruiting

The two years between the Integration Act of June 1948 and the start of the Korean War in June 1950 proved critical to the development of the WAF. While all the other services retained female World War II veterans, the women who chose to switch to the Air Force had to not only help stand up their new service but also develop methods of operation, administration, and logistics, such as recruiting, training, uniforms, housing, supervision, and so forth, associated with employing women. While the services initially templated their women's programs off the British military's women's programs, each service soon adjusted its own program according to needs and social customs.[20]

As female enlistments began stalling toward the end of World War II, the AAF Corps' schools and training centers also started closing down. Women who were still serving in the Army as WACs were left to their own devices but allowed to continue working if they wished while the battle over women in the military raged in Congress. Most WACs did not believe the bill would pass and elected to accept a discharge and return to civilian life. With the enactment of PL 625, Air WACs still on active duty were given to option to go back to the Army (WAC), transfer to the new USAF, or revert to civilian status. Of those Air WACs, 168 line officers and 1,433 enlisted women had signed on with the new Air Force, far below the 300 officers, 40 warrant officers, and 4,000 enlisted women permitted by law.[21] For the first few years of its existence, almost all WAF personnel were former WACs or WASPs who had served during WWII.

Another factor to contend with when standing up the Air Force was the recently passed executive order mandating desegregation in the services. Prior to 1948, African-American men had traditionally been assigned to segregated "Negro" combat and noncombat units commanded by White officers. During WWII the Army set a goal of 10 percent African-American men and then carried that rule over the WAAC after it was established in 1942.[22] The WAAC/WAC was the only service to accept African-American women for most of the war and remained entirely segregated until the executive order in 1948. Discrimination and segregation policies created many difficulties in terms of effectively recruiting, assigning, and employing African-American women throughout the war; however, approximately 1,100 African-American women served as WAAC/WACs during WWII (approximately 3,000 women shy of the 10 percent goal).[23] After Truman issued the executive order in 1948, the Air Force decided to integrate immediately over the objections of many commanders who were adamantly opposed to the idea. Of course, an official policy mandating racial integration did not solve the problem of institutionalized racism and systemic discrimination. However, as of 1948 discrimination based on race was no longer tolerated while discrimination based on sex was still alive and well. This placed female African-American Airmen and their service in a precarious situation. Against most odds, by 1949 the Air Force had 17 women serving as the first female African-American Airmen.[24]

The WAF officially began recruiting on 1 September 1948 and planned to accept approximately 100 enlistments every month until it reached authorized end strength.[25] Because the purpose of the female force was to provide a group of ready-to-serve women in the face of war, most active duty WAF officers were given regular commissions.[26] In 1948 the first call out for WAF officers was opened to any woman who had held a commission in any service during WWII. However, only 409 applied, an early indication that recruiting women in a postwar era might prove more difficult than imagined.

In August 1948, Capt Marjorie O. Hunt, WAF staff director for Headquarters, Air Defense Command, which then supervised the Air Reserve Forces, issued a revised training plan based on work begun in January 1947 for the training of women in the Air Force Reserve. Any WAC officer currently on active duty, those who had served with the AAF, former WAC officers who had served at any time in the top three grades, and civilians with particular specialties needed by the Air Force were all encouraged to commission in the WAF Reserve. A WAF reservist could be assigned to any vacancy in an organized unit for which she was qualified and where a mobilization assignee position was available.[27] The initial WAF training plan welcomed all former WAC enlisted women and offered a variety of paths for a reserve commission in the WAF program.

A few months later, in January 1949, Cochran, now a WAF reservist herself, wrote to all former WASPs encouraging them to take advantage of the Air Force Reserve offer for second lieutenant commissions. Cochran stressed that it was "very important for each of you to avail yourself of the privilege of being in the Reserve and there is always a hope that at a later date you may be put on a flying status. If there is a war, and we are still of a proper age, I am reasonably certain that we would be assured of flying status."[28] Using names and addresses supplied by Cochran, WAF director Colonel May also sent 700 letters to former WASPs encouraging them to commission in the WAF Reserve. By June, six WASPs joined the Reserve, with 84 cases pending. The June 1950 WASP newsletter discussed the opportunity to join the Air Force Reserve as an officer, explaining that reservists served 15 days on active duty plus a maximum of 48 training periods with pay status. However, on the question of entitlement to flying time, the answer always came back from the military: "NO! Ex-Wasps with Reserve commissions may fly only as passengers in military aircraft."[29] Additionally, while Air Force representatives urged WAF reservists to apply for active duty (regular billets), Mary "Sandy" Saunders Wilson reported that when she applied, "they were full-up and therefore could take only those with a college degree and legal training." Nonetheless, 150 WASPs signed on for nonflying duty in the new service with 26 receiving reserve commissions by 1950.[30]

Though the Integration Act allowed for approximately 7,000 WAFs, with 400 officers, the Air Force chose to implement an interim ceiling of 4,300 women with 300 officers, until June 1950. These conditions were likely put into place as a way to gauge the full impact of having women in the service. By June 1950, the regular WAF had only grown to 303 female officers and 3,782 enlisted women, short of even the interim ceiling goals.[31] The WAF Reserve stood at 1,127 women with 491 officers and 636 enlisted personnel, comprising approximately 1.6 percent of the total positions in the organized air reserve.[32]

Fig. 6. The first Air Force uniforms, early 1950s

The Cochran Affair

As the initial two-year WAF integration phase ended in June 1950, the future looked promising for the fledgling force. Thirty-six squadrons were already in the field, and there was talk of significantly enlarging the women's program.[33] However, displeased with lower-than-expected and -authorized WAF numbers, Chief of Staff Gen Hoyt Vandenberg skipped Colonel May and went straight to an outside source for counsel: Cochran.[34] On 25 October 1950 General Vandenberg wrote a letter to Cochran thanking her for accepting an assignment as a "special consult" to him on issues pertaining to Air Force Women.[35] Being a tough and outspoken woman, famous pilot, and WAF reservist with many powerful connections in Washington, Cochran gladly accepted the invitation to involve herself heavily in the WAF program. She was a known player around the new Air Force and a personal friend of most of its top officials, including Secretary of the Air Force Stuart Symington. Despite her failed efforts to get the WASPs commissions in the regular Air Force as pilots, she was accepted to have some credibility on women's matters.[36]

Despite the inadvertent yet obvious offense aimed at May, Cochran's primary target was the Air Staff. On 6 December 1950 Cochran submitted a formal, 10-page report to Vandenberg criticizing many aspects of the WAF program, focusing primarily on the contention that WAF recruits were not the caliber of women the Air Force needed to be an elite force.[37]

> Just as the Air Force as a whole should use every proper means to keep its male personnel, both in the flying and the ground branches of service, . . . it should do so with its WAFs. The Air Force, indeed, should be doubly attentive in respect to the quality of the WAFs because they will set a standard of public appraisal of the Air Force far out of proportion to their numbers in the whole of the personnel. The WAFs should be equal to the best among women's services. It should be the aim to make them the best. They are not so now.[38]

Cochran charged that about one-third of all enlisted WAF were not fit for the image the Air Force was trying to establish and that the recruiting service was attempting to fill quotas by bringing in "misfits."[39] Cochran believed the solution lay in the Air Force creating and training its own recruiters, eliminating quotas, and changing physical standards for women, both in terms of grooming and medical requirements. She criticized the overall lack of WAF supervision and how the WAF director position was buried within the Air Staff. Cochran proposed a permanent special assistant to the Chief of Staff or Secretary of the Air Force head the WAF program, presumably to be filled by Cochran herself, since she understood the WAF director position to be merely symbolic. Regardless of Cochran's intentions, it became clear to Air Force leadership, specifically General Vandenberg, the program needed to be strengthened and treated more as a separate personnel component to succeed.[40]

In response, Air Force Headquarters set up a committee of six officers—four male colonels and two WAF lieutenant colonels—to study and reply to Cochran's report. Despite the committee's complete discount of the claims, Vandenberg sent a message out to all Air Force commanders stating that the appearance of some women was "not up to the required standards of the USAF."[41] After Cochran's report was leaked to the press, columnist Drew Pearson commented that General Vandenberg believes the WAF could go for taller women who are more feminine and stick to secretarial work "instead of trying to be mechanics, truck drivers and grease monkeys," as they did in World War II.[42]

The Korean War, 1950–1953

When North Korean communist troops marched across the 38th parallel into the Republic of Korea (ROK), a US ally, on 25 June 1950, the brand-new Air Force and Air Force Reserve were unexpectedly put to the test.[43] Soon after, the Department of Defense announced its plans to double the size of the armed forces, with the goal of 3 million men in uniform. At the time there were 22,000 women in uniform (across all services) with a third of them in the health professions. The remaining 15,000 in the line comprised less than 1 percent of total force and legally allowed strength.[44] Over the course of the war the number of women in uniform more than doubled, and by 1953 approximately 12,800 WAF officers and enlisted women were serving worldwide.[45]

In September 1950, three months after the war started, the first WAF squadron of 48 women arrived in Tokyo and took over jobs such as control tower operators, cryptographic operators, and finance clerks. As the war progressed, WAFs were assigned to numerous support bases in Japan, on Okinawa and Iwo Jima, and in the Philippines as air traffic controllers, radar operators, weather observers, and photo interpreters directly supporting the war. Despite numerous requisitions for women, the Air Force did not send any to the combat zone, with the exception of nurses. In 1952, Air Force and Army commanders in Korea cosigned a memo to the DOD requesting units of servicewomen. This request was denied, citing poor recruitment and low personnel numbers.[46]

Most Air Force nurses also served stateside, though some were assigned to Japan and a few others flew as flight nurses in the Korean theater during the conflict. At the start of the war the Air Force Nurse Corps was 1,088 strong with 83 of those women already in theater.[47] Some flew as many as three evacuation missions per day during emergencies, and in an attempt to lighten their load the Air Force eventually assigned general nurses to aid evacuation flights. The Military Air Transport Service (MATS) was responsible for evacuating sick and wounded soldiers from Japan back to the United States.[48] In total, the WAF had three casualties during the Korean War, all of whom were nurses killed in plane crashes while on duty.[49]

As was the case in World War II, most American military women, including WAFs, were assigned stateside "freeing a man to fight." US planners assumed Europe, in its postwar fragility, would be the place where communism would take hold and so believed it was necessary to reinforce troops there, including a limited number of female troops in support roles. As of 1950, more than 100 women were serving in NATO, with 13 of them WAFs.[50] By 1953, approximately 200 WAFs were serving overseas, mainly in Germany and Newfoundland. However, assignments commensurate with rank and experience were rare. WAFs were assigned to more than 20 Air Force bases around the country, with more than half doing technical work. During the war, the Air Force was forced to slowly increase the number of women assigned to the USAF Headquarters at the Pentagon, replacing men as they were sent to combat.

DOD Women's Recruiting Campaign

By August 1950, both officer and enlisted reserve women of all services were caught up in their first military recall on both a voluntary and involuntary basis.[51] Each service quickly discovered the rules regarding a woman's eligibility to serve during peacetime now prevented them from doing so in wartime. A large number of women in the WAF Reserve were World War II veterans who now exceeded the age limit or had gotten married and/or had children since joining. Unmarried female reservists were suddenly in high demand, making it easier for a male reservist to get a deferment from service in Korea than an eligible female reservist.

Initially, each service took responsibility for recruiting more women, and there was little sense of urgency or concern when numbers failed to increase as quickly as expected. According to a July 1950 *Washington Post* article, the Korean crisis had found 22,000 American servicewomen (7,000 of them nurses) already back in uniform, backed up by an estimated 25,000 in the Reserve.[52] The article claimed that "if a woman can fit into a specialist grade the services says she's as welcome as a man."[53] In keeping with the Integration Act, no WAFs were assigned to flight duty because "flying [was] a job better left to men."[54] Initial monthly recruiting ceilings for Air Force enlisted women were raised from 175 per month to 350 per month and in the fall to 500 per month. However, by the end of the year the Air Force was facing major supply issues and, unable to adequately house or outfit all its female recruits, backed off to 250 per month. In December 1950, the Air Force took no new enlisted women because it was out of uniforms.[55]

Optimistically watching the women's programs steadily grow during the first year of the war, Assistant Secretary of Defense Anna Rosenberg projected the military forces could recruit and use even more women. While Congress approved her request to remove the 2 percent ceiling, by mid-1951, it was apparent individual service recruiting was not as productive as hoped. Rosenberg strongly suggested a committee be created to help focus the effort. In response, Secretary of Defense George Marshall created the Defense Department Advisory Committee on Women in the Services (DACOWITS) in August 1951 to "give advice and guidance on policies relating to women in the service."[56] The DOD appointed 44 civilian women, including the four former wartime women's directors in addition to well-known female doctors, philanthropists, scholars, and politicians to fill the committee. DACOWITS met for the first time 18 September 1951 with the mission to "help develop policies and standards for military women in areas such as recruiting, utilization of women, expanded career opportunities, housing, education, and recreation."[57] The first committee was assigned four focus areas and required to report their findings to Rosenberg:[58]

- How to inform the public of recruiting needs.
- How to reassure parents of young women who wish to serve.
- How to convey career opportunities to young women.
- How to raise the prestige of military women in the mind of the public.

As public resistance to the draft began to increase, the Department of Defense decided to launch a nationwide military women's component recruiting campaign in November 1951 to help offset calls for men. The Air Force subsequently planned the largest increase of all the services, aiming to grow its female force to 10 percent of the total projected force, with an end goal of 4,000 officers and 44,000 enlisted women by July 1952.[59] Typical press coverage during the first year of the recruiting campaign featured Air Force women who held especially exciting or glamorous jobs. The most popular of these was the MATS flight attendant position—a coveted job available only to women in the enlisted force.[60] The 543rd Band (WAF) was another highly visible recruiting aid, as were women's patriotism slogans, such as "American's Finest Women Stand Beside Her Finest Men."[61]

In the spring of 1951, former World War II WAVES member Col Mary J. Shelly replaced Colonel May as WAF director. Having had to be convinced to take the job, Shelly quickly realized her new position was a tenuous one. She found the WAF in complete disarray, filled with low-quality recruits and declining morale. By 1952 Shelly reported to the chief of staff and secretary of the Air Force that the end strength would likely level off around 12,000 instead of the projected 48,000 recruiting goal. By the time DACOWITS held its second meeting in 1952, it was clear the DOD women's recruiting campaign was not working. However, the campaign continued until multiple women's directors, upset at the low quality of women who were being admitted in order to hit quotas, demanded a halt to the program in 1953.

Ultimately, the campaign was a complete failure in two ways. The first was that the Air Force was unable to recruit anywhere near the number of women needed or desired. This was due to four reasons: unrealistic goals, high recruiting standards, social values of the time, and the overall national mood towards the Korean War.

Unrealistic Goals

While all services were working through their own growing pains related to integrating and utilizing women, the WAF had to work through its process within the parallel context of a brand-new service also undergoing its own growth—and during a period of war no less. Following the success of recruiting Air WACs in World War II, Air Force leadership believed recruiting women to their new, elite military service would be simple. The Air Force projected the highest female recruiting goals of any service, making it nearly impossible to reach desired end strength and ultimately setting itself up for failure. Overburdened recruiters resorted to falsifying test scores and records in an attempt to increase their numbers, which seriously undermined the quality of recruits and ultimately negated any increase in numbers. Because recruitment numbers were so far below projected goals, the fledging WAF was put under a microscope at a critical time when it was still struggling to establish itself and gain credibility.

Recruiting Standards

Women were required to meet higher educational and health standards than men and were also subject to additional, special processing to include background investigations and psychiatric examinations.[62] As was the case with male Airmen, women who were educated or skilled often found better paying civilian jobs than the military offered. Many who did join found little job satisfaction or few opportunities for advancement. In an attempt to mitigate the influx of low-quality recruits, Shelly insisted enlisted criteria be raised even higher, which effectively improved quality but also reduced already low intake numbers. The focus on quality of WAF recruits would continue into the 1960s, revived by the "why WAF?" debate.

Social Values

Despite efforts to glamorize service, most young women who were interested in the WAF largely viewed military service the same way they would a civilian job: a temporary stop along the road to marriage and motherhood. At first, most WAFs were veterans of World War II and therefore older, likely single, and a low attrition threat. However, new Korean War recruits were young and of marriage age. A temporary ban was placed on the option to separate upon marriage in 1950,[63] but when lifted a year later as a recruiting incentive, WAF attrition rates skyrocketed, hitting 24 percent per year in 1952.[64] In keeping with American culture during the 1950s, there was little the Air Force could or would even want to do about WAF members getting married and having children. It was largely assumed and accepted that marriage and motherhood were simply incompatible with military service.

National Mood

Another important factor was the underestimated difference in national mood surrounding World War II and Korea. Americans were largely war weary and resented another reason to take women out of the home. By the time the recruiting campaign was in full force in 1952, public attitude towards the war had turned sour and the services could not compete with the civilian labor market. Low birth rates during the Depression years were becoming evident as there were fewer young women than there had been a decade prior in

World War II, and shifting cultural values towards female responsibility within the nuclear family created a palpable barrier to those few women who might have been otherwise interested in military service.[65] Lingering rumors from war-era smear campaigns concerning servicewomen's morals, or lack thereof, also prevented an unknown number of women from enlisting. American men in general resisted the idea of women in uniform, fearing military life made their wives, girlfriends, sisters, or daughters less feminine and more prone to immorality.[66] Likewise, female veterans of WWII had mostly returned to civilian life and found their service was not universally appreciated. Many programs or offices meant to assist returning veterans were unaware or unwilling to help servicewomen who were entitled to the same benefits as men.

The second failure of the recruiting campaign, and more important in terms of long-term impact, was the damage done to the credibility of the Integration Act. The spirit of the act—that women could and would play a significant role as supplemental manpower in a time of war—was put under the spotlight. Both the Korean War and the failed recruiting campaigns reinforced the fact that women in the military were volunteers and that without a significant improvement in opportunity, training, employment, and motivation, the women's services were doomed to be a small, token force if they managed to exist at all. As the primary beneficiary of Eisenhower's "New Look" defense strategy, the Air Force had no problem recruiting all the high-quality men it needed, which even further disqualified the argument that women would be needed to backfill men if necessary. Bureaucratic inertia, rather than any sort of conviction that women were capable of and necessary to national defense, is likely the only reason the military women's programs survived this decade.[67]

Notes

1. Millett, *For the Common Defense*, 440.

2. As a prominent lobbyist for the Air Force, Cochran was recommended for promotion to the rank of colonel in spite of DOD regulations limiting women officers to only one colonel per service. The legislative liaison officer who recommended her cited her close association with certain key personnel on Capitol Hill. Rich, *Pilot in the Fast Lane*, 205.

3. The foundation of the Air Force Reserve originated with the Preparedness Movement and National Defense Act of 1916, which authorized an or-

ganized reserve corps for each service. In July 1946, the War Department established the Army Air Force (AAF) Reserve program as part of the Army Air Corps, at the time an acknowledged flying club with the almost sole purpose of allowing Reserve pilots to fly. According to Air Force Reserve historian George Cantwell, the Army Air Forces was never entirely sure how to structure or use their Reserve forces and so developed an umbrella program to cover all air reservists. Air Force Reserve Command, "History."

4. Millett, *For the Common Defense*, 451.

5. Witt, "*A Defense Weapon*," 62.

6. Nurses already had become permanent fixtures of the Army with the creation of the Army Nurse Corps in 1901. Holm, *Women in the Military*, 9.

7. "Women's Armed Services Integration Act."

8. While no limitation was specifically placed on women in the Reserve, due to the statutory limitation on Regular WAF, the 2 percent figure was also made applicable to the organized air reserve. Holm, *Women in the Military*, 133.

9. However, women were allowed to serve in the ranks of major and lieutenant colonel two to three years longer than male officers before mandatory retirement.

10. The Air Force chose to integrate officer promotion lists.

11. Women serving in World War II could have dependents. WAC Director Oveta Hobby had two children herself. This new policy would force the discharge of selected women who had served continuously since World War II with dependents but now were not allowed to continue doing so. *Los Angeles Times*, "Women of the Air Force Reserve."

12. This policy was put in place and rescinded multiple times throughout the 1950s and 1960s and often only applied to enlisted women.

13. The primary purpose of this provision was to terminate service of women who were pregnant (or chose to adopt), an idea that became law with EO 10240 in April 1951. Holm, *Women in the Military*, 124–25.

14. Being a brand-new service, the Air Force was able to create new systems with regard to managing women, instead of trying to fit them into old traditions and personnel structures. One such example was the Air Force decision to establish career fields rather than corps as the best way to manage skills needed in modern military service (with the exception of medical, chaplain, and judge advocates). Holm, *Women in the Military*, 122–23.

15. The Air Force was the only service where men and women were actually integrated and competed with one another for promotion to grades they were authorized to hold. The other services maintained gender-segregated promotion lists in which women competed with one another for the available promotion vacancies, not with the men. Holm, *Women in the Military*, 123.

16. *Washington Post*, "Colonel May Heads Women of Air Forces." May started her service when she was accepted into the first Women's Army Air Corps (WAAC) office training class (1942) and served as a Women's Army Corps (WAC) staff director in the Air Transport Command, 1942–46, commanding 6,000 enlisted women and officers. May had decided to separate and was on terminal leave when she received a phone call from WAC director Mary Hallaren informing her the WAF wanted her in their service. Soon thereafter, never having been asked to apply or interview, May was selected as the first WAF director and promoted to full colonel.

17. Air Force Regulation 35-20, "Administration of Women in the Air Force."

18. Holm, *Women in the Military*, 132.

19. Holm, interview. The Chief of the Nurse Corps was different. She was chief of the nursing function of the Air Force and had direct control over the nursing functions of the Air Force.

20. According to Holm, all of the US military women's programs stayed in close touch with their British counterparts, both officially and informally. An officer exchange program ran for years between the Women's Royal Air Force (WRAF) and WAF in which a WRAF officer served in the WAF directorate for a full tour of duty and vice versa. Holm, interview.

21. Holm, *Women in the Military*, 133.

22. Holm, 77–79.

23. Holm.

24. *Chicago Defender*, "Sister Airmen Training in Texas." Though units were desegregated, quarters and mess integration would take longer to fully implement. The first three African-American female Air Force officers were commissioned in 1951. Ibid.

25. *Washington Post*, "Colonel May Heads Women of Air Forces."

26. When the Air Force was established, there were three types of commissions for officers: temporary, Reserve, and regular. Most officers were commissioned in Reserve billets and were essentially in a probationary status until they reached 12 years of service. Reserve commissioned officers could still serve on active duty full-time, side by side with regular officers, but if reductions in force came around, those in Reserve billets were typically the first to be involuntarily forced out of the service. At the 12 years of service mark, Reserve officers were screened for selection in a regular billet. If they were selected, they were able to continue serving and be eligible for promotion to major, and if they were not selected they were released. Mitchell, *Air Force Officers*, 319.

27. Cantwell, *Citizen Airmen*, 83.

28. Holm, *Women in the Military*, 140.

29. *Washington Post*, "Women Are as Welcome as Men."

30. Carl, *A WASP among Eagles*, 111.

31. Witt, *A Defense Weapon*, 102. Of the 303 female officers, 211 held regular billets, almost all of whom were former WAAC/WAC.

32. McConnell, memorandum.

33. Witt, *A Defense Weapon*, 49.

34. Holm, *Women in the Military*, 140.

35. Vandenberg, memorandum.

36. Holm, *Women in the Military*, 141.

37. Witt, *A Defense Weapon*, 49.

38. Vandenberg, memorandum.

39. Vandenberg.

40. Witt, *A Defense Weapon*, 49.

41. Witt.

42. Witt.

43. From 1948 to 1949 the US had withdrawn troops from Korea as the Joint Chiefs of Staff determined the country had no strategic value. After the invasion, President Truman believed the US needed to take a firm stand in order to lessen the chances of Soviet communist expansion in Europe. Thought of as a "preventative and limited war," the US still needed to build up its military forces to cope with the immediate crisis while preparing for what at the time seemed to be an increasingly possible World War III. Millett, *For the Common Defense*, 453.

44. Holm, *Women in the Military*, 149.

45. Lockwood, "Women's Legacy Parallels Air Force History."

46. Witt, *A Defense Weapon*, 221. It is interesting to note that while the Air Force was very hesitant to send servicewomen (other than nurses) to Korea, civilian women, such as Red Cross and United Service Organizations (USO) volunteers, were in and out of Korea the entire war. Ibid.

47. Witt, *A Defense Weapon*, 181.

48. The MATS was a unified joint command that fell under the Air Force and eventually became what is now the Air Mobility Command. During the Korean War, individual WAFs were assigned to the MATS mission. The evacuation route started in Tokyo or Haneda to Guam, to Kwajalein (an atoll in the Marshall Islands), to Johnston Island, to Hickam Field (Hawaii), and ended at Travis AFB, California. Witt, *A Defense Weapon*, 181.

49. The Women's Memorial, "Highlights in the History of Military Women."

50. Witt, *A Defense Weapon*, 155.

51. The same recall procedures applied to both men and women in which 10 days' notice was given by telegram. The first year of the war required drafting 585,000 men and calling 806,000 reservists and guardsmen back to duty. Between July 1950 and June 1953, the Air Force mobilized nearly 147,000 Air Force reservists to active service for periods from one to three years. *Washington Post*, "Officer Grades Offered Women in Air Force."

52. "Officer Grades Offered."

53. *Washington Post*, "Women Are as Welcome as Men."

54. *Washington Post*, "Women's Services Calling 80,000."

55. Witt, *A Defense Weapon*, 102.

56. Throughout the history of women in military service, DACOWITS has been critical to pushing for further integration and equality of women in the military, often proposing measures years, if not decades, before their passage. Women in all services owe much to the committee.

57. Holm, *Women in the Military*, 151.

58. Holm, 141.

59. Witt, *A Defense Weapon*, 73; and Holm, *Women in the Military*, 152. The total force WAF numbered around 8,200 at that time.

60. Witt, *A Defense Weapon*, 74.

61. Holm, *Women in the Military*, 152. Over its 10-year lifespan, from 1951 to 1961, the 543rd Air Force Band (WAF) was served by 235 women musicians, with approximately 50 members at any one time. The women performed in countless parades and ceremonies throughout the country and at the time was one of the few places women could perform as professional musicians. Lockwood, "Women Play Huge Role."

62. Witt, *A Defense Weapon*, 110.

63. Holm, *Women in the Military*, 156.

64. Witt, *A Defense Weapon*, 111.

65. Holm, *Women in the Military*, 154.

66. This resistance was often likely a case of "mirror-imaging," as men who might have otherwise not had their own morals corrupted, succumbed to temptation during their own service.

67. Holm, 158.

Chapter 3

Survival
The 1950s and 1960s

The same issues that plagued the Korean War recruiting campaign would continue to affect recruitment and retention of women in the Air Force through the two next decades. What was proving to be a small, token force operating in a relatively peaceful Cold War military structure resulted in a barely surviving WAF with all-time low personnel numbers and opportunities. Because there was no immediate "crisis" to contend with, career options for women continued to shrink as more emphasis was placed upon their feminine responsibilities and roles.[1] All the services slowly shifted women into jobs they could do 'as well as or better than men' (meaning administration and nursing), ultimately duplicating their potential civilian status and employment. As the 1950s and 1960s progressed, Air Force women found themselves increasingly isolated and segregated from the rest of the force.

Acceptance vs. Equality

Service policies during the 1950s reflected the larger cultural stereotypical thinking regarding proper gender roles in the workplace and society. For women, they also reflected the goals of women's military leadership: to survive and be accepted in (not equal) to the male dominated world of the military.[2] While each successive WAF director continued to push for expanding the use of and opportunities for women, the unspoken rule was to avoid rocking the boat. According to Holm, the early women directors seldom questioned their secondary status in the military, both because they recognized women in the military received a better break than many other male dominated professions and because the general consensus was that women were not put into combat, thus their needs and desires were less important than those of men.[3] Higher female enlistment and officer accession standards were officially justified because relatively few women were required, or allowed, into the service. The argument was that higher quality women resulted in fewer personnel problems, and that since women were performing skilled labor it made sense they had higher education standards.[4] Unfortunately, in many cases women were assigned to jobs where they were overqualified, resulting in boredom, low job satisfaction and morale—none of which helped retention numbers. The female service directors pushed to uphold the higher standards, worried about repeating the Korean War–era recruiting mistake of having a small *and* unqualified force. As every service continually failed to meet their recruiting goals for women, the female standards only seemed to become more stringent.

Feminine Appearance

As the 1950s WAF lurched from one crisis to the next, numbers, opportunities, and morale continued to decline. DACOWITS brainstormed ways to make military service more appealing to women, and, in keeping with current American values, all the services began to focus more on the physical appearance of the women already in service. Salad bars started showing up in mess halls while WAF newsletters provided guidance on food selection and uniform wear. The DOD started working with cosmetic manufacturers to create and recommend specific shades and types of cosmetics for service women. In its second annual meeting, DACOWITS's final report included a recommendation for a six-week training and indoctrination class on the role of women in the military and why they serve for both service women recruiters and male recruits.[5] A course in personality development, added to officer professional development curriculum in 1956, focused on social and official relationships, feminine conduct in general, selection and wear of military and civilian clothing, proper grooming, and related topics.[6]

In a decade of relative peace, cultivating the most attractive—rather than most useful—women's force became the highest priority. The booming prosperity of postwar 1950s America created a nationwide feeling of stability, optimism, and cultural consensus. Between 1945 and 1960, the gross national product more than doubled, growing from $200 billion to more than $500 billion, kicking off "the Golden Age of American Capitalism."[7] Government spending skyrocketed in part due to the distribution of veteran's benefits. The GI bill subsidized low-cost mortgages, encouraging the growth of suburbs and the accompanying baby boom. Military spending was also high, creating a well-stocked and well-staffed force with the time and resources available to spend on personnel issues. The Air Force alone consistently numbered over 900,000 personnel throughout the entire decade, with only about 10,000 of those being women.[8]

With such small numbers, the women's programs across all services during the 1950s were still seen as auxiliary rather than a serious personnel resource. Women were also viewed as "pawns in the continuing game of interservice one-upmanship."[9] In 1966 physical appearance became a key criterion in the officer and position selection process when the Air Force Chief of Staff told the Recruiting Service commander to "get a better looking WAF."[10] Each applicant was required to pose for and submit four profile photographs for final selection and approval by the Recruiting Service commander. All the services were in the practice of handpicking the most attractive women to work as receptionists, protocol officers, or secretaries. Preferential treatment was certainly given to attractive WAF personnel, with weight or appearance issues sometimes barring women from certain leadership positions.[11] In the freely distributed *Handbook for Air Force Women*, produced by the Air Training Command in 1957, cheerful vignettes illustrated how cooperation, tears and laughter, compassion, and stamina made a girl into a WAF. Female readers were reminded that a proper WAF "keeps her humor up, her gripes down."[12] Thirty-eight of the 87 pages in the handbook were dedicated exclusively to grooming and appearance tips, with articles such as "Operation Hair-Do," makeup application for daytime and evening, civilian fashion advice, and the "A B C Ds of keeping beautiful skin," overpowering the few articles concerning Air Force education opportunities and policies regarding marriage.[13]

Military pinups, sometimes featuring willing WAFs, were a tradition that continued into the early 1970s. WAFs even had the chance to compete for titles such as "Miss Lackland Air Force Base," "Miss Air Power," or "Miss Ground Safety," and while still running, Air Force Officer Candidate School (OCS) had a graduation dance in which one WAF was chosen "Queen."[14] By regulation, women were prohibited from serving in the honor guard because they were forbidden to bear arms and their presence was believed to lessen the honor and solemnity of the occasion.[15] Instead, a separate female "color escort" accompanied the honor guard and, keeping with the rules, did not bear arms.[16]

Fig. 7. Excerpt from 1957 WAF handbook offering makeup application routines for both day and nighttime. Caption for left-side photo reads: "Lucky girl. Your make-up problem is the simplest on earth since your costume color is not only invariable but so becoming it's like a cosmetic itself. Most effective if you play up the light, aerial shimmer." Caption for right-side photo reads: "Objective—glamour. This is the time for make-up to make your eyes look bigger, your skin fairer, your smile sparklier—and for some complete illusions." Reprinted from USAF Air Training Command Manual 35-2, *A Handbook for Air Force Women*, 1957.

According to WAF director Col Emma Riley, "one of the biggest problems was the constant crying about the fat WAF." She explains that although there was an all-around problem of overweight Airmen, the WAF stood out because they were easy to pick on.[17] A July 1959 IG inspection found an "alarming trend towards obesity" among WAF personnel. As a result, Lackland Military Training Center revised the WAF basic course including greater emphasis on diet and maintenance of proper weight.[18] Fitness was viewed as a way to keep the women fit and trim rather than to prepare them for any physical labor. Most WAF team sports were eliminated in 1957 (swimming, golf, and bowling were encouraged as the more socially acceptable options), accompanied by a force-wide recommendation that WAF supervisors take more responsibility for the physical appearance of their enlisted women.[19] Another significant portion of the WAF handbook dealt with maintaining proper weight, warning women that "the opportunity for excess weight lurks in every impulse for second helpings" and "the active WAF should eat 1,200 [fewer calories] than active airmen or she'll get fat! . . . Thank your lucky stars and stripes that the Air Force, with a kindly glance at the WAF, has authorized 60 salads a month!"[20]

Just as emphasized as physical appearance was the focus on a woman's "mental health"—or their propensity to be categorized as emotional, weak, sensitive, or worst case, hysterical. Before attending initial basic or officer training, women were required to take the Air Force Women's Selection Test (AFWST). This test determined aptitude for technical training as well as the recruit's mental health. Multiple years' worth of WAF director summaries, memorandums that reviewed the previous six months to one year of WAF-specific issues, kept an updated interest in developing a test for measuring personality traits. Ideally, "every person in the armed forces should be a well-adjusted individual: assured, but not egotistical, ambitious, but not irritatingly so, adaptable, likable, and dedicated to the service."[21] DACOWITS also sponsored a selection manual prepared by a psychiatrist in collaboration with women recruiters and civilian consultants as a way to best qualify female recruits.[22]

Officer Accessions, Training, and Utilization: 1948–1969

Unlike the other services, the Air Force chose to fully integrate women into its officer corps from the start. Seven months after the Integration Act was signed, the Air Force enrolled 19 women in the first gender-integrated OCS class; 16 of them went on to commission in July 1949. Women were required to meet the same academic requirements as men and received the same instruction, with the exception of physical training and field exercises.[23] Though it was expected OCS would produce 60 female graduates each year, the first two years produced 34 and 39 respectively. When the women's recruiting campaign kicked off in 1950, the Air Force tentatively upped the quota for its two annual OCS classes from 25 women each to four classes per year allowing 15 women in each, netting 10 more female officers. By mid-1951 the number had jumped to 40 women per class, creating 160 officers that year (a 400 percent increase).[24] Another officer procurement option available, though rarely used, was for a WAF reservist to volunteer for recall to active duty.[25]

To meet female officer recruiting goals, the Air Force began fast-tracking WAF commissions through direct appointment, a process in which qualified women (i.e., a college graduate who fit all other requirements—age, mental and physical health, no dependents, etc.) were appointed as second or first lieutenants in the Reserve then moved straight to active duty, bypassing the traditional congressional review. This method, also used in the Army and Navy, became the primary procurement source of WAF officers for the rest of the decade as accessions continued to decline. The direct appointment program kept the WAF officer corps afloat during the 1950s. Producing 250 new officers between fiscal years 1957 and 1960, it was also unfortunately the least helpful option for the Air Force. The women from this program were all civilians with little prior military exposure and once in the force often failed to demonstrate necessary leadership qualities. Despite its numerical success, the direct appointment option was phased out with the last class graduating in November 1959. As a means of replacement, the gender-integrated Officer Training School (OTS) program began that same month with the new requirement of a baccalaureate degree for entrance.[26] OCS was still considered a commissioning source until the program's end in 1964; however, with the creation of OTS it became a program only for enlisted women wishing to become officers, few of whom ever qualified for or even requested attendance.[27]

Persistently lower than expected and desired WAF officer recruiting numbers encouraged the Air Force to consider ROTC as a possible path to commissioning. The idea was that not only would a woman in college already be comfortable with a nontraditional life and career path, but she would also be college educated, making her an ideal candidate for an officer commission. Under WAF director Col Phyllis Gray, the Air Force ran a trial WAF ROTC program at 10 university Air Force Reserve Officer Training Corps (AFROTC) detachments starting the fall semester of 1956.[28] Considered a distinct entity from regular AFROTC, a regular WAF officer was assigned as assistant professor of air science to recruit, screen applicants, and supervise training. The female cadets were required to take advanced air science courses to complete the two-year program and upon graduation received a commission as a second lieutenant in the Air Force Reserve.[29] According to Riley, who took over the program from Gray, the program had little to offer women beyond a commission. The women were expected to complete the required courses for no credit and were not considered officially enrolled in AFROTC, nor did they receive scholarships, stipends, or other typical ROTC benefits and opportunities.[30]

Fig. 8. Members of the Officer's Training School at Lackland AFB, Texas, 1960

Only 54 women joined the program during the first semester, and when the DOD abruptly dropped its effort to amend legislation to allow women in ROTC in early 1957, it became apparent the program was to be short-lived.[31] Though Air University wanted to keep the program going, Air Staff support waned, and, unable to justify the expensive program any longer, Secretary of the Air Force James Douglas ordered WAF ROTC canceled immediately at colleges where no women were enrolled in the advanced air science classes.[32] The first attempted WAF ROTC program ended in June 1960 having produced only six officers.[33] The outgoing WAF report explained that Air

University believed better college selection would have yielded better results.[34] Air Force ROTC did not start accepting women again until 1969 when new legislation made their participation legal.

By late 1954, the regular WAF component was 67 percent below authorized strength, with 80 percent of WAF officers in field grades.[35] The number of WAF officers in the Reserve was more than double the number on active duty.[36] There were simply not enough regular company grade officers to effectively uphold the WAF program. Though one-third of all WAF Reserve officers were eligible for a commission in the regular component, there was low interest in doing so. Of the approximately 700 WAF officers (regular and Reserve), the bulk still chose to serve in personnel and administration fields.

A select few women officers (ranks unknown) stepped out of the status quo; as of 1957 there were 13 female judge advocate generals, eight in weather, 33 in intelligence, one on the Air Force Academy staff, and one on the Armed Forces Staff College staff.[37] In 1959, the selection criteria for Air War College changed to allow lieutenant colonels, thus opening the door for women to also attend.[38] However, anecdotal evidence illustrates that even though women were legally allowed to attend they were often denied so as to not "waste a good school quota on a woman."[39] Progress was still slowly made, and by 1962 there were nine WAF officers enrolled in Air Force Institute of Technology programs (in public relations, motion picture science, and meteorology programs).[40] Overall, the education level of WAF officers was higher than their male counterparts, with 75 percent of WAF officers having a baccalaureate degree or higher compared to 46 percent of all Air Force officers, including doctors, dentists, and chaplains.[41] While procurement remained low, so too did attrition, which is what saved the WAF officer corps from disappearing altogether. As opposed to the enlisted WAF corps, officers expressed great job satisfaction; however, very few showed an interest in regular commissions (and by implication a military career). By 1956 only 167 WAFs held regular billets.[42]

Until 1965, WAF officers were selected by different boards and against different selection quotas than men, but after 1965 they began competing for promotions against men. Promotion rates and the number of women selected for regular commission remained low in each situation. In 1969, Holm launched an investigation as to why WAF officers were being promoted at such a low rate. An examination of over 700 WAF officer efficiency reports—a primary tool used in promotions, special assignments, and determining regular status—found few remarks that were unfavorable. However, about 20 percent contained remarks such as "she is the picture of efficient femininity," or "she is a lady at all times," or "I would not hesitate to put her in any position to which a lady officer could be assigned." While innocent, these comments implicitly conveyed the idea that women needed special treatment, were weaker than men, and were hopelessly limited in their effectiveness. By 1970, gender-oriented remarks in efficient reports were forbidden.[43]

According to Air Force policy, WAF officers had equal promotion opportunity among men and women through the rank of major (O-4). Until 1967, no more than 10 percent of regular component women could hold the rank of lieutenant colonel (O-5), and only one woman could hold the temporary rank of colonel (O-6), given to the WAF director position. Once this woman finished her assignment she could either retire as a colonel or take another assignment and revert back to lieutenant colonel.[44] Many WAF officers filled positions which called for grades higher than they were permitted to hold, such as a female lieutenant colonel serving in a position that had always been held, and would resume being held after her tenure, by a male colonel. Once a WAF officer reached major, her opportunities for responsibility were limited to the small WAF hierarchy, since women traditionally did not supervise men. To complicate the issue, the Air Force initially established too many WAF squadrons. With only 40 to 50 women each, these squadrons were too small to be administered efficiently, especially considering that low officer recruiting numbers failed to provide appropriate leadership for them.[45] Many of the newest officers were assigned directly overseas, leaving higher-ranking, veteran officers stuck in squadron assignments unable to move on or progress in their career. When Colonel Shelly began consolidating squadrons in 1952 to free up some officers, it became apparent there were male officers who felt women should only be allowed to supervise other women. Major commands frequently resisted assigning senior major and lieutenant colonel females in the field, regardless of their qualifications. This attitude applied to female NCOs as well.[46] Together, these factors resulted in a growing rank bottleneck and career stagnation problem that forced experienced women out of service during what should have been their most productive years.[47]

Despite all of these personnel management challenges, the quality and existence of the WAF officer corps generally went unchallenged. The WAF enlisted corps was another story.

Enlisted Accessions, Training, and Utilization: 1948–1969

In 1947, planners for the Army and proposed Air Force decided the WAC and WAF would train together in a combined WAC/WAF basic training at Camp Lee, Virginia. However, soon after her appointment as WAF director, May convinced the Air Staff that the Air Force should train its own women. In 1949, WAF basic training was first moved to Kelly AFB, and then quickly re-established at nearby Lackland AFB in San Antonio, Texas. Though WAF basic trainees were incorporated into the men's training wing, they remained assigned to the separate 3741st WAF Training Squadron. While gender-integrated basic training had been considered initially, women were only required to complete 11 weeks compared to the men's 13, because they did not take the extra combat and small arms training required for men. Additionally, female recruits were generally better quality because of the higher education recruitment standards and so needed less time for academics.[48]

Fig. 9. Esther Blake McGowin, the first woman to enlist in the Air Force, 1948

Once the basic training process was established, the next question became how to supervise and administer enlisted women—a highly discussed and disagreed upon subject. Wherever enlisted women were stationed, the base commander was responsible for establishing and designating a WAF squadron, with only one allowed per base. Initially, enlisted women were administered similarly to Air WACs in World War II, in which women were assigned to Air WAC squadrons but performed duty in other units, while a female WAAC commander had complete authority and responsibility over the women's administration and management. However, as the force started operating, a majority of male Air Force staff and field commanders advocated for total integration of women into their units and the elimination of any WAF supervision by WAF officers.

May was opposed to this full integration, as were most enlisted women who had served in World War II (which was almost all of them at this point in the early WAF), who felt the need to identify with a WAF unit and female commander. A compromise was found in 1949 in which enlisted women were assigned to a duty organization, commanded by a male officer, and attached to a WAF squadron, commanded by a female officer. The WAF squadron commander was responsible for the off-duty administration, inspection, counseling, guidance, health, welfare, and discipline of her assigned WAF personnel.[49] She shared *Uniform Code of Military Justice* authority with the male commander; any punishment required coordination and approval by both male and female supervisors. Assigned (male) duty commanders were responsible for job performance, training, and promotion and required to evaluate female Airmen "on the same basis as male airmen."[50] Ultimately, this system of dual responsibility did not help women become more integrated into the Air Force or gainfully employed by their units.

Though male recruitment also stalled during the postwar 1950s, female enlisted recruitment proved more difficult than males' for various reasons. First, women were required to score higher on the Air Force Qualification Test (AFQT) and hold a high school diploma to be eligible for enlistment.[51] Most women who were qualified often elected to take one of the numerous civilian job opportunities available, particularly as there was a nationwide shortage of teachers and nurses—the preferred and acceptable female career choice. Perhaps most importantly, the social expectation and goal for most women at the time was to get married and raise a family as soon as possible.[52]

While many women participated in the workforce prior to marriage and children, the social expectation was that she would leave her job to attend to her home and family full time. This idealized standard was made possible by a booming postwar economy in which most families could live off one person's wages.[53]

Women who did choose to enlist in the WAF often did so to pursue higher education, to travel, and to take advantage of unique career opportunities.[54] However, choosing military service was still an incredibly unique choice for a woman during that time. Most young women either still did not know the military allowed women to enlist or were simply not interested. General public apathy or even disapproval toward women in uniform trumped most efforts to recruit more women into the force.

Utilization

Despite May's determination that enlisted women could and should be employed widely in the Air Force, in 1949 the Air Staff commissioned a study to determine how to best employ them. Four criteria were developed to test the appropriateness of a career field for women: physical demands, psychological and environmental appropriateness, career opportunities, and an opinion poll.[55] Of the 43 enlisted career fields, the Air Force determined only 13 were "fully suitable" for women and 14 "partially suitable."[56] Soon after, the Air Force closed 158 of its 349 enlisted specialties with no plan for how women would be trained and integrated into these "off-limits" fields during the inevitable crunch of wartime.

During the Korean War the number of enlisted WAF working in administration actually dropped to around 26 percent, while more than twice as many women began working in more technical fields. By 1953 almost 40 percent worked in weather observation and forecasting, air traffic control and warning, radio and radar maintenance, and statistics.[57] Unlike their WWII predecessors, WAF were not allowed to drive trucks, taxi aircraft, staff airborne radios, or repair engines. The Pentagon insisted women's work must be "psychologically, physiologically and sociologically suitable."[58]

As the war ended and the decade progressed, doors were shut and opportunities dwindled. Of the 34 total Airmen career fields available in 1956, 30 were authorized in part or in whole for enlisted women. Of those 30, WAFs were assigned to 28 (although in 16 of those 28 fields there were fewer than 100 women each). Two-thirds of WAF strength was still concentrated in administration, personnel, supply, communications, and medical fields.[59]

When Maj Gen Curtis LeMay took over Strategic Air Command (SAC) in 1948, one of his first orders was to take women out of air control towers, stating that their voices were too hard to understand.[60] LeMay, a world symbol of airpower after essentially rebuilding SAC from 1947 to 1957 (reaching four-star rank in 1951), became the USAF vice chief of staff in 1957 and chief of staff in 1961. It was widely believed that LeMay was "anti-WAF," particularly the enlisted women. Whether or not this was true, the Air Staff was under the impression it was and so acted accordingly.[61]

Beginning in 1958 women were no longer allowed to enter fields such as weather, flight attendance, information, or intelligence. Those who were already serving in those fields, approximately 4 percent of the enlisted force, were retrained.[62] Despite numerous WAF director attempts to expand career opportunities for enlisted personnel, there was not much interest from women to enter technical fields. According to Riley, there was considerable Air Staff resentment against women doing any kind of "hands dirty" work, and by the end of the decade they were not sure what to do with the small female force that was left.

Though they had similar recruiting, accession, and attrition difficulties as the officer corps, the WAF enlisted corps were always the ones facing criticism. A common sentiment, iterated by LeMay during his time at SAC, was that WAF officers were useful but WAF enlisted were more trouble than they were worth and should be made into civilians.[63] Maintaining suitable quarters and uniforms for such a low number also proved expensive and another reason to question the validity of the WAF program. As foreseen by Cochran's report to Vandenberg, mid-decade concerns over a "slippage in quality of recruits" was corroborated by the discovery that WAF enlisted recruits were cheating on their AFWST. When forced to retest under controlled conditions at Lackland (under the AF Personnel and Training Research Center), many did not pass, indicating they were receiving help from recruiters during their initial test.[64] This situation did not help the growing argument for eliminating women, especially enlisted women, from the Air Force.

In a self-sustaining loop, high attrition and low recruitment encouraged the Air Force to lower WAF ceilings, which in turn took away their ability to have impact on the mission. Women grew bored, were underutilized, and had little opportunity for advancement, and so they separated—again encouraging lower WAF ceilings. By 1954, over 80 percent of the women leaving the service did so because of marriage or pregnancy.[65] Retention of female enlisted WAFs was so poor that many senior officers questioned whether they were worth keeping on staff.

"Why WAF?"

Five years after the Integration Act was signed, the new deputy chief of staff for personnel, Lt Gen Emmett O'Donnell, raised the question of whether it was worth maintaining a force of enlisted women during peacetime.[66] The next year, in 1954, an Air Force colonel submitted an Air War College paper entitled "Why WAF?" giving a name to an idea that would persist for the next decade. Heavily influenced by the latest "New Look" strategic doctrine, the author concluded that the continued use of women as members of the Air Force could not be justified, as "there will not be time to cope with WAF when D-Day comes with all its fury and destruction of fission and fusion weapons."[67] Though nothing came of this paper, it was an oft-cited reference throughout the next decade in discussions pertaining to the WAF's validity.

In a 1989 interview, Riley remembered that as WAF director during the 1950s, "Why WAF" "was a recurring subject. I don't doubt that today somewhere in the Pentagon is a paper about 'why women in the service?' "[68] The question almost always pertained specifically to enlisted WAF and primarily ended with staff studies. According to Riley, "If people didn't have something else to think about or worry about they would pick on WAF Airmen."[69]

When LeMay became Vice Chief of Staff of the Air Force in 1958 amid a protracted force reduction, the WAF entered into its biggest test yet.[70] Revered as a human symbol of airpower and an outspoken critic of the WAF, LeMay—within months of his arrival at the Pentagon—ordered Riley to reevaluate the WAF program to determine its validity for existing. Riley's response focused on countering the three primary arguments made for disbanding the WAF: manpower billets, job performance concerns, and the cost difference of male and female Airmen.[71]

Manpower Billets

A popular, and incorrect, rumor was that manpower billets were separated by gender, and so one could take away female billets and make them male billets. Riley proved that elimination of the WAF program would actually save only about 155 manpower spaces, and, since women held validated billets, they would have to be replaced by men, thus creating no reduction in strength.

Job Performance

While it was generally accepted there were some jobs women did just as well as, if not better, than men, Riley provided reports from a 1958 study citing commanders who preferred women working in air defense combat control centers, passenger air transport operations, statistical analysis, and data processing, even over some men.[72] This was in addition to the assumed superior performance in administration and nursing positions, jobs most men were uninterested in doing.

Cost Difference

While female Airmen were expensive to recruit, males were more expensive to train and retain because of associated dependent costs.[73] Female Airmen often elected to separate upon marriage and were still not allowed to serve if they had any dependents under the age of 18. The few WAFs who had male civilian spouses were not allowed dependent privileges.[74] The collective and proportional cost of male Airmen far outweighed that of female Airmen.

Though Riley's successful argument kept the WAF in existence, she would still be required to pay a price. Regardless of Air Staff opinions, legally the Air Force secretary was the one responsible for determining the end-strength ceiling of the WAF. In October 1958, Secretary of the Air Force James Douglas approved a staff study recommending WAF Airmen strength be reduced to 5,000 by the end of FY60.[75] Despite her best efforts, Riley was forced to concede to the suggested 5,000 ceiling, a 30 percent WAF reduction within little over a year. Soon thereafter, the Air Force decided to phase women out of "nontraditional fields," such as intelligence, weather, flight attendants, control tower operation, or maintenance, and close more bases to enlisted WAFs, resulting in an all-time low in 1965 of 4,700 total women in the Air Force.[76]

Morale and Attrition

The general public and military attitude toward female service members in the late 1950s and early 1960s was apathetic at best. The Korean War was a doubled-edged sword for the WAF. Because it came so quickly on the heels of the Integration Act, there was not enough time to dwell on the idea of using the women that were now allowed in the Air Force. However, because the force was so new, small, and largely unregulated, its inability to fully utilize women during the Korean conflict—a tall order given the fact they had only even been allowed in the force for two years when hostilities began— nevertheless provided ammunition for those who opposed the idea that women could be a genuine force of supplemental manpower, let alone equal service members in their own right.

During the 1950s, American culture was firmly rooted in the notion that women were only needed in the military in times of dire crisis. Both men and women largely disapproved of women working outside the home, viewing the ability to stay home and tend to the household and children as a sign of wealth and status. Women who might have chosen to serve or remain in service were likely dissuaded by the lack of military career opportunities, personnel numbers and rank caps, varied levels of hostility from male service members, and the channeling of most women into dead-end clerical jobs. Witt summarizes it well, pointing out that "discrimination against women simply because they were women was, in the 1950s, as widely accepted in the military as it was in society."[77] A woman's social obligations as wife and mother were placed above all other responsibilities, including military service, and were a primary reason for the high attrition rate of first-term enlisted Airmen. While the average age of female recruits fell, attrition rates increased as the majority of women completed their minimum service and took advantage of the voluntary discharge offered because of marriage.[78] Both male and female military leaders accepted and even encouraged this plight as well as the values underpinning it.

During and after the Korean War expansion, some male commanders did view women as a potential source of high-quality personnel to supplement their forces, pushing for their employment in more technical career fields. Others wanted more restrictions placed upon women, limiting them to a few tightly defined roles. Ultimately the latter perspective won, and a steady stripping of job options and opportunities commenced. In many cases, women were overqualified for the jobs they were allowed to do. For those women who did choose to stay in the service, dwindling opportunities, job dissatisfaction, and career bottlenecks often resulted in frustration and early separation.

Secondary, yet significant, contributors to both low morale and the "Why WAF" crisis were inadequate uniforms and housing. Since the advent of the WAF, uniform shortages proved to be a massive logistical issue and often contributed to the perceived poor quality of the women. When the Air Force became a separate service in 1947, the need for new Air Force and separate women's uniform were important topics of conversation. Initially, the women wore World War II Army men's uniforms with neckties; however, one of May's first actions as WAF director was to design and order women's uniforms. The cut of the winter uniform was modeled after those of airline flight attendants, using the same material as the men's winter uniforms. Instead of a necktie, tabs were worn on the collar and were considered professional and contemporary. Uniforms and ranks did not switch over from Army Air Corps to the current Air Force standard until October 1951. During the first push for WAF recruits in 1951, the Air Force could not adequately house or outfit all its new female recruits.[79] Air Force contractors had difficulty making their delivery schedules and those uniforms that were delivered were often such poor quality they could not be issued. For example, of the 5,100 women's uniforms delivered to Lackland AFB in 1951, only 1,200 were usable after alterations.[80] If needed for an interview or special duty, a community uniform was often shared. These type of women's uniform issues continued into the 1960s. When slanted pocket deficiencies in the female tropical uniform prevented proper alignment of ribbons, the WAF director ordered all 10,000 uniforms be issued to basic and OTS trainees and sold exclusively out of Maxwell and Lackland to newly commissioned officers.[81]

Likewise, the lack of suitable female housing proved detrimental to morale and career sustainability. In a 1959 USAF sponsored personnel survey, 98 percent of WAF officers indicated housing as their number one complaint. The Air Force was the hardest hit of all services by the housing shortage that plagued the military after World War II. Most air bases had been hastily constructed during the war, meaning that the limited housing that was available was bare bones and not the best quality. A housing boom in the early 1950s led many Air Force bases to report "ample housing" suitable for female Airmen. However, much of this potential housing was soon converted to family quarters, leaving the leftover, older, substandard quarters for the women. There was little incentive to fix this issue, as the lack of female housing provided an ever-available reason to prevent women from being stationed on a base or sent to a certain location (particularly overseas). Despite, or perhaps because of, these continued shortages and issues, base housing was one of the first areas to see gender equalization in the military. In the early 1960s, there was still not enough on-base housing for men, and women's quarters were only filled at about 65 percent.[82] In an effort to better utilize base housing, officer quarters became desegregated by gender in 1964 to fill empty women's quarters with men who needed them; however, older facilities with shared restrooms retained separation.[83] Additionally, women gained the ability to stay off base and still receive basic allowance for quarters (BAQ) when there was insufficient lodging.[84] Before this directive, male lieutenants were authorized to reside off base and draw BAQ, while female captains were required to occupy government quarters. WAF director Col Elizabeth Ray brought this issue to attention, arguing off-base quarters were a privilege based on seniority, not gender.[85]

In a speech at a recruiting conference in 1961, the deputy WAF director announced that "WAF will no longer be assigned to jobs where they create resentment, or are termed a 'nuisance.' We think that individually and as a whole they will be accepted more than ever as part of the Air Force."[86] Two years later, during the 1963 WAF director's conference, Ray defined the WAF program as "the little-understood and imprecise reference to some 5,000 individual enlisted Women in the Air Force, plus a few officers who are necessary to their welfare, and their management. They constituted a program only because the Air Force must take cognizance of their special needs in a few areas."[87] Tolerated but not taken seriously, the WAF and its female leadership were as, if not more, concerned with their image than their male counterparts. Few women questioned their second-class role, believing in its fundamental rightness not only because that had been a woman's legacy for generations but also because women were not allowed in combat, which was widely understood to mean they did not deserve the same benefits and treatment as their male counterparts.

From the beginning of the 1960s to the end, the roles, expectations, and opportunities for the women of the Air Force and America looked very different. With President John F. Kennedy's inauguration in 1961 came the commission on the status of women, and with that came recommendations for expanded opportunities for women in both federal service and the public sector. Presidential commissions in 1963 and 1964 started to seriously consider ending or reducing the draft through a focus on better and more inclusive recruiting—of which women were considered a part. In 1940, only approximately 25 percent of the workforce had been female, but by the end of the 1960s that figure was over 40 percent and rising.[88] While the number of women in the Air Force was at its lowest point in history, American women were undergoing a revolution concerning their place and possibilities in the workforce and society as a whole.

Notes

1. Witt, *A Defense Weapon*, 85.
2. Holm, *Women in the Military*, 179.
3. Holm, 178.
4. Holm, 180.
5. As historian Linda Witt points out, this marks the beginning of a DACOWITS tradition in which the group's recommendations are repeated numerous times, across years and decades, until the military acts upon them. Witt, *A Defense Weapon*, 85.
6. "Annual Report of the WAF Program for 1956."
7. HISTORY, "The 1950s."
8. USAF Statistical Digest, 236.
9. Holm, *Women in the Military*, 180.
10. Holm, 181.
11. Mitchell, *Air Force Officers*, 319.
12. ATC Manual 35-2 (ATCM 35-2), *A Handbook for Air Force Women*, 19.
13. ATCM 35-2, 20.
14. Mitchell, *Air Force Officers*, 322. All these traditions disappeared from print during the 1960s.
15. This was a policy across all military services into the 1970s.
16. Mitchell, *Air Force Officers*, 322.
17. Riley and May, interview.
18. "Historical Summary: 1 Jul 1959–31 Dec 1959."
19. Annual Report of the WAF Program for 1956.
20. ATCM 35-2, 25.
21. "Report of WAF Program, 1 August 1954–15 February 1955."
22. "Report of WAF Program, 1 August 1954–15 February 1955."
23. OCS was a primary commissioning program for enlisted personnel, graduating 300–600 reserve officers per year, with a spike during the Korean

War years, until its termination in 1964. A college degree was not required for OCS selection or to commission, but it was generally required for promotion once within the officer ranks.

24. Witt, *A Defense Weapon*, 103.

25. Only approximately 20 WAF reservists volunteered annually to go on active duty.

26. "Historical Summary: 1 Jan 1959–1 Jun 1959."

27. During the 1950s, very few enlisted women had any interest in a commission, let alone in a career in the military. Most wanted to serve one tour of active duty before attending college or getting married and starting a family. The attrition rate for WAF enlisted personnel topped 20 percent almost every year until the mid-1960s.

28. Director of WAF, Historical Summary: 1 Jan 1956–1 Jun 1957. The participating universities were Butler University, University of Maryland, University of Texas, Miami University of Ohio, University of California–Los Angeles, Southern Illinois University, George Washington University, University of Omaha, University of Florida, and Pennsylvania State University.

29. "Historical Summary: 1 Jan 1959–1 Jun 1959."

30. Riley and May, interview.

31. Mitchell, *Air Force Officers*, 314. When the Reserve Officer Training Corps (ROTC) was established by the National Defense Act in 1916, the language of the law could be interpreted to specifically exclude women from participation. To start the trial program, the Air Force drafted amendatory legislation, and while the other services were not enthusiastic about its possible implementation, there was a general agreement among them to not oppose the trial program.

32. Mitchell, *Air Force Officers*, 314. The college campuses were also unsupportive. Likely due to a war-fatigued generation of students, ROTC was not popular in 1957 for either gender, in any service. In the years that followed, many universities removed the requirement that made ROTC mandatory for male students.

33. Mitchell, *Air Force Officers*, 315.

34. After a slow start, AFROTC commandant Maj Gen T. C. Rogers recommended an additional 35 colleges be added to the program, especially in areas where women students appeared interested. His recommendations were not approved, and due to lack of interest the Air Force removed two colleges from the program in 1958.

35. In the massive Air Force–wide conversion of reserve personnel into regular ranks beginning in 1958, only 200 women were among the 60,000 Reserve officers who applied for a regular commission.

36. Harrison, "Integration of WAF Procurement," memorandum. There were 209 regular, 492 Reserve officers.

37. "Historical Summary: 1 Jan 1957–1 Jun 1957."

38. "Historical Summary: 1 Jul 1965–31 Dec 1965."

39. Holm, *Women in the Military*, 194.

40. "Historical Summary: 1 Jul 1962–31 Dec 1962."

41. At this point, a baccalaureate degree was not required for a commission. The Air Force made a major push for education for both enlisted and officers during the 1960s. However, generally those who were educated left the force and those who were not stayed in. As the Air Force ended commissioning programs that did not require college degrees, such as the Aviation Cadet program, OCS, and direct appointment, the number of officers with degrees organically increased. Many of the officers commissioned without degrees to meet the emergency during World War II were also leaving the service, helping to reduce their numbers across the force.

42. Mitchell, *Air Force Officers*, 316.

43. Mitchell, 323.

44. The Integration Act also set age limits that forced women to retire earlier than men ostensibly so that they would not be in uniform during menopause. Retirement age would not be made equal to men until 1967 with the passage of Public Law 90-130. Witt, *A Defense Weapon*, 118.

45. Women were grouped in only five of the 13 major air commands to ensure sufficient numbers to form WAF squadrons. Each squadron required a minimum of 120 women.

46. Witt, *A Defense Weapon*, 109.

47. A major factor in career stagnation across the entire Air Force Officer corps was what was referred to as "the hump." This term refers to the influx of officers commissioned at the start of World War II who crossed into the Air Force and were now field grade officers. After an unimpeded slew of temporary officer promotions during the Korean War, Congress passed Public Law 83-349, the Officer Grade Limitation Act of 1954. Popularly known as the OGLA, the new law placed ceilings on field grade officer ranks and centralized the temporary promotion system.

48. Holm, *Women in the Military*, 136. Enlisted women had to pass entrance exams with a higher score than the average male entering the Air Force.

49. The role of WAF squadron commander was considered a primary duty only once the WAF population reached 75 or more women. Any number less than that made the position an additional duty.

50. Air Force Regulation, 35-20, Administration of Women in the Air Force.

51. Colonel Shelly had the minimum AFQT score for female enlisted raised in 1952 from 49 percent to 65 percent. A high school diploma was also required for women to enlist, though not for men.

52. The median age of marriage was 20. US Census Bureau, "Historical Marital Status Tables."

53. Riley and May, interview.

54. "WAF Program, 1 August 1954–15 February 1955," memorandum.

55. If any factor proved questionable, "experts" (often men who had never worked with women) were consulted for their recommendations on whether their job might be suitable for women. Holm, Women in the Military, 138.

56. Ironically, prior to the results of the study, the Air Force trained a much higher percentage of women in radio, radar, intelligence, photography, weather, and flight operations between 1948 and 1951 than the Army Air Forces had during World War II.

57. Witt, *A Defense Weapon*, 112.

58. Holm, *Women in the Military*, 183.

59. "Annual Report of the WAF Program for 1956."

60. The Air Force continued to train Army enlisted women as control tower operators. Riley and May, interview.

61. Holm, *Women in the Military*, 172.

62. Holm, 184.

63. Riley and May, interview.

64. "Annual Report of the WAF Program for 1956."

65. Mitchell, *Air Force Officers*, 319.

66. Holm, *Women in the Military*, 170.

67. Holm, 171. At this time most Airmen believed that nuclear weapons had revolutionized warfare. The idea of mass mobilizations appeared to be obsolete and so using women to boost the personnel count, as was necessary in WWII, seemed entirely unnecessary now. In a nod to O'Donnell's argument, if the assumption was nuclear war, then employing women would nearly guarantee they would become combat casualties—an idea that was abhorrent to most men and women at the time. Though his conclusions proved wrong and certainly detrimental to women in the Air Force over the next few decades, his opinion was likely shared by many.

68. Riley and May, interview.

69. Riley and May.

70. A second attempt to terminate the program came a few years later in 1961 with an Air Force query to Representative Carl Vinson, chair of the House Armed Services Committee, about possible congressional reaction to amending PL 80-625, the statutory foundation on which the WAF rested. Vinson's reply was so strongly negative that the idea was immediately dropped.

71. Holm, *Women in the Military*, 172.

72. Holm, 172–73.

73. Holm, 251–54. Additionally, a DOD study led by Navy commander Dr. Richard Hunter in the early 1970s revealed that high-quality women and low-quality men were cheaper to recruit than high-quality men. Though the

Air Force had the smallest differential of all services, based on service-provided data it still cost an estimated $870 to recruit a high-quality man versus $150 for a high-quality woman or lower quality man. Therefore, by substituting women, the services could save an extraordinary amount of money (estimated by Martin Binkin and Shirley Bach at $1 billion annually, as Holm notes in *Women in the Military*).

74. The military regarded servicewomen as single, regardless of marital status, and not entitled to dependent benefits unless they could prove their husbands were dependent on them for more than 50 percent of their support.

75. "Historical Summary: 1 Jul 1958–31 Dec 1958."

76. Holm, *Women in the Military*, 174.

77. Witt, *A Defense Weapon*, 236.

78. Upon marriage a WAF could request separation after having met her minimum service commitment: 12 months after basic, 18 months after technical training, or 12 months after an overseas assignment. Officers were eligible to separate two years after commissioning.

79. Witt, *A Defense Weapon*, 80.

80. Witt.

81. "Historical Summary: 1 Jan 1964–30 Jun 1964."

82. Wilson, "Designation of Bachelor Officers' Quarters."

83. Young, "Officers' Quarters."

84. As provided in Air Force Regulation 30-6.

85. Wilson, "Designation of Bachelor Officers' Quarters."

86. "Change of WAF Airman Utilization."

87. Ray, WAF Director's Conference remarks.

88. Mitchell, *Air Force Officers*, 319.

Chapter 4

Revolution Stirring
Public Law 90-130 and Vietnam

By the mid 1960s, women's programs across all the services were very different from what was envisioned when the Integration Act was signed. Transformed into "typewriter soldiers," the WAF and other women's components were at their lowest personnel levels since before the Korean War.[1] As the defense budget rose and reservists were slowly called up to face a series of crises in Berlin, Cuba, and Laos as well as a gradual build-up in Southeast Asia, the women's programs continued to decline. A 1966 *Washington Post* article entitled "Should We Send Our Women Soldiers to Vietnam?" declared "more attention is paid to the rise and fall of hemlines than to the ebb and flow of battle lines."[2] In 1965, only 15 career fields and 151 Air Force Specialty Codes (AFSC) were open to women in the Air Force.[3] Seventy percent of enlisted women and 75 percent of officers were serving in clerical or administration positions, while 23 percent worked in medical facilities.[4]

Meanwhile, as the nation was knee-deep in the civil rights movement, historical precedent would indicate a push for women's rights was not far behind. The 1963 and 1964 presidential commissions studied the feasibility of ending or reducing the draft through increased military compensation and expansion of recruitment, with better (and potentially greater) use of women considered as an option. Paralleling the rise of the feminine mystique in popular culture, the Commission on the Status of Women's report, Equal Pay Act of 1963, and formation of the National Organization for Women (NOW) by 1966 the second wave of feminism was upon the American public.[5] With the US on the precipice of war once again following the Gulf of Tonkin Resolution in 1964, the increasing inevitability of military conflict provided the leverage needed to overlook tradition and crack the door for women to integrate a little further into the force.

In 1964 Secretary of the Air Force Eugene Zuckert asked the Air Staff for a study relative to eliminating, or at least reducing, the use of the draft. Increasing "womanpower" was an included option; however, the staff concluded holding the WAF at 5,000 under a "highly selective minimum-force concept" was appropriate. A few months later, director for manpower and organization Maj Gen Bertram Harrison ordered a similar study. However, this one concluded the WAF could and should be doubled—to 1,500 officers and 10,000 enlisted women—as soon as possible. Additionally, Harrison recommended Air Force personnel policy regarding the recruitment, retention, and utilization of women be amended to be more in line with the civilian sector. WAF director Col Jeanne Holm supported these conclusions and reassured the deputy chief of staff for personnel, who disagreed with Harrison, that the increase of women in support roles would free men to fill combat roles.[6] In 1965 the Office of the Secretary of the Air Force recommended doubling the size of the WAF, and the following year the assistant secretary of defense for manpower, Thomas Morris, asked the Air Force to consider raising WAF strength to 10,000 with 930 officers. Despite the enthusiasm, none of these recommendations had an effect.[7]

Fig. 10. The directors of women for the four US military branches pose at a DACOWITS meeting in Washington, DC, in October 1966. WAF director Col Jeanne Holm stands at far right, with, from left, Col Emily C. Gorman, director of the Women's Army Corps; Capt Viola Brown Sanders, director of Women in the Navy; and Col Barbara J. Bishop, director of the Women Marines. (Reproduced with permission from Viola Brown Sanders Papers, WV0323.6.020, Martha Blakeney Hodges Special Collections and University Archives, University Libraries, The University of North Carolina at Greensboro.)

Toward the end of the decade, personnel policies started changing to allow more comprehensive gender integration into the force as well as to improve the overall quality of life for WAFs. Most major changes happened or were started during Holm's tenure (November 1965–February 1973). According to the opinion of many, she was "articulate, forceful, and convinced that women could contribute more toward national defense; she was the right officer to manage the WAF during this critical period."[8] Holm was willing to challenge Air Force policies she felt were obsolete or unfair and played an important role in many of the policy changes that affected women during the late 1960s and 1970s. One of the first changes was Holm's push to get more career fields opened to women. After becoming deputy chief of staff for personnel in 1970, Lt Gen Robert Dixon revoked the right for major command commanders to arbitrarily exclude women from certain jobs, something Holm had been personally advocating to him for some time. Instead, he required exclusion be approved on a case-by-case basis—which ultimately proved difficult and helped bring a revolution in assignment policies.[9]

Public Law 90-130

After years of growing pressure from DACOWITS, Congress, and the White House,[10] a reluctant DOD eventually drafted legislation seeking to remove rank ceilings on women in the military, though, Holm said, they "never seriously envisioned, ever, that women would be able to perform in those senior roles in their own right without heading up a woman's program."[11] Signed in November 1967, PL 90-130 effectively removed restrictions on female officer careers and was the first major policy change concerning women in the military since the 1948 Integration Act.[12] Specifically, the new law opened promotions to colonel and general ranks, removed the 10 percent limit on the number of regular officers who could serve as a permanent lieutenant colonel, equalized retirement rules for men and women, and removed the 2 percent strength ceilings on the regular line strengths.[13] The law also authorized women to enlist in the Air National Guard.[14]

The most immediate effect of PL 90-130 on the WAF was a relief in officer promotion bottlenecks. The Air Force was the first but also most cautious service to act under the new law, and in 1968 with 41 WAF lieutenant colonels on active duty and more than half eligible for promotion to colonel, the Air Force elected to promote one. A few months later, the Army promoted seven, Navy six, and Marine Corps eight women to colonel/captain.[15] Two years later, in 1970, the Army awarded women their first stars, and in 1971 the Air Force followed suit with the promotion of Jeanne Holm to brigadier general.

Though PL 90-130 was a major step forward, cultural change did not immediately accompany legislative change. Fearing it to be a women's promotion law, the Air Force strongly opposed allowing women to serve in positions that authorized general officer rank. It is important to note that most male and female officers truly believed lieutenant colonel to be as much rank as a woman could handle, given that they were noncombatants. Additionally, the Air Force had long associated high rank with aviation, particularly combat aviation, an elite network barring most men and certainly all women. Some feared that removing rank restrictions would create a pressure to promote women, a thought often deemed unthinkable at best and a threat to national security at worst.

WAF in Vietnam, 1967–1973

As of 1961, President Kennedy's flexible response defense strategy and accompanying single integrated operational plan (SIOP) meant the Air Force was now responsible for anything ranging from all-out nuclear war to supporting the Army in limited ground conflicts.[16] As a force that had been born amidst a shift in international power dynamics as well as US military structure and policy, airpower was not prepared for the type of limited warfare that would come to characterize the Vietnam War.[17]

Unlike in the Korean War, personnel shortages during the Vietnam War stemmed largely from national reluctance of men to volunteer. The Pentagon's war plans were contingent on calling upon the Reserve and National Guard both before and after the Gulf of Tonkin incident. However, despite augmenting strategic airlift, rescue, and recovery and serving as intelligence analysts, medical specialists, aerial porters, maintainers, lawyers, and chaplains, the Guard and Reserve were also avenues for well-connected, college-educated, and mostly white men to avoid service in Vietnam.[18] In an attempt to increase volunteerism, Johnson ordered military pay raises, increased GI benefits, and improved services for dependents. When incentives failed, Defense Secretary Robert McNamara mandated the services lower enlistment standards for men and accept over 100,000 men who would not have qualified for service under previous standards. Known as "Project 100,000," this program ran for almost a year (1966–67) before the DOD announced it would augment the number of military women by approximately 6,500 total members.[19]

During the spring 1966 DACOWITS meeting, members were shocked to learn that thousands of qualified female volunteers were being turned away from serving in Southeast Asia (SEA) and many new recruits were being delayed for reporting due to a "gentleman's agreement" between the personnel center and field commanders who had banned women from deploying to theater.[20] The narrative and belief at the time that conflict in Vietnam would be brief and limited helped rationalize the public's expectation that men should "protect" women from the harshness of this war. Less than one month later, the DACOWITS chairman pushed for the creation of an interservice working group, chaired by Colonel Holm, to examine the use of women in the military with a goal to increase numbers to the legal 2 percent limit. The group concluded that the ceiling could be reached in three to five years without lowering quality by expanding recruiting efforts and better informing the public on the role and importance of women in the military.[21]

In June 1967 the first WAF personnel, one officer and five enlisted, arrived for duty at the headquarters in Saigon at the request of the Military Assistance Command, Vietnam.[22] Additional women soon followed and were assigned to the Seventh Air Force headquarters and Tan Son Nhut Air Base on the outskirts of Saigon. A few officers were subsequently assigned to duty at Bien Hoa and Cam Ranh Bay air bases.[23] The most often used rationalization for denying WAF requests to serve in SEA was the concern of having to use additional resources on women's safety, housing, and other special needs. This reasoning might have kept women out of SEA altogether were it not for growing public resistance to the draft, DACOWITS, and the persistence of servicewomen. According to Holm, realistically "female officers required little or no special arrangements. They could easily be accommodated in bachelor officer quarters (BOQ) much as the female officers of the other services and the civilian women (civil service employees, Red Cross workers, librarians, teachers, etc.) working in the theater."[24] However, Air Force policy required enlisted women be quartered in all-female dormitories supervised by a WAF squadron with a female officer, ultimately preventing many enlisted WAFs from deploying to South Vietnam. Those who did make it overseas were assigned to units with the Thirteenth Air Force in Thailand at Korat, Udorn, Ubon, Nakhon Phanom, Takhli, and Don Muang, as well as the Military Assistance Command, Thailand in Bangkok and at U-Tapao.

Approximately 600–800 WAFs served in SEA during official US involvement, with over half of them officers and the vast majority nurses. Both enlisted and officer WAFs rotated with male personnel for regular one-year tours, serving in jobs women had been barred from during the previous decade. WAF officers worked in a variety of noncombat fields, such as intelligence, public affairs, aircraft maintenance, supply, personnel, and meteorology and were fully integrated into the units of which they were a part. Despite serving alongside the men, each WAF in SEA "realized that she was on trial. In addition to adapting to the combat theater environment, she was conscious of living in a fishbowl where her professional competence, her personal character and her courage were always subject to critical scrutiny."[25] By the time US forces withdrew from theater, both male and female Air Force officers were serving in comparable proportions. While the number of deployed enlisted WAFs remained small, those who did deploy primarily served in traditional female roles, such as administration, clerical, personnel, and data processing.

The biggest test for the WAF in SEA came in January 1968 when the Vietcong launched a coordinated attack on US installations in what came to be known as the Tet Offensive. Shortly after the attack, in a report to the chief master sergeant of the Air Force, a male senior master sergeant reported, "What impressed me the most, with respect to the conduct of our personnel during the Tet Offensive, was the calm [with which] female service members went about their duties. That belief that the frail (or fair) sex will tremble at the first sign of trouble is not true. I observed female military members performing their duties no different than anyone else. If they had fears . . . they did a terrific job of concealing them. . . . Air Force women are doing an outstanding job here."[26]

Regardless of their performance, both the Seventh Air Force and Pacific Air Force commanders requested all WAFs be pulled out of theater following the attack. With few exceptions, the women refused. One WAF major insisted: "I want to stay and finish my tour. I'm not a fool and I'm not saying this because I'm patriotic. I feel we have a job to be done and we'd best get on with it." A female staff sergeant echoed the same sentiments in a letter to the WAF director: "Don't let them send us home. I came here to do a job and I want to see it through." In a controversial and precedent-setting decision, Air Force chief of staff Gen John McConnell decided to let the women stay.[27]

As was often the case, WAF nurses never had the option to leave, especially as fighting and casualty rates intensified. Initially, only male nurses from the Air Force Nurse Corps were deployed to combat in theater, but it quickly became apparent female nurses would have to join them. In 1966 the first 16 female nurses arrived for duty at the new 12th USAF Hospital on the USAF base at Cam Ranh Bay in Vietnam. Additional female medical personnel, such as physical therapists and dieticians, soon joined them. Flight nurses were assigned to the 903rd Aeromedical Evacuation Squadron at Tan Son Nhut, and crews from various operating locations hopped from base to base, airlifting casualties to in-country medical treatment centers.[28] According to Holm, it was not uncommon for a flight to stop at 10 different locations in one day.[29]

WAF flight nurses conducting air evacuation of casualties provided one of the most valuable contributions to the war effort. Vietnam proved to be the perfect stage for the Air Force to test its newly designed global aeromedical evacuation system, connecting the battlefield with the most modern medical facilities in the world. In the new age of jet-powered aircraft, it became possible to move a casualty from the battlefield back to a hospital in the US in as little at 72 hours. Air Force flight nurses were instrumental in designing, operating, and improving this system, saving the lives of many men who, at any point earlier in history, would have died on the battlefield. One of these flight nurses was Capt Mary T. Klinker. On 4 April 1975, Captain Klinker became the last American military woman, and the first and only WAF, to die in Vietnam during the ill-fated Operation Babylift. The effort cost the lives of 138 of the 314 South Vietnamese and Cambodian orphans, flight crew, and caregivers as the C-5A they were on crashed shortly after taking off from Tan Son Nhut Air Base.[30]

Many Air Force men and women alike were never sent to the combat zone in SEA but were still essential to the overall war effort. WAFs were assigned to air bases just outside the combat theater, to bomber-launching SAC bases in the US and overseas, and to Military Airlift Command bases preparing personnel, supplies, ammunition, and equipment for airlift to bases in the western Pacific. Others served in Air Force communications units providing the global communications link vital to every phase of the operation. Still others worked at secret electronic listening posts on isolated mountaintop sites in Taiwan, Japan, and the Philippines. Enlisted women controlled air traffic landing and taking off from bases in Hawaii, California, Alaska, and the Philippines flying to and returning from SEA. At terminals on the west coast they processed passengers boarding flights bound for SEA and off-loaded returnees rotating back to the "real" world and home. At USAF hospitals in Japan, Europe, and the US, female nurses, enlisted WAF medical personnel, and biomedical sciences officers worked side-by-side caring for war casualties and returning POWs.

Fig. 11. 1st Lt Linda V. Bowser, a nurse with the 8th Tactical Fighter Wing Med Cap Team, examines a child in Bong Song Village, Thailand, 1974.

In 1970, Congress repealed the Gulf of Tonkin Resolution in order to reassert control over presidential power during war, and in 1973 the Paris Peace Accords were signed, removing the US from theater. Of the 58,000-plus Americans who lost their lives during the war, 13 were military women and one an Air Force woman. The Air Force invested over 1.2 million fixed-wing sorties, 6.2 million tons of explosives, 2,118 dead, 599 missing in action, and 2,257 aircraft, at the total cost of $3.1 billion.[31] The US dropped three times as many bombs in SEA between 1965 and 1974 as it did in all of World War II. Despite the relatively small numbers of Air Force women to deploy and serve in theater, Vietnam was significant because it was the first time female Airmen, other than nurses, deployed overseas in support of a war effort.

However, upon their return from SEA women faced a greater sense of alienation than men. Though all WAFs who served in theater received combat pay, many earned decorations, some were injured, and one died, most Department of Veterans Affairs (VA) programs and studies entirely ignored women. Though it is generally agreed upon that approximately 7,500 military women served in SEA, neither the VA nor DOD has reliable data on the actual count. To date, no data accurately reflects the exact number of Air Force women who served in SEA during the war. Additionally, no one has compiled a list of the citations and decorations awarded to the military women who served during this time.

But perhaps more important to the story of women in the Air Force is that a generation of future Air Force leaders walked away from Vietnam convinced that "body counts, sortie rates, and tons of bombs dropped were all poor means for judging air power's effectiveness."[32] In retrospect, Vietnam was a turning point—and a major external influence on the integration of women into the service. All the ways the war had played out made it clear the Air Force was no longer living in an all-out strike, Cold War climate. The character of warfare had changed and so had the way the Air Force was mobilized and used to fight. These major perspective shifts would soon be accompanied by the switch to an all-volunteer military force, which would affect everything from doctrine and tactics to personnel management—and specifically the use of "womanpower."

Notes

1. Holm, *Women in the Military*, 177.
2. Holm, 175.
3. "Change of WAF Airman Utilization."
4. Holm, *Women in the Military*, 177.
5. Betty Friedan's 1963 book *The Feminine Mystique* is often credited with lighting the ready match of the second wave of American feminism. Initial reformers early in the decade, such as Friedan, did not want to change the world itself, they just wanted in on it. They also had little interest in changing the rules and dynamics of private relationships. Essentially, they wanted to marry, have children, and have the career. "Radicals" on the other hand, coming of age a few years later, wanted to go much farther than leveling the playing field. They wanted to "overthrow the hierarchy" and allow women to be everything they could be, often encapsulated in the slogan: "the private is the political." Collins, *When Everything Changed*, 59. One of the most well-known symbols of the women's movement is the National Organization for Women (NOW). The group was founded in 1966 by 28 women who were frustrated with the way in which the federal government was not enforcing new antidiscrimination laws. NOW membership took off, with chapters in all 50 states addressing issues in their own communities. Dicker, *A History of U.S. Feminism*, 72.
6. Holm, *Women in the Military*, 189.
7. Mitchell, *Air Force Officers*, 317.
8. Mitchell, 319.
9. As commander of the USAF Military Personnel Center in the late 1960s, Lt Gen Robert Dixon helped persuade Air Force Chief of Staff McConnell not to withdraw women from Vietnam after the Tet Offensive. Holm, *Women in the Military*, 237.
10. According to General Holm, the president had a personal interest in PL 90-130. One of his favorite staff members was a female Reservist lieutenant colonel in the Army; he wanted to promote her to full colonel but was told he could not because of the existing law. Holm, interview.
11. Holm, interview.
12. An amendment of PL 625 titles 10, 32, and 27.
13. The 2 percent ceiling on regular strength women in service was designed to keep the numbers small. However, at no time during the existence of the law was the 2 percent limit ever reached. In fact, until the late 1960s women rarely constituted even 1 percent of their service.
14. The Air National Guard allowed female officers starting in 1956.
15. Holm, *Women in the Military*, 202.
16. Millett, *For the Common Defense*, 496. Flexible response called for mutual deterrence at strategic, tactical, and conventional levels, giving the

United States the capability to respond to aggression across the spectrum of war, not limited only to nuclear arms. The single integrated operational plan (SIOP) was the US's general nuclear plan from 1961 until 2003. Highly classified, the first SIOP, titled SIOP-62, was implemented on 1 July 1961 and updated annually thereafter.

17. The US officially became involved in the Vietnam War following the North Vietnamese response to the implementation of a March 1964 covert sabotage program known as OPLAN 34A. This policy provoked the Gulf of Tonkin incident in August 1964, followed shortly by the Gulf of Tonkin Resolution permitting the president to "take all necessary measures to repel any armed attack against the forces of the US and to prevent further aggression." Johnson invoked this resolution to justify larger war, and from late 1964 through 1968 the US waged a progressively larger war in Vietnam. The strategy in Vietnam was: "don't lose [the] war, but don't win it either"; the US was to hold off North Vietnam until South Vietnam could defend itself. Millett, *For the Common Defense*, 516.

18. From 1964 to 1973, approximately 27 million men reached draft age. Of that number, about 60 percent of personnel were waived from service, and out of the remaining 40 percent who wore a uniform, only about a quarter went to Vietnam. This meant working class men who lacked the money to attend college or hire lawyers bore the disproportionate burden of fighting the conflict. Millett, *For the Common Defense*, 526.

19. Holm, *Women in the Military*, 187.

20. In her book *Women in the Military: An Unfinished Revolution*, Holm tells an anecdote of one African-American Air Force lieutenant colonel who, after completing a highly classified counterintelligence course in preparation for assignment to Vietnam, saw her orders abruptly cancelled. "Initially, she was uncertain whether her rejection was based on her race or her gender. She eventually learned that her race had nothing to do with the decision to hold her back. It was simply that her superiors were uncomfortable with the idea of sending a woman to Vietnam." Preventing her assignment based on race would have been illegal; however, on the basis of sex it was allowed. Holm, *Women in the Military*, 210.

21. Holm, *Women in the Military*, 191.

22. These assignments were the direct result of Holm's work to get women in theater, even though the entire country was designated as a combat zone.

23. Mitchell, *Air Force Officers*, 317.

24. Holm and Wells, "Air Force Women in the Vietnam War."

25. Holm and Wells.

26. Holm and Wells.

27. Mitchell, *Air Force Officers*, 317.

28. The treatment centers were located at Cam Ranh Bay, Da Nang, Pleiku, Qui Nhon, Nha Trang, Vung Tau, and Phu Cat. Holm and Wells, "Air Force Women in the Vietnam War."

29. Holm and Wells.

30. Holm and Wells.

31. McFarland, *A Concise History of the U.S. Air Force.*

32. McFarland.

Chapter 5

Turning Points
The 1970s

The 1970s were a turning point for military women due to greater equality and opportunity through legislation and a change in perception of how American women saw themselves, their roles, and their potential in the Air Force. Together, the effects of the Vietnam War, the equal rights movement, and the expanding numbers of women in the labor force created the opportunistic boost necessary to break the WAF's stagnation—and arguably regression—of the previous 15 years. By the end of the decade, the US had become the world leader in use of military womanpower, both in total number as well as proportion to the total force, with the Air Force leading the way.[1]

Specific civilian and military leaders proved vital to pushing reform in areas that no longer served the military's best interest, in particular the effective use of personnel. DACOWITS in particular was critical to pushing the DOD, and going around the institution when necessary, to recommend legislation creating opportunities specifically for military women. In her 2003 Library of Congress oral history interviews, Holm remembered that she "set about trying to open up as many fields as I could to women, using any gimmick I could . . . it was about equality . . . and it was about overturning traditional roles and what women could do in society."[2] General Dixon, commander of the USAF Military Personnel Center in the late 1960s and deputy chief of staff for personnel in 1970, was another major force for change. According to Holm, previous chiefs of personnel were conservative and mostly negative toward any policy changes she believed were necessary. "They were against women going to the service academy, against women in ROTC, against retaining women with children, against expanding numbers or job opportunities. The list is endless. It was General Robert Dixon who came in, in my final years as director, WAF, who broke the logjam."[3] As was the case with the initial integration of women into the force, the primary motivation for further inclusion of women was not necessarily inspirational or altruistic but because they were needed to solve a potential personnel problem: the viability and sustainability of an all-volunteer force (AVF).

The All-Volunteer Force

Shortly after the Paris Peace Accords were signed in 1973, effectively ending US participation in Vietnam, male career officers and NCOs left the service in droves as the US military underwent a dramatic personnel reduction from 3.5 million in 1968 to 2.1 million in 1975.[4] The DOD tried to compensate for the anticipated readiness shortfalls in two primary ways. The first was to improve reserve units through the new "total force" concept, introduced in 1970 and made policy in 1973.[5] The second was to eliminate the draft and create an all-volunteer military, the effects of which would have a major impact on the use and eventual full integration of women into the Air Force.

Soon after his election to office and at the height of public backlash toward the draft during the Vietnam War, President Richard Nixon directed a commission be established to develop a plan for eliminating the draft. On 27 March 1969 former Secretary of Defense Thomas Gates was appointed as head of the commission to develop a comprehensive plan for eliminating conscription and creating an AVF.[6] Concluding it would be in the nation's best interest to eliminate the draft and focus on recruiting individuals with higher education, intelligence, and technical skills than the average population, the Gates commission also seriously reconsidered the requirements for an adequate reserve program. Initially, as the services began searching for alternative labor sources, they largely ignored women. For example, when asked to develop a plan to implement the new AVF, the Gates commission never mentioned (or, likely, considered) the need for or feasibility of expanding the role of women in a voluntary military.[7]

Before the Vietnam War, Air Force leadership could generally rely on a steady flow of reasonably fit and mentally stable young men to join the service. However, shortages after the withdrawal from Vietnam combined with the passage of the Equal Rights Amendment in March 1972 made clear it was time for the services to re-examine their practices and policies concerning women. That same month a special subcommittee on military manpower held hearings concerning the role of military women. In its published conclusions, the subcommittee stated: "We are concerned that the Department of Defense and each of the military services are guilty of 'tokenism' in the recruitment and utilization of women in the Armed Forces. We are convinced that in the atmosphere of a zero-draft environment or an all-volunteer military force, women could and should play a more important role. We strongly urge the Secretary of Defense and the service secretaries to develop a program which will permit women to take their rightful place in serving in our Armed Forces."[8] In response, the head of the AVF task force ordered the services to develop plans to increase the use of women. As was the case during the Korean War, the Air Force was targeted as the service most able to expand its roles for women.

Despite the relatively rapid increase in benefits, use, and opportunities for servicewomen during this decade, the perceived value and effectiveness of women in the Air Force—and military writ large—were still consistently up for debate. The Brookings Institution, an independent research entity, issued a report in 1976 stating, "The trade-off in today's recruiting market is between a high-quality female and a low-quality male. The average woman available to be recruited is smaller, weighs less, and is physically weaker than the vast majority of male recruits. She is also much brighter, better educated, scores much higher on the aptitude tests, and is much less likely to become a disciplinary problem."[9] A report to Secretary of Defense Melvin Laird in December 1971 stated, "Every time a woman was enlisted, it saved the DOD over $10,000. . . . Servicemen cost many times more than Servicewomen."[10] This report spurred the creation of the Central All-Volunteer Force Task Force in early 1972, which concluded by the end of that year that women were a potentially underutilized market for military manpower. In April 1972, the services were instructed to "take action to eliminate all unnecessary [restrictions] applying to women."[11] The Air Force submitted the most aggressive plan of all the services, aiming to triple the number of women by the end of fiscal year 1978.[12]

In 1972, one in every 30 recruits was a woman; by 1976, the rate was one in every 13.[13] The sudden increase in WAF numbers and their accompanying demands stretched the director and her staff more than they were built to handle, and when WAF director Col Bianca D. Trimeloni retired in June 1976, her position, staff, and office were unceremoniously dissolved. According to Trimeloni, she "thought the timing was bad [to eliminate the WAF director position] but there was really no other practical solution under the circumstances."[14] Free from their WAF association for the first time, women in the Air Force were now on their own in the new, totally volunteer Air Force.

Family Policies

As the American economy slowed after the Vietnam War, a world in which the nuclear family could live on one income began to disappear. Whether by need or by choice, many married women started to join the workforce, and by 1969 more than half had jobs outside the home.[15] Although on average women received less than 60 percent of pay than men, they found it easier to get work since growth sectors, such as health care and service industries, were traditionally feminine fields and most employers did not have to provide equal pay or benefits to that of a male employee.[16] While Air Force women had always received pay equal to that of their male counterparts, there were significant discrepancies between male and female service members when it came to benefits and family policies. As the population of women in the Air Force grew, the need for greater gender equality in these categories could no longer be ignored.

Legislative changes during the 1970s affected family policies and officer commissioning, opening doors some may have never fully realized were shut. DOD family policy evolved organically after World War II, and until the 1970s, the role of women in US society and the military largely rested on the "natural" assumption that a woman's primary responsibility was as a wife and mother and that military service was inherently incompatible with those duties. Traditionally, the courts had deferred to Congress and the executive branch in issues involving military personnel. Despite the limitations of her position as WAF director, during her long tenure Holm still was able to achieve changes "despite a lot of opposition. Not just from the power structure, not just from the people in power who were always men in those days—male generals, but often from women as well. The only way [to] . . . get anything done was to deal directly with the men in authority to convince them of the need for change."[17] Because military readiness and operational policies were largely structured in terms of men, they almost automatically ignored women. According to Holm, "it was very difficult to get policy makers when they made policy, to think in terms of how that policy would affect women."[18]

Before 1971, the Supreme Court had never found a sex classification law to be in violation of the equal protection clause of the Constitution.[19] When a challenge arose, the courts only required the government to provide a "rational reason for treating men and women differently" for the statute to be upheld. This leniency changed when the Supreme Court struck down a sex-based classification in Reed *v.* Reed (1971), setting a legal precedent for military women who were already challenging the services' policies on constitutional grounds.[20] By the end of the decade there were over 400 pieces of legislation in Congress addressing women's issues, with some of these directly affecting military women. Faced with mounting external and internal pressure to update policies regarding women, each service began its own review of sex discrimination rules; the Air Force found 32 laws and policies treating men and women differently.[21]

The first policy to be overturned was one that discriminated against men: the law allowing women to separate voluntarily due to marriage. This policy revision immediately reduced attrition rates and produced new demands for joint assignment of military couples. Consequently, the suddenly larger number of married women in the force spurred demands to equalize dependency entitlements.[22] Holm explained how every time she would talk to women in the Air Force on her field trips, they would raise the issue of unequal dependent benefits:

> Why can't we have the same (military) benefits as men when we marry, they'd ask . . . . They were very upset about this. I would tell them that we're not going to win this until we have some woman or man who has a civilian husband who is willing to challenge the ruling in a court of law. If we do that, I was convinced we would win. I said if anyone wants to take it upon themselves to fight, either for their benefit or their husband's benefit, be my guest. That I would send them all the information that I had in my files to bolster their case.[23]

In December 1970, Air Force physical therapist and 1st Lt Sharron Frontiero at Maxwell AFB, Alabama, took up that challenge and filed a class-action suit in federal court claiming the denial of equal spousal dependent benefits for women was unreasonable sex discrimination.[24] Until this point, Air Force servicewomen were considered single in regards to dependent benefits, regardless of marital status, and were not entitled to those benefits unless they could prove their husbands were dependent on them for more than 50 percent of their support. Through Frontiero's appeals, on 14 May 1973 the Supreme Court declared it was unconstitutional to require female service members to prove their dependents are reliant on them for over 50 percent of household support before they could receive benefits such as medical care and commissary access. Soon after, the DOD revised its directives and replace the words "wife" and "husband" with "spouse" in all documents concerning dependency and entitlements.[25]

The rules concerning servicewomen and minor dependents and pregnancy were next to change. Executive Order 10240, signed by President Harry S. Truman in April 1951, had allowed the services to terminate the commission, warrant, or enlistment of any woman (regular or Reserve) if she was the parent, by birth or adoption, of any child under age 18, had personal custody of any child under age 18, was the stepparent of any child under age 18 and said child lived in the same house as her for more than 30 days per year, became pregnant, or gave birth to a living child while serving. During the 1950s waivers were rarely granted, but by the late 1960s the process started becoming more liberal, though a waiver still required the woman to prove she could provide for a child without interfering with her official responsibilities (a rule that did not apply to military men, even single fathers).[26] Holm openly questioned the Air Force policy of discharging women who became pregnant and denying permission of women to adopt based on the grounds that it was unfair to force women to choose between the military and motherhood; the practice was causing the Air Force to lose highly qualified personnel. She argued the choice should be up to the individual who was actually carrying the responsibility for dependents and their military duties.[27]

When Capt Susan Struck, an unmarried Air Force nurse at McChord AFB, became pregnant while serving in Vietnam in 1970, she was given two choices: have an abortion at the base hospital or leave the service. Struck took the issue to court and in her testimony stated, "I do not want an abortion; I want to bear this child. It's part of my religious faith that I do so. However, I will use only my accumulated leave time for the childbirth, I will surrender the child for adoption at birth, and I want to remain in the Air Force. That is my career."[28] When a lower court ruled against her, she appealed. Though the Air Force initially wanted to see the case through and prove their point that they should not be required to retain pregnant women, three service judge advocate generals (JAG) advised the service to back off rather than risk the Supreme Court ruling in her favor. Struck was allowed to give birth, surrender the child for adoption, and remain on active duty.[29]

Soon after the Struck case, the services became increasingly inundated with litigation concerning pregnancy, and the Air Force realized it could not go on waiving individual cases based on risk mitigation. Military women themselves were split, with some seeing pregnancy and readiness as incompatible while others openly resented having to choose between a family and a career while their male coworkers were not required to make that same choice. In March 1971 the Air Force announced a new policy that provided waivers for discharge (or re-entry within 12 months for women who were discharged) for pregnancy and birth.[30] By 1973, 60 percent to 86 percent of waiver requests were being approved, but annual attrition due to pregnancy was still around 6 percent in the enlisted corps.[31] On 1 June 1974 the DOD told the services involuntary separation due to pregnancy was no longer viable and that all separations would now be voluntary effective 15 May 1975.[32]

Soon after, recruiting rules were changed so they no longer excluded women with children from joining the force.[33] One of Holm's biggest battles was to reverse the practice of involuntarily discharging women who acquired minor children via adoption or marriage. Though she "found support from many of the men," her boss General Dixon "was the key."[34] He ordered his staff to change the policy, even though Holm's women's program director counterparts in the Navy and Army desperately fought the change knowing they would also have to change their policy if the Air Force did first.[35]

Despite policy changes and more support structures available for women working outside the home during the 1970s and 1980s, women did not necessarily lose any traditionally female responsibilities at home. Many motivated women soon found themselves overburdened with a career, house, husband, and children to balance. Military women often experienced this burden on another level, as they were the first to hold and navigate both family and a demanding, nontraditional career. Until the Military Child Care Act of 1989, there was very little support from the Air Force for child and family care. Most Air Force mothers, particularly those who did shift work, had to forge deals with other female coworkers or male coworkers with spouses to trade childcare. The issue of child rearing as "women's work" would continue to disproportionately affect female recruitment, retention, and morale for the next few decades.

Officer Accessions

While there were no documented issues concerning the management of female Air Force officers, until this point a major shortcoming within the realm of female recruitment and integration was the lack of a consistent WAF officer procurement process or official end-strength objectives. After terminating the direct appointment option and slowly phasing out officer candidate school in the 1950s, the only option available for women to commission was Officer Training School. A decade after the failed trial WAF ROTC program in the late 1950s, a new law allowing women to commission through ROTC passed in 1969 and produced immediate success as the women performed beyond anyone's expectations.[36] Air science professors even reported the presence of women had improved the perception and acceptance of AFROTC on campus.[37] By the fall semester of 1971, 154 campuses offered coed AFROTC and enrollments had doubled.[38] The next year all AFROTC detachments were open to women with over 1,800 enrolled in the program.[39] Similarly, the Armed Forces Staff College admitted women for the first time 1969, and the first woman to attend the Air War College, Col Letha Willingham, entered in 1970.[40] The next major Air Force tradition in sight was the Academy.

In addition to basic equal opportunity, the fight for women to be allowed in the US Air Force Academy (USAFA) was significant because graduates were traditionally singled out for faster promotion, selection for schools, and command positions. In 1972, two congressmen introduced a resolution stating women nominated to a service academy should not be denied admission based solely on gender. After several failed attempts to get the bill through the House, enough internal friction on the issue built that House Armed Services Committee Chair F. Edward Hebert promised to hold hearings on the topic.[41] Starting in May 1974, the three military departments, DOD, and President Nixon all opposed admitting women to the service academies, citing the common argument that academies were training grounds for combat, and since women were not allowed in combat, they had no place at the academy.[42] This was an interesting argument, since the USAFA accepted men who were not qualified to fly and therefore could never qualify as an Air Force combat leader. Of all the graduates from 1964 to 1973, fewer than 40 percent participated in combat jobs, and of the 24 career fields open to graduates, only three were closed to women.[43]

Though the hearings ended unresolved, the issue did not disappear from DOD discussion. The services began planning for the inevitable next step of female integration. Assistant Secretary for Manpower and Reserve Affairs J. William Doolittle seemed to anticipate the inevitability of an increased role for women in the military and approved a plan submitted by the WAF director to, for the first time, set a fixed floor for WAF officer accessions with no ceiling. In mid-1975 the

House added an amendment to a DOD appropriation authorization bill that authorized women at the service academies, and after a number of unsuccessful counterproposals the bill was passed.[44] The first USAFA women enrolled in the 1976 fall semester, and the class of 1980 became the first coed class in the history of all service academies.

Fig. 12. A photograph from the 1980 US Air Force Academy yearbook highlights the first 157 females to graduate from the academy, 1980.

Though the Air Force was officially opposed to women's entrance into the academies, as were all the other services, it had been quietly considering the possibility for a few years, with some leadership even tacitly supporting the idea. After PL 94-106 was passed, the Air Force took the most active role of any service in bringing women into its academy. Letters were sent to every high school in the nation showing interest in recruiting the best female students. The Air Force also set up a program with 15 female lieutenants who were given an abbreviated version of academy training and then used as acting upperclassmen for the first class of incoming women. At the end of the first summer of training, the attrition rate of women from USAFA was the lowest of all services (and lower than that of the men).[45] When asked about her experience, Marianne Owens, a member of the first class of USAFA women, stated: "Needless to say, it's been no picnic here. Yet many of us have made it through under the same conditions as the men. Therefore, we say: Don't point us out; don't applaud us, or you'll be ruining what we've been trying to establish. We've come so far in fighting the hard feelings. . . . It is the goal . . . for us, to simply leave this institution, not as the first women graduates, but as deserving, hardworking graduates to enter the Air Force."[46]

Opportunity Expanded

The repeal of PL 90-130, the overhaul of significant personnel policies involving women, particularly marriage and pregnancy, and the political impulse to keep the AVF afloat seemingly flung open the doors for women to not only enter the service but also make it a viable career choice.[47] The Air Force soon started eliminating gender-based criteria for the enlisted corps, first adopting a single set of enlistment standards and then consolidating basic training at Lackland AFB, Texas. In 1977, after a two-year study on women in the military, the Brookings Institution concluded that without radically departing from current policies and practices, 76.1 percent of Air Force enlisted jobs could be filled by women.[48] Though the idea of women as drill instructors still met with resistance, weapons training became a new norm for women during the mid- to late 1970s. Separate housing was gradually phased out as motel-like dormitories that made it easier to accommodate both men and women replaced World War II barracks. Enlisted women were integrated into their units, and women officers were gradually given command of mixed units. By 1974, 21 Air Force women were commanding mostly male organizations, and by the end of the decade two female major generals were commanding large training installations.[49]

By the time Colonel Holm's tenure as WAF director ended in 1973,[50] only four Air Force specialties remained closed to women: pilot, navigator, missile operations, and security forces. All would open within the next decade. In 1976, the same year the WAF director's position and office were quietly dissolved, pilot training was opened to women. A year later women became eligible for aviation duty in noncombat aircraft, and the Titan missile crew duty was opened to women. Generally, the Air Force was more willing to open doors to women than the other services, but according to Holm, "when the decision was made in the '70s to open pilot training to women, that cut close to the Air Force's heart."[51]

In March 1972, Holm briefed the Air Force Secretary and Chief of Staff at the Pike subcommittee hearings,[52] suggesting the Air Force open flying training to women.[53] Though the Navy opened aviation to women in 1973 and the Army in 1974, the Air Force lagged until 1976 presumably because flying was the essence of the service and pilots were considered the elite branch, making the exclusion of women from rated (and therefore preferred) slots more symbolic than practical.[54] Until this point, the availability of qualified men and exclusion of women from combat were reasons enough to keep women out of the cockpit.

Fig. 13. The first 10 female officers to graduate from the Air Force Undergraduate Pilot Training Program, Class 77-08, with a Northrop T-38A Talon, 2 September 1977: from left, Capts Connie Engel, Kathy La Sauce, Mary Donahue, Susan Rogers, and Christine Schott; 1st Lts Sandra Scott and Victoria Crawford; and 2nd Lts Mary Livingston, Carol Scherer, and Kathleen Rambo.

In 1975, the Air Force Chief of Staff announced a three-year test program in which 28 women were trained as pilots and navigators for noncombat flying "to identify training or utilization problems associated with women in previously all-male careers." Considered a success, upon its conclusion the Air Force decided to open assignments for female pilots to C-141 cargo planes around the world as well as on refueling tankers. Additionally, the Air Force committed to enrolling 150 women into flying training annually through 1982. In 1976, the first 20 women, already commissioned officers, went to the 49-week Undergraduate Pilot Training (UPT) at Williams AFB, Arizona, and a year later, in 1977, the first six women were sent to navigator training. According to 1st Lt Shirley Popper, a former weapons loader, the first group of women were accepted into the UPT program without any major issues. The women went through the exact same training as the men and by all accounts fared just as well. The combined effect of PL 90-130 and allowing women to become pilots was that, for the first time, female Airmen would be able to legitimately fill staff and command positions, making them much more competitive for promotion.[55]

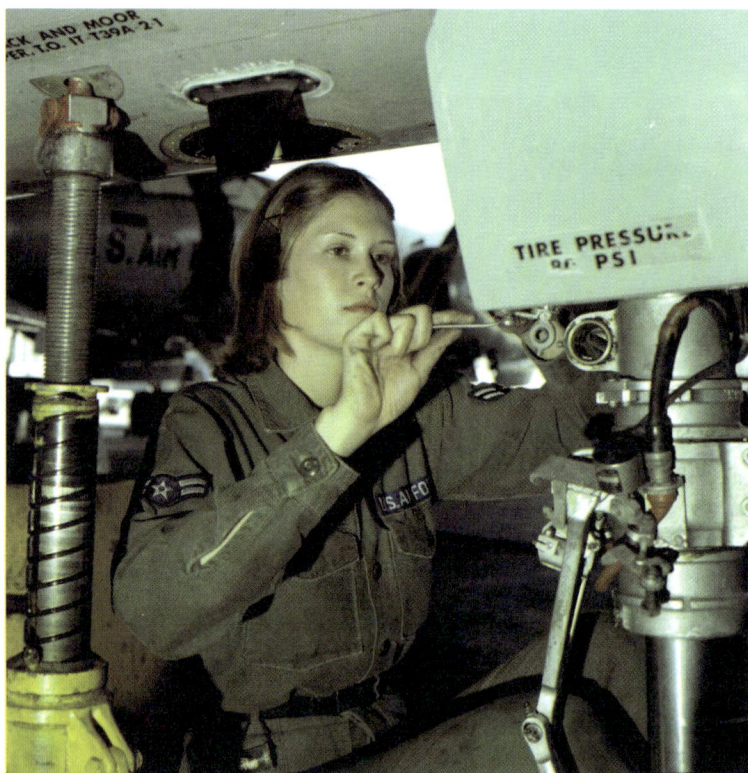

Fig. 14. A1C Janet E. Wuco, aircraft mechanic, works on the wheel well of an aircraft. 1974. (Source: NARA)

In 1978, the DOD asked Congress to remove the ban on women flying fighter aircraft, but it was ignored. When asked, General Davis said the Air Force "remained uncertain about retention patterns of women pilots, as well as how they would behave in an emergency situation. . . . He noted that it cost $225,000–$500,000 to train an Air Force pilot, who is then committed to six years. He expressed concern that in that six-year span some women were likely to get medically grounded or pregnant."[56] However, even with the combat restriction, the Air Force soon made 30 percent of pilot, 18 percent of navigator positions, and 20 different types of aircraft available for women.[57]

The same tentative integration of pilots carried over to female aircrew. Charlotte Eschmann, one of the first female aircraft mechanics, was one of just three women assigned to the 1st Tactical Air Command's 1st Organizational Maintenance Squadron and the only woman assigned to the actual flight line. When she arrived at MacDill AFB, Florida, on 4 April 1974, she was not allowed to step foot on the flight line and instead ordered to clean latrines and urinals (there were no separate bathrooms for women). "We were told in tech school that . . . no female would ever be allowed to actually work on an aircraft."[58] After some time, Eschmann was finally given the chance to work on the F-4 Phantom, eventually becoming crew chief. "Once I had a chance to prove myself, the other Airmen began to see that I could carry my share of the load. . . . In just a few months, I went from not being allowed to step on the flight line to being named Airman of the Month."[59] Despite her performance, there was still some resistance to her presence. She remembered one pilot who came back from Vietnam and refused to have a female crew chief because he did not think she could do the job. On a hot, humid day in Tampa, Eschmann decided to remove her "fatigue shirt" so she could work in her white t-shirt as all her male counterparts were doing, and she was written up because women were not allowed to remove their uniform top.[60]

As pilot, navigator, and aircrew training and positions opened to women, pressure grew on the intercontinental ballistic missile (ICBM) community to similarly allow women into their ranks. Launch officers were considered rated and combat positions, but when the Integration Act was written, ICBMs were only just being developed and thus not considered under the listed exclusions. As a compromise, Secretary of the Air Force John Stetson opened Titan II to women, primarily because the older facilities already had bathroom doors with latches.[61] All 13 women who entered Titan missile training completed it, and by mid-1979 four were assigned as combat crew commanders and nine as deputy commanders. Lt Gail Adams graduated from OTS in 1982 and was assigned as one of the first female launch officers on the Titan II at Little Rock AFB, Arkansas. According to Adams, it was a "very stressful career field," where women were under a microscope not only to do their job right but also to prove they could do it as women.[62] The training was severely technical, with a high washout rate regardless of gender. Adams was the only woman on her crew as both deputy and commander for four years. Though as a female she was not allowed in combat, she was in a combat role and therefore received a combat medal for her time there. In a 2008 interview, Adams recalled:

> I think initially with so few women in the nuclear business . . . they looked at us pretty hard as women, the few of us that were around. I don't know if they were wanting us to fail or not, but they were definitely really watching us pretty closely. I did feel that way. But over time I had proven myself, and obviously proved myself to the point that I became a commander of an instructor crew. And I earned my way there. It wasn't somebody trying to fill a quota. I never felt that way. I did feel that anything I ever did, it was I earned my way to that. Someone felt that I would be good at that, or that I would succeed at that, or that I could contribute something by doing that.[63]

Strategic Air Command leadership eventually admitted that the primary issue precluding opening positions to women was the concern over mixed crews, specifically the percentage of Air Force spouses who objected to their husbands working in close, isolated, and unsupervised quarters with women.[64] According to an Air Force survey, of the 1,200 Minuteman officers, 841 were married, and 67 percent of their wives disapproved of the idea of their husbands serving with a woman.[65] The "risk rule" would ultimately open all Minuteman launch crew positions to women in 1988.

By the end of the decade it had become clear the removal of the draft and the increase in number of servicewomen had actually increased the quality of recruits. The percentage of women in traditional jobs had dropped from 90 percent (1972) to 54 percent,[66] and female officers were now flying jets, teaching flight skills, and sitting at the launch controls of ICBMs, while enlisted women were maintaining fighter aircraft, missiles, computers, operating large equipment, refueling aircraft on the ground and inflight, and controlling air traffic.[67]

Fig. 15. An air traffic controller assigned to the 2021st Communication Squadron, Air Force Systems Command, monitors air traffic at Tyndall AFB, Florida. 1974. (Source: NARA)

Adjustment Period

Before joining ROTC in 1971, Dr. Yardley Nelson Hunter's college advisor, a former WAC, gave her some hard-won advice:

> People have a certain thought about women going into the military. That they are going in to find a husband, or blend in because they are so tomboyish they'll never get married anyway. You're none of that, and so you're going to have to make it very clear to them that you're none of that. Besides that, I don't want you ever to walk into a meeting with a pad or a pen, because you're nobody's secretary. You're going to be an officer, so you don't take minutes. So don't get into the habit of being assumed that you're a secretary, and don't learn how to make coffee . . . because everyone is going to think that you should be the one making coffee.[68]

Despite the majority of men being outwardly accepting of increased gender integration, most women interviewed who served during this time frame had at least one male supervisor or coworker who made it clear he did not feel she should have the same opportunities and income as he did. When Adams took paperwork to her boss, a male chief master sergeant, to get signed permission to take a night class off base he told her, "Look, I know why you came in the Air Force. You came in the Air Force to get married, find a husband to get married. I need you . . . and I can't have you distracted and going to school, and that sort of thing." She eventually went above him to his boss to get the form signed.[69] As for the men on base, Adams laughed. "Well, you never longed for a date. So—it was okay. I mean we were welcomed with open arms, so they were happy to have us. More and more women trickled in over time, and we got to where we had . . . I guess probably 60, 80 women [on Rhein-Main Air Base in Germany, 1972–1974]."[70] Adams retrained to become a professional military education (PME) instructor in 1982, and despite rave reviews from her NCO students, she remembered one male who ended up being discharged from the school because he refused to be taught by a woman, claiming "there isn't anything any woman has to say that I'm going to listen to."[71]

Because the reserve component is, by design, filled with Airmen who spend most of their time in the civilian sector, the difference in attitudes toward female integration from the 1980s onward was noticeable, particularly in nontraditional fields. Cherise Miller March, one of the first 100 females allowed in the security specialist field, remembers her male coworkers in the 917th Tactical Fighter Wing (Shreveport, LA) as brothers. She said "they embraced us (herself and the other woman in their unit), and there was no discrimination in that unit as a reservist. Active duty was a different story."[72] MSgt Patricia Wicks, an active duty enlisted WAF, was assigned to the 7th Special Operations Squadron, Rhein-Main Air Base, Germany, working ground communications. Upon her arrival to the unit, she found out her commander had been trying to cancel her assignment up until the day she arrived. As one of the first active duty women assigned to an Air Force special operations unit in the early 1970s, Wicks remembers having to learn to demand support from her male coworkers.[73]

Civilian and military men were not alone in their period of adjustment to women having more domestic and economic rights and opportunities. By 1969, women had been in the Air Force for an entire generation, and their status, rules, and roles had settled into tradition. As the 1970s brought massive legislative changes concerning women in the workforce, women across the services, including members of DACOWITS, were often split on whether their further integration into their service would benefit or harm their careers or the mission. Most women (and men) were trying to cope with social evolution they may have desired but for which they were not necessarily prepared. As Holm remembered, "most of us weren't prepared for the changes that were coming. Everyone had to adjust. We women had to adjust our thinking, to ask ourselves some rather profound questions about what we were raised to believe or things that we thought were true that don't withstand objective analysis, one of them being women's roles in this nation as citizens."[74]

With equality and opportunity come responsibility and obligation. When considering social history, it is easy to categorize any changes as inherently progressive, positive, and desired. However, it is important to remember some women resisted these new rights and opportunities, seeing them as burdens of additional responsibility they did not want or need. This was true of women's integration into the military as well, particularly women in the 1970s who were transitioning from a world of minimal military opportunity, equality, responsibility, or obligation to one in which they had to embrace all of it. Many women did not believe the military should accommodate the special needs of women or that they (especially enlisted women) should be truly integrated into the military organization. Women who had served during the 1960s, 1950s, and World War II were used to the protection and guidance provided by the women's support structures, sometimes referred to as "petticoat channels." However, while the strict division between male and female service members might have once been helpful, as the social and political climate changed during the 1970s this division began to outgrow its usefulness.

Despite exponential numerical growth during the late 1970s and 1980s, the number of women in the Air Force was still very low compared to the number of men. As women were able to branch out into nontraditional jobs and assignments, they often found themselves isolated from other women. Because the power structure, particularly in the military, was still largely male, most career-minded women simply did not have many, if any, women to look up to. Female mentors were often not given equal weight as male mentors, as it was understood that without a man's support or guidance "you [weren't] going to make it in most organizations."[75]

Networking among women was generally discouraged, as women themselves believed they needed to fit in with the men if they were to be accepted. Culturally, women in the 1970s and 1980s were still trying to adapt to the new social order, and there was a bias against "women's issues," making most women hesitant to speak out on behalf of themselves or other women or to help mentor them. This reluctance was partially based on the fear of reminding male coworkers or bosses that they were female, which might then stir up their biases or assumptions about what women could or should be doing in the Air Force.[76] Smith, who served in the regular component and Air National Guard from 1975 to 1998, remembers some men being irritated by women caring about hygiene and makeup while in the field because "they wanted you to be a soldier. They didn't want you to be a girl, and when you became a girl, all the stereotypes of being a girl . . . surfaced. Weak, crybabies, that you whined a lot, you weren't strong enough to handle certain things, and always wanted someone else to help you."[77] The lack of mentorship and networking and its effect on morale and retainability translated to female veterans as well. While men had numerous veterans' organizations as well as more peers to share their military experiences with, women remained isolated and often excluded from veteran support services or acknowledgment. This exclusion intensified for women who belonged to any other minority group.[78]

Another important factor in female morale was the issue of sexual harassment and assault. Culturally, sexual harassment was not even categorized and recognized as a term until the late 1970s. Some military women interviewed for this study claimed that they did not remember anything inappropriate directed toward them during their service, but almost always added a disclaimer, such as "that's just the way things were back then." However, other women did have strong memories of sexual harassment and assault, with few Air Force reporting channels or support options available. March remembers "a lot of sexual comments and stuff . . . went on during that time at night in the [nuclear weapons] alert facility. There was a gag order back at that time. If anything happened, the women had to be quiet. Like, you were not allowed to say a word, because of reprisals back then, it was the good ol' boys club. . . . There were things that happened to women . . . and you didn't talk about it; you were labeled whores and such, so you didn't talk about anything back then."[79] These issues continued well into the 1990s and became part of the argument to prevent the integration of women into combat during the 2010s.

TSgt Kimberly Galloway, a Morse systems operator from 1974 to 1979, remembers not feeling as if she were trailblazing the path for future Air Force women but more as if she was just sticking it out, improvising, and surviving.[80] This sentiment was a common one among women during this time frame. Still receiving uniform and makeup lessons during Air Force PME into the late 1980s, women found themselves navigating a cultural cognitive dissonance in which they were expected be perceived as just the right amount of feminine and masculine at the same time; a futile effort to say the least. The ability to value and integrate feminine qualities in the domains of war and war fighting, culturally perceived as strictly masculine realms, was a unique task the Air Force grappled with in the coming decades.

Notes

1. Holm, *Women in the Military*, 246.
2. Holm, interview, 2003.
3. Holm, interview, 1998.
4. Millett, *For the Common Defense*, 568. At the close of the war, the Reserve was at full strength with men who joined to fulfill service obligations with a minimal risk of going to Vietnam.
5. Millett.
6. Specifically, the president did not charge Gates with determining whether or not an all-volunteer force *should* be implemented but instead to plan *how* such program would be implemented. Holm, *Women in the Military*, 247.
7. Holm, *Women in the Military*, 250.
8. Holm, 251.
9. Holm, 258.
10. Rostker, *I Want You!* The report was focused on how to successfully implement the AVF.
11. Rostker.
12. "Triple the number" meant having up to 50,000 women in the total Air Force. Holm, *Women in the Military*, 250.
13. Mitchell, *Air Force Officers*, 317. WAF officer strength stood at 1,300 and enlisted at 12,600 by the end of 1972. These numbers were well ahead of schedule to meet the quotas demanded by 1974.
14. Holm, *Women in the Military*, 283.

15. Mitchell, *Air Force Officers*, 317.

16. Blau and Kahn, "The Gender Pay Gap." The gender pay ratio between men and women in the United States held at about 60 percent until the late 1970s when the gap started to decrease. The gap decreased substantially during then 1980s but then leveled off during the 1990s.

17. Holm, interview, 1998.

18. Holm.

19. Holm, *Women in the Military*, 266. In Reed *v.* Reed (1971) the Supreme Court ruled for the first time that the Equal Protection Clause of the Fourteenth Amendment to the United States Constitution prohibited differential treatment based on sex.

20. Holm, *Women in the Military*, 266.

21. Holm, 267.

22. DACOWITS and the women's service directors had previously tried to get dependent entitlement rules overturned without success.

23. Holm, interview, 1998.

24. When General Holm heard about the lawsuit, she sent Frontiero all the information and case files she had to help bolster her case. The case went all the way to the Supreme Court, where Ruth Bader Ginsberg represented Frontiero and won. Holm, interview, 2003.

25. Holm, *Women in the Military*, 290.

26. In her book, *Women in the Military: An Unfinished Revolution*, Holm speaks of two cases showing the inconsistent treatment between men and women regarding dependent policies. The first example was a sergeant who was lauded in the press for volunteering for an assignment to Vietnam, even though he was the sole parent of several children following the earlier death of his wife. If he had been a woman, he would not have been allowed to serve—let alone volunteer for a deployment. In the second example, an unmarried male chaplain was praised for adopting two Vietnamese boys, which would also not have been allowed if he were a woman. Additionally, if either of these men ever married a military woman, her career would be the one in danger—not his. Ibid., 290–94.

27. Mitchell, *Air Force Officers*, 317.

28. *New York Times*, "Ginsburg Nomination."

29. Holm, *Women in the Military*, 299.

30. Women were also allowed the option of taking a one-year, unpaid leave of absence after which they could return to active duty in their same grade.

31. Holm, *Women in the Military*, 300.

32. Holm.

33. The other services, most notably the Army, continued to push back against allowing service women to stay in the military during and after a pregnancy. In 1976 Crawford *v.* Cushman ruled the Marine Corps's regula-

tion requiring immediate discharge of a pregnant Marine violated the Fifth Amendment, because no other temporary disability also resulted in immediate, mandatory discharge. The next attempted argument focused on time lost for pregnancy and childcare. In 1977 the DOD conducted a study on this subject and found that the difference between time lost for men and women was not significant because on average men lost much more duty time than women for absence without leave, desertion, alcohol/drug abuse, and confinement. Holm, *Women in the Military*, 302–3.

34. Lt Gen Robert Dixon, commander of the USAF Military Personnel Center in the late 1960s, was a strong advocate for equal rights for female service members. Holm, *Women in the Military*, 294–95.

35. Holm.

36. In 1971, Jane Leslie Holly became the first woman to commission through an AFROTC program via Detachment 005 at Auburn University in Alabama. Holm, *Women in the Military*, 267.

37. Holm, 269.

38. Holm, 270.

39. Mitchell, *Air Force Officers*, 318.

40. The Armed Forces Staff College name later changed to Joint Armed Forces Staff College. Prior to attendance at Air War College, Colonel Willingham served as deputy director of the WAF and was the first woman to assume a position at the major air command level.

41. Though it passed in the Senate, the resolution died in the House. The next year, in September 1973, a woman who desired to enter the Air Force Academy brought a lawsuit against the Air Force. A similar lawsuit was also brought against the Navy, and another by four members of Congress who objected to being required to discriminate on the basis of sex on academy recommendation letters. Holm, *Women in the Military*, 306.

42. Holm, *Women in the Military*, 308. Interestingly, none of the senior women from any service were invited to testify in the hearings. However, retired Air Force Reserve lieutenant colonel and former WASP director Jacqueline Cochran did make an appearance, testifying that women should not be permitted to enroll in USAFA for the same reason provided by leadership: academies teach combat and women should not go into combat.

43. Holm, *Women in the Military*, 309.

44. On 7 October 1975, Public Law 94-106 passed the House by a vote of 303 to 96, and the Senate by a voice vote, requiring the services to admit women into their academies the following year.

45. Holm, *Women in the Military*, 310.

46. Little, "A Look at Women Cadets after Four Years."

47. Despite manpower data indicating women could fill a majority of positions with their services without "disturbing combat effectiveness," each service still found its own technique to slow the inclusion of women. The Air

Force chose to retain informal strength quotas and continually cited a lack of adequate facilities as barriers to assignment and utilization of women. Holm, *Women in the Military*, 255.

48. Holm, 252.

49. Holm, 279.

50. After her retirement from the Air Force, Holm served as the Special Advisor for Women to President Gerald Ford and continued to advocate for policy changes regarding women in the military. Following the social revolution of the previous decade, Holm's office would largely look to and cite trends or examples from the civilian workforce as to how to be better employ women in the military. During her tenure her small staff, including Karen Keesling, was able to get President Ford to sign a letter to the Justice Department instructing them to examine all federal laws and regulations that treated men and women differently and to make recommendations for changes (either through legislative initiative or policy changes). President Ford was an active participant and supporter of getting the ERA through Congress, and everyone postured for what they assumed would be its passage through the states. The task force was set up and underway when the Carter administration came in in 1977. They liked the initiative so much they claimed it as their own and followed through on the process. National Women's Hall of Fame, "Jeanne Holm."

51. Holm, interview, 1998. The Air Force generally led the way in social policy change, due largely to the efforts of General Holm and also because the other services were not interested in changing their women's programs and policies. The Army and Navy directors wanted to retain control of their recruiting, commissioning, and training programs as well as their women's policy related issues. Because the Vietnam draft had drastically lowered recruiting standards, the Army and Navy's women's components felt pressure to maintain much higher quality and standards than the rest of their service. Because the Air Force was the newer, preferred service, it did not have to take draftees and so did not have the same problem.

52. On 6 March 1972, a special subcommittee chaired by Representative Otis Pike examined the use of military personnel. The subcommittee, of which Holm was a part, held hearings on the role and use of military women. The subcommittee's final report was highly critical of the policies and attitudes of the services and the DOD concerning the status of, and opportunities available to, military women, stating: "We are concerned that the Department of Defense and each of the military services are guilty of 'tokenism' in the recruitment and utilization of women in the armed forces. We are convinced that in the atmosphere of a zero draft environment or an all-volunteer military force, women could and should play a more important role." Holm, *Women in the Military*, 249–50.

53. Holm, 317.

54. Unlike the Air Force or Navy, the Army was not restricted by the law on the use of women in either combat or noncombat missions. Army policy allowed women to be assigned to combat support units, meaning there were no major hindrances to training and using women as Army aviators.

55. Though the Air Force boasted a "whole-man" concept, it was common knowledge the promotion system was weighted to favor the rated officer, academy graduate, unit commander, combat service, professional school graduate, and the regular (vs. Reserve) officer. In every category, women were either barred or at a significant disadvantage. In the 1973 the DOD developed the Defense Officer Personnel Management Act (DOPMA), calling for uniform laws to manage officers across the services and more specifically to abolish separate male and female promotion lists. Though the Air Force had practiced integrated promotion lists from its inception, this did not give heart to the women of its sister services, as Air Force women historically fared the poorest in the promotion process. For example, in 1978 of the 48 female line colonels in the military, only three came from the Air Force. Holm, *Women in the Military*, 277–78.

56. Weinraub, "Air Force to Assign Women as Noncombat Pilots."

57. Holm, *Women in the Military*, 323.

58. Humphrey, "Niceville Woman Has Fond Memories of F-4."

59. Humphrey.

60. Humphrey.

61. Holm, *Women in the Military*, 323–26.

62. Adams, interview.

63. Adams.

64. This issue primarily affected the Minuteman integration because those were two-person crews as opposed to the four-person crews on the Titan II.

65. Holm, *Women in the Military*, 326. The implication soon became the Air Force cared more about the morale of spouses than that of active duty female officers.

66. Holm, 275.

67. After initial policy changes early in the decade, Air Force women were still only being assigned to 70 percent of the noncombat jobs that were technically open to them. While some women did not know certain jobs were now open to them, others preferred traditional jobs that they knew would help get them hired for future civilian job positions. In response, the services created mandatory "sex-based, affirmative-action" quotas for nontraditional occupations (mechanical, electronic, etc.) and caps on easy-to-fill traditional occupations (administration, medical, personnel, etc.). Though well intentioned, the quotas resulted in overly ambitious recruiting goals for nontraditional jobs, while caps on traditional jobs sent many qualified women away

from service. Women in nontraditional jobs often experienced low morale as they lacked interaction or support with fellow servicewomen. Holm, 274–75.

68. Hunter, interview.

69. Adams, interview.

70. Adams was one of the first women assigned to the base in Germany. There were no dormitories for women, so the few women that were assigned there had to stay off base in a hotel until the base commander took one floor of one wing of a dormitory and designated it for women. There were only two bathtubs (no showers) for about 30 women. Many women started writing complaints and got senior women involved, even reaching General Holm. Eventually they got another wing, a kitchenette, and some showers. Adams, interview.

71. Adams.

72. March, interview.

73. Wicks, interview, 2018.

74. Holm, interview, 2003.

75. Holm, interview, 1998.

76. Hunter, interview.

77. Hunter.

78. Hunter.

79. March, interview. While serving overseas in Japan, March had a supervisor who told her that if she wanted a good evaluation she had to sleep with him.

80. Galloway, interview.

Chapter 6

Having It All?

The 1980s and 1990s

In a February 1984 testimony before the House Armed Services Committee, Army general John Vessey Jr., then Chairman of the Joint Chiefs of Staff, stated, "The greatest change that had come about in the U.S. Armed Forces in the time that I have been in the military service is in the extensive use of women. . . . I am not against it. We have wonderful servicewomen doing extraordinary things and doing very well, but we have taken a male institution . . . and turned it into a coed institution, and it has been a traumatic exercise for us."[1]

The culmination of nearly two decades of social change, and subsequent breakthrough of women into formerly sacrosanct service academies and rated positions, created widespread apprehension in 1980s that the military was being "feminized" under a liberal agenda that cared more about politics than national defense. Parts of the military community held fast to the belief that reliance on women was a temporary condition that would pass with the demise of a misguided Carter administration.[2] More often than not, military leadership sought to defend the status quo or even reverse progressive trends, while civilian leadership sought to press women's inclusion forward, often for political reasons, with Congress in the middle forced to make decisions. As for the servicewomen themselves, they too were caught as pawns in a political game, with little say in the outcome or quality of their life or careers. Both enlisted and officer women often found themselves isolated in predominantly male organizations without other female friends or mentors and certainly without networks to fall back on. DACOWITS was the primary method for women to communicate their concerns to the power structure; however, the services often resented this intrusion into their affairs.[3]

"Woman Pause"

As the first group of women graduated from USAFA in June 1980, the decade started with new opportunities and new concerns.[4] Shortly after Ronald Reagan's election, the Army and the Air Force secretly submitted proposals to the Reagan transition team to scrap the Carter administration's strength goals for enlisted servicewomen until women's impact on force readiness could be determined. This was most likely a reaction to the recently passed Defense Officer Personnel Management Act of 1980, which established ceilings on the number of field grade officers and codified rules concerning promotion criteria, separation, and retirement.[5] Both services asked to maintain the enlisted recruiting minimum for 1981 and 1982 in order to assess the situation.[6] According to Holm, many military women feared this was an anti-women campaign, as backlash for all the progress made during the 1970s.[7] The Air Force was largely motivated by a fear that if the Army's request to hold female recruiting was honored, they might be required to take up the slack (implying all the quality men would go to the Army). As a rationale for limiting the recruitment of enlisted women, the Air Staff devised a mathematical model combining affirmative action goals and ceilings with estimates of women's propensity to enlist in each career field, producing a basis for female recruiting objectives. Of course this model could be, and was, manipulated to meet internal Air Staff recruiting "goals."[8]

While this "woman pause"[9] was initially given credibility, once the new administration settled in and got a grip on the realities of the personnel situation, it became clear the hiatus on recruiting women was ill founded. Secretary of Defense Caspar Weinberger issued a memo to the service secretaries on 14 January 1982 to set the record straight on the administration's view of women in the services:

> Military women are a very important part of our total force capability. Qualified women are essential to obtaining the numbers of quality of people required to maintain the readiness of our forces. This administration desires to increase the role of women in the military, and I expect the Service Secretaries actively to support that policy. While we have made progress, some institutional barriers still exist. I ask that you personally review your service policies to ensure that women are not subject to discrimination in recruiting or career opportunities. This Department must aggressively break down those remaining barriers that prevent us from making the fullest use of the capabilities of women in providing for our national defense.[10]

In March 1982 the woman pause ended, although specific recruiting goals were still not set. Some senior Air Force women agreed that an assessment of women in the force might be beneficial to avoid the recruiting mishaps of previous decades. There was a concern that increasing female recruiting numbers would also increase attrition rates and so damage the image of the new female Airman, which they had worked hard to cultivate over the last decade. Some believed the recent emphasis on assigning women to nontraditional fields had backfired, arguing that in moving too quickly to force change, both men and women largely resisted—"hurting recruiting, reducing acceptance, lowering retention rates, and contributing to growing problems of sexual harassment."[11] Additionally, the services still had not fully worked out pregnancy and childcare policies, one of the core causes of female attrition. Ultimately, because the Air Force applied the same recruiting and training standards to both men and women, there was no internal incentive or advantage to recruit more women. However, elected on a promise to rebuild the perceived understaffed, underequipped, and underpaid "hollow" military force, the Reagan administration planned the largest defense buildup since the Vietnam War, and for the first time with all volunteers. Civilian leadership recognized the importance of women to this buildup and the sustained viability of the AVF.[12]

Operational Assets

The late seventies and early eighties were a highlight reel of firsts for women in the Air Force. In 1976, three years after the first female naval officers earned their military pilot wings, the Air Force allowed women into pilot training. After placing the first woman on operational crew status in 1975, SAC assigned the first woman aircrew member to alert duty in 1978. In 1982 the Air Force selected its first female aviator for Test Pilot School, and the following year an Air Force Reserve (AFR) officer was selected as the first woman in any reserve component to be promoted to brigadier general. A major policy landmark for women came in 1983 when Congress passed Public Law 98-160, establishing a much-needed female veterans' commission. This law further legitimized females in the military, acknowledging women should be treated as equals, not as men, in respect to their military service.

According to Holm, part of the reluctance to allowing women more roles in aviation was the unspoken but deep-seated doubts about how they would perform under stress in combat.[13] It wouldn't take long for those doubts to start being resolved. In 1983, Air Force women serving on aircrews conducted strategic airlift missions to Grenada as part of Operation Urgent Fury. By chance, Lt Celeste Hayes, a C-141 pilot out of Charleston, South Carolina, delivered troops from the Army's 82nd Airborne Division to Salinas Airfield while combat operations were in progress around the field because she was listed on the duty roster for that day.[14] In that action, Hayes technically broke the law and joined the list of women who have served in combat simply by doing the task at hand. Two-and-a-half years later in April 1986, women participated in a strike against Libya in support of counter-state terrorism policies, known as Operation El Dorado Canyon. Six Air Force women served as pilots, copilots, and boom operators on KC-135 and KC-10 tankers that refueled FB-111s during the raid.[15]

Fig. 16. Airman 1st Class Scott works on an auxiliary power unit that she removed from an A-10 Thunderbolt II aircraft during Exercise Bold Eagle, 1982.

As women demonstrated their proficiency in different types of aircraft and mission environments throughout the 1980s, it became increasingly difficult to continue denying them flying assignments. Under pressure from Congress, service secretaries, and some of their own service commanders, each service gradually relaxed their restrictions on flying opportunities for women.[16] The E-3 Airborne Warning and Control System (AWACS) was opened to women in 1982 and the new KC-10 in 1984, and in 1986 the Air Force opened 1,645 additional aircraft positions, including pilot and aircrew positions on the new RC-135 and EC-130, U-2, and RS-71, all of which were previously closed to women.[17] The ban on women performing airdrops was lifted, and previously closed assignments, such as pilot, navigator, flight engineer, loadmaster, and flight crew chief, on the C-130 and C-141 were opened after Operation Just Cause in 1989.[18] Though the gains were minimal numerically, the impact on women's advancement in the Air Force was major.[19]

The 1980s proved to be an era of expansion for almost every aspect of the Air Force as President Reagan's defense policies required a substantial increase in military funding and readiness. In response to requests from the services to allocate more funds for recruiting higher quality men, Congress required 19 percent of the new Air Force recruits in 1987 be women, 22 percent in 1988, and prohibited the force from setting minimum or maximum gender-specific related recruiting goals in 1989.[20] After the Goldwater-Nichols Act in 1986,[21] increased cash flow coupled with multiple contingency operations across the globe provided opportunities for women to redefine their roles and further integrate themselves into the force. As all the services were being encouraged, if not directed, to focus on eliminating barriers for women in the military, it became clear the combat exclusion law was the primary remaining barrier to integration.

Combat Exclusion and the Risk Rule

Advancements in aviation, sensor, and weapons technology paralleled by the changing character and scope of warfare made it increasingly difficult to draw distinctions between combat and noncombat aircraft and missions. Through the 1980s, the services still operated under the widely held assumption that combat exclusion laws excluded all women from all forms of combat, when in reality no such law existed. Sections 6015 and 8549 of Title 10 US Code provided the basis for these policies and by the 1980s were the last remaining pieces of the 1948 Integration Act still enforced. Unforeseen changes in technology, post–World War II military use, and the altered cultural perception of women left many legal technicalities on the use of women up for debate. While the law only specifically barred women from serving on "aircraft engaged in combat missions," historically Air Force policy had gone above and beyond to exclude women from any job or unit assessed to have a "high probability of exposure" to direct combat, hostile fire, or capture.[22] If the Air Force wanted to bar women from any job, unit, aircraft, or mission, all it had to do was designate it combat or combat-related. Entire classes of combat aircraft were closed to women, primarily fighters and bombers, even when only used for training and testing missions. Women were also excluded from the crews of noncombat aircraft whose mission might take them over enemy territory and nonflying units with missions that might deploy to combat areas (such as aerial port and civil engineering).[23]

Both the Carter and Reagan administrations had attempted to define combat more clearly so a DOD standard could be created, but a common stumbling block was the difference in service missions. Repeated DACOWITS reports led Defense Secretary Caspar Weinberger to establish a DOD Task Force on women in the military to address a wide range of issues impacting female careers, morale, utilization, and quality of life.[24] The 1987 task force report found that inconsistent application of combat exclusion policies across the services was harming female careers, morale, and quality of life and recommended the DOD adopt a universal definition and standard, stating that "the risks of exposure to direct combat, hostile fire, or capture are proper criteria for closing non-combat positions or units to women, provided that . . . such risks are equal to or greater than that experienced by associated combat unit in the same theater of operations."[25] The result was the DOD Risk Rule. Made official in 1988, the rule introduced a standard interpretation of combat exclusion laws and effectively opened 30,000 noncombat positions across the services, with over 2,700 of those being Air Force positions, to women.[26] These new roles included mobile civil engineering units, aerial port, aircrew in reconnaissance and electronic warfare support aircraft, and the Minuteman launch crew.[27] A year later, the 1989 DACOWITS report recommended women be allowed to enter all military fields, including combat.[28]

Though a major step forward, real world application of the law quickly proved difficult. The spirit of the law was inherently ironic: to protect women from risk in a risky occupation. Even within the newly expanded limitations, women filled positions that made combat exclusion policies difficult to define and enforce. Women received weapons training, served as military police and embassy guards, launched missiles, and served in other positions that blurred differentiations between combat and noncombat positions. For example, women in the Air Force could launch intercontinental ballistic missiles with nuclear warheads to eliminate enemy targets but could not serve in air-to-air combat.

During the 1989 Operation Just Cause in Panama, the risk rule was tested as Air Force women flew cargo and refueling missions, frequently under enemy fire, and worked in combat zones doing intelligence, finance, special operations, and signals.[29] After Army Captain Linda Bray led 30 soldiers of her 988th Military Policy Company in a routine police-operation-turned-infantry-style firefight to seize an enemy objective, she lit a fire under the controversy of new roles for women in the military.[30] Interestingly, the American media and public did not seem concerned over whether women should be in combat; instead the discussion turned to how inconsistent and pointless combat exclusion laws were in the face of modern combat.[31] These realizations would develop more fully in the next major test for women in the military: The Persian Gulf War.

"Mommy War"

As the Berlin Wall fell in late 1989 followed by the Union of Soviet Socialist Republics in 1991, the US was left momentarily standing as the only global superpower.[32] By 1990, just over 40 years after the Integration Act was signed, there were 223,000 women on active duty in the DOD, nearing 12 percent of the regular force. Additionally there were approximately 151,000 women in the Reserve and Guard, composing 13 percent of the reserve forces. Together with the Coast Guard (under the Department of Transportation), which had another 2,700 women in active units plus 1,200 in the Reserve, women collectively totaled approximately 378,000 in the US military.[33] The Air Force had the highest percentage of women among all the services, with over 77,000 female personnel making up 14 percent of the service and had 97 percent of Air Force jobs open to women, at least in theory.[34] At this point, women were so integrated into the Air Force, as well as the other services, they would be unable to deploy forces to war without them, as was proven in the Persian Gulf War.

On 2 August 1990, the Iraqi Army, under the orders of Saddam Hussein, invaded and occupied Kuwait. This action immediately drew international condemnation, and together United Kingdom Prime Minister Margaret Thatcher and US President George H. W. Bush deployed forces into Saudi Arabia.[35] Known as the Persian Gulf War, this conflict was the "most significant operational challenge since outbreak of war in Korea," and was the first real test for the total Air Force.[36] With Cold War fears all but eliminated, the US military was able to put full effort into the conflict, and the Air Force was able to test modernized technology and doctrine according to the unique components of the war.

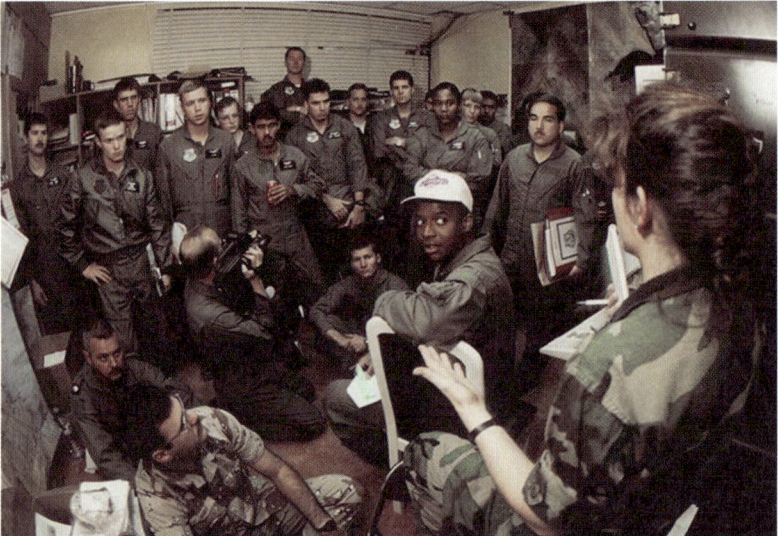

Fig. 17. TSgt Tony Tesori, weather forecaster, Detachment 6, 17th Weather Squadron, Hill Air Force Base, Utah, briefs aircrews on local and Iraqi weather conditions during Operation Desert Storm.

The Gulf War was the largest deployment of military women in US history up until that point. After facing initial difficulties convincing the conservative Saudis to allow female military service personnel into the country, approximately 40,782 women, constituting 7.2 percent of US forces, ended up deploying in support of the war in the largest call up of women since World War II. Of the total number of women deployed, 4,246 (just over 7 percent) were women in the Air

Force.[37] Similar to the men, the majority of women deployed were in the regular component, but the highest proportion of women deployed were in the reserve.[38]

In a first true test of the total force concept, the Air Force Reserve mobilized over 22,000 volunteer personnel (approximately 22 percent of all reservists) to support operations in the Persian Gulf. By the summer of 1990, the Air Force Reserve was at a high state of operational readiness, with most units meeting or exceeding manning goals and training requirements. On 22 August 1990, President Bush called up an additional 200,000 Reservists for 90 days, marking the sixth major call up of Reserve units and personnel since its activation in 1948. Reserve units and personnel provided 50 percent of the Air Force's strategic airlift and aerial port crews and capabilities, 33 percent of its aeromedical evacuation aircrews, and 25 percent of its tactical airlift forces during the war.[39] In November the recall was extended to 180 days, and in January 1991 Bush declared a national emergency and ordered the partial mobilization of the Ready Reserve for up to 12 months. The Air Force was authorized to mobilize 52,000 of its personnel, although it never reached that number. By February 1991 approximately 16,500 Air Force reservists were on active duty (3,800 officers and 12,700 enlisted). Mobilization peaked in March 1991 with almost 23,500 Air Force reservists on active duty, mostly medical personnel.[40] Of those mobilized Air Force reservists, 5,390 (24.5 percent) were women, and of the 7,209 deployed reservists, 2,148 (29.8 percent) were women.[41] Across the DOD, nearly 21.3 percent, or more than one in five, reserve officers sent to the Gulf were women.[42] In total, 13 military women died during the conflict (none Air Force) and two were taken captive as the first female prisoners of war (POW) since World War II.[43]

During her time in Saudi Arabia, Therese Robinson, an air weapons controller, recalls female service members having to follow specific rules in accordance with Saudi customs concerning women. These rules included the requirement to wear the full body cover *abaya*, always have three male escorts with her, ride in the back of the bus, and sit in a separate room from the men in restaurants. Saudi women were often intrigued by the American military women, wanting to touch their light hair for good luck. Robinson, as most other female service members, took the unique female military experience in stride because "that was what was required while in their country."[44] This general acceptance did not last, however, as illustrated when

Martha McSally successfully sued the US Department of Defense in 2001, challenging the military policy requiring US and United Kingdom servicewomen stationed in Saudi Arabia to wear the *abaya* when traveling off base.

During both Desert Shield and Desert Storm, American military women did almost every mission except engage in physical combat (although the line was often blurred). Air Force women were routinely assigned to tactical air bases in Saudi Arabia where they serviced, repaired, and armed combat aircraft in preparation for strike missions. These air bases were frequent targets for surface-to-surface missile system (Scud) attacks, often taking direct hits. After the conclusion of conflict, military leaders acknowledged that excluding women from the mission would have impacted combat readiness. For the first time, national leaders began regularly referring to the "men and women" of the armed forces and using the term "service personnel" rather than servicemen.[45]

Significantly, the Gulf War marked the introduction of live news broadcasts from the front lines of battle. The news, and more importantly video, of military women facing equal danger as military men became a focus of the press, serving to drive home the full extent of women's involvement in the armed forces.[46] The press initially grabbed on to the "wife and mother going to war" as a twist on the old "husband and father going to war" theme, dubbing the operation as the "mommy war." In a September 1990 issue of People magazine, the front page featured an Air Force captain in uniform hugging her young child with the headline: "Mom Goes to War. With tears and brave smiles, Air Force pilot Joy Johnson and thousands of American mothers are saying goodbye to their families to face unknown dangers in the Gulf. One 10-year-old's question: 'Mommy, what if you die?'"[47] Many men resented the implication that leaving their families and lives to go to war was less painful than a woman doing the same. Likewise, many women resented the implication that they were weak, unprofessional, and that childcare and parenting was solely a woman's concern.[48] Ultimately, certain long-held theories about women serving in war were finally proven to be myths, showing that, when the action started, no one cared if a service member was a man or a woman. All that mattered was whether or not they could do the job.

The Kennedy-Roth Amendment

At the conclusion of the Gulf War, civil rights and women's advocacy groups renewed efforts to expand the use of women in the military. Despite continued senior military leader resistance, at their spring 1991 meeting DACOWITS recommended (again) the repeal of combat exclusion statutes, arguing the services should be able to utilize all qualified personnel based on ability rather than gender.[49]. Desert Storm had exposed the public to the contradictions in policies concerning women in combat. Women were barred from flying fighters or bombers but were allowed to fly lucrative unarmed targets (refueling tankers and AWACS) over enemy territory. They were being assigned to launch ICBMs with nuclear warheads but not allowed to deliver conventional weapons from an aircraft. Additionally, most of the challenging and career-rewarding flying assignments remained off limits, as combat flying experience was still rewarded above all else. Lawrence Korb, former assistant Secretary of Defense for manpower, installations, and logistics during President Reagan's first term, stated: "Women are being put in danger, but denied the rewards that those in direct combat positions are entitled to in the service. Who gets promotions in the Air Force? The fighter pilot. The woman [who] is flying the tanker—she's in just as much danger, but she can't get the promotions."[50]

The first congressional move to repeal the combat exclusion law came on 8 May 1991 when the House Armed Services Committee voted to allow women to fly combat missions in the Air Force, Navy, and Marines. The committee report noted that lifting the combat restrictions did not necessarily imply women would perform combat missions, but instead passed the decision to the service secretaries.[51] When the bill was passed to the Senate, Senators McCain and William V. Roth (R-Del.) took the lead in advocating changes to the combat exclusion laws.

Meanwhile, House approval had generated a national public debate. While the DoD remained officially neutral on the topic, both male and female military officials fought the combat repeal, fearing it would open the floodgates to removing all barriers for women and effectively undermine combat readiness.[52] Though female aviators had previously flown in Panama, Grenada, and Kuwait, opponents began seriously and effectively lobbying against the Kennedy-Roth bill. Replaying emotional arguments heard 50 years prior, the narrative was that allowing women to fly in combat would "threaten the American family because it would lead to the drafting of women and sending mothers to die in foxholes."[53] All four service chiefs spoke against making any changes to the laws preventing women serving in combat. The Air Force Chief of Staff, Gen Merrill McPeak, a career fighter pilot and combat veteran of Vietnam, was the most lenient, testifying that while he personally was not "eager to increase exposure of our women to additional risk . . . the Air Force does not believe in artificially barring anybody from doing any job."[54]

At the Senate Armed Services Committee hearings in June 1991, Senators Roth and Edward M. Kennedy (D-Mass.) were the only senators present who actively favored repeal. Conflicting testimony during the hearings opened the debate from combat flying to all gender-based assignment policies, effectively stalling the repeal momentum entirely. The Senate Armed Services Committee version of the 1992–1993 defense authorization bill emerged in July with no mention of opening combat flying to women. Senator Roth's proposed bill (similar to the one passed by the House) had been tabled while the committee proposed that Congress direct the President to appoint a commission to study the assignment of women in the military.[55] Roth replied in a press release that favoring a commission was "hogwash. As we have seen in the Persian Gulf, women have already proven themselves capable of flying in combat situations. . . . I am simply talking about giving women pilots equal opportunity for equal capability—no less, and no more."[56]

Roth decided to persist and was joined by Kennedy as the two cosponsored an amendment to the defense authorization bill when it came up for debate on the Senate floor. To combat the opposition's effectiveness, Roth's and Kennedy's staff advised that those who wanted a repeal would need to organize and fight for it. Word went out to active and retired military women, former DACOWITS members, and the vast network of national women's organizations to encourage their senators to vote for the Kennedy-Roth bill. The public debate that ensued highlighted many of the problems, both real and imagined, concerning women in combat.

Despite all the fears and concerns, ultimately no neutral evidence could continue justifying women being barred from flying in combat. Examples of successful performance as operational, test, and instructor pilots were combined with weighty testimonials, such as those from Senator John McCain, a decorated Navy fighter pilot, and Lt

Gen Charles Horner, USAF, who stated that restricting women in combat was "contrary to individual freedoms the military is sworn to uphold."[57] On 25 July 1991 Senators Roth and Kenney held a joint press conference announcing their intention to introduce an amendment to the 1992 defense authorization bill that would repeal the 1948 law barring women from combat flying. In his opening statement to the press, Roth stated: "We are here today to talk not about gender but about excellence. We are here to talk, not about whether we want women pilots flying combat missions, but whether we want the best pilots flying combat missions."[58] Kennedy went on to say that "the issue is not whether women should fly high-performance aircraft. They are already do as instructors of combat pilots. The real issue is whether we select our combat pilots based on ability or on gender," particularly based on a law that is "no longer relevant in today's world."[59] Though at the surface level the debate was whether or not women could perform the job, the deeper issue was that most men were still wrapped up in their perceived masculine responsibility to protect women from whatever they regarded as harm. Throughout the history of women in the military, whenever a push for more opportunity is met with resistance this cultural belief is often the source of that tension. Adding more fuel to the debate was the recent experience of Maj Rhonda Cornum, an Army flight surgeon who was shot down over Iraq in 1991 and subsequently tortured and sexually assaulted as a prisoner of war. Cornum testified about her treatment to the Presidential Commission on the Assignment of Women in the Armed Services in 1992, making her story still fresh in the mind of both the military and the public.

While everyone expected a "floor fight" on the women in combat issue, in the end the bill passed the House quickly, and when the Senate came together to vote on the bill in July 1991, the measure was approved on a voice vote.[60] On 5 December 1991 President Bush signed National Defense Authorization Act for FY 1992–1993, which included the Kennedy-Roth bill, meaning women could now serve aboard combat aircraft engaged in combat missions. He also established a commission on the assignment of women in the armed forces and authorized the Secretary of Defense to waive remaining combat exclusion laws in order to conduct test assignments of female service personnel in combat positions.[61] The President's Commission on the Assignment of Women in the Armed Forces leader Robert Herres, retired Air Force general and former vice chairman of the Joint Chiefs of Staff (JCS), told the panel there was no reason to ban women from flying combat aircraft and that the debate was more aligned with social than military considerations.[62] In early 1993 Secretary of Defense Les Aspin directed all services to open combat aviation to women, including enlisted aircrew. On 28 April 1993 General McPeak announced that women would be eligible to fly any aircraft in the Air Force inventory.[63] In 1994, the risk rule was rescinded and replaced by the Direct Ground Combat Definition and Assignment Rule (DGCDAR). This new policy directed that women were eligible to be assigned to all positions for which they qualified, except for units below brigade level whose primary mission was to engage the enemy in direct combat. During her deployment to Kuwait in 1995, Martha McSally flew combat patrols enforcing the no-fly zone over southern Iraq in support of Operation Southern Watch, becoming the first American female to fly in combat.[64]

Fig. 18. On 28 April 1993, Gen Merrill McPeak announced the selection of, from left, Sharon Preszler, Martha McSally, and Jeannie Leavitt as the Air Force's first female combat pilots.

Closing Out the Millennium

Though the USAF came home from the Gulf War on a high, personnel cuts and base closures continued as had been planned prior to the war.[65] The Clinton era (1993–2001) was characterized by decreased defense spending and low-risk military interventions, particularly in power vacuums left by the dissolution of the USSR. As the focus shifted from communism to the rise of international, nonstate threats, investments in missile defense and space-based information systems increased.[66] In 1991 Chief of Staff McPeak and Secretary of the Air Force Donald Rice outlined a new direction for the service in a policy paper titled: "The Air Force and US National Security: Global Reach—Global Power." As determined by the paper, the new version of the Air Force needed to streamline the chain of command, reduce organizational layering, and clarify and decentralize responsibility and authority. Under McPeak the Air Force downsized and reorganized almost every major command in order to centralize command and create a more effective force.[67]

Meanwhile, the AFR became heavily involved in humanitarian relief efforts in the former Soviet Union, Eastern Europe, the Persian Gulf region, and Somalia, as well as natural disaster-relief efforts, making it appear the military was more like an "armed Peace Corps mission than the world's unchallenged military power."[68]

Fig. 19. Amn Anne Moor, 24th Security Police Squadron, Howard AFB, Panama, stands guard while a C-130 is unloaded during Operation Green Clover, 1996.

As the Air Force responded to hot spots around the globe, women were a vital component of the smaller, more flexible, total force.

Working alongside other nations, US military personnel deployed to Bosnia-Herzegovina, Macedonia, Haiti, Rwanda, Guatemala, and other countries to perform peacekeeping, humanitarian, and disaster-relief missions. At home they fluxed in concert with the largest military downsizing in five decades. Some were promoted to senior officer and enlisted ranks, and, for the first time, the services promoted women to three-star rank. By 1999, 99 percent of all Air Force occupations were open to women. Though women had made incredibly significant strides toward full inclusion over the previous two decades in particular, the next two decades brought unforeseen challenges that eventually required women to finally be fully integrated into the Air Force.[69]

Notes

1. Holm, *Women in the Military*, 381.
2. Holm, 282.
3. Holm, 383.
4. The defeats of both the Equal Rights Amendment and President Jimmy Carter, a supporter of women's rights, were popularly perceived as a blow to the waning women's rights movement. Holm, 387.
5. In the mid-to-late 1970s, Secretary McNamara convened a joint service group, known as the Officer Personnel Study Group, which collected and analyzed data for two years, ultimately producing the Defense Officer Management System (DOMS). The DOMS recommended a single promotion system instead of the current temporary and permanent structures, used officer baseline strengths to calculate the rank structure, and placed limits on the number of colonels and lieutenant colonels. For the Air Force that meant 112,000 baseline strength for officers, 6,150 colonels, and 11,070 lieutenant colonels. No limit was placed on the number of majors, increasing promotion potential to that rank and thereby allowing a 20-year career (but only if one made the cut to become a regular officer). The DOMS never became law but was tentatively approved by all services and used to mold their officer corps. The draft did, however, form the basis for a major officer personnel act: the Defense Officer Personnel Management Act (DOPMA) of 1980, which effectively consolidated the Officer Personnel Act (OPA) of 1947 and Officer Grade Limitation Act (OGLA) of 1954. The DOPMA standardized, for the first time, officer personnel management across all services. Ultimately the DOPMA created predictable career paths for officers as well as clear lines concerning whether an individual was allowed to stay in or be separated from the force. Mitchell, *Air Force Officers*, 269–75.

6. Most of the service's discontent was with enlisted women. The Air Force, as well as the other services, expressed no issues recruiting and managing quality female officers.

7. Holm, *Women in the Military*, 387.

8. Holm, 387–97.

9. The term was coined by Jeanne Holm in her book *Women in the Military: An Unfinished Revolution*. Holm, 387.

10. Holm, 396.

11. Holm, 388.

12. Holm, 384.

13. Holm, 426.

14. Holm.

15. Holm, 427.

16. A 1988 GAO report considering job restrictions imposed on military women concluded that the Air Force set arbitrary limits on the number of women it thought would be interested in or could qualify for noncombat pilot and navigator positions. At the time, 315 (1.4 percent) of more than 22,000 active duty pilots were women. Of 480 eligible noncombat pilot positions, women were only allowed to fill 40. Holm, 424–29.

17. Holm, 282.

18. Holm, 337. This decision had actually been made years earlier but institutional inertia had prevented it from being implemented before Operation Just Cause started.

19. Holm, 425.

20. The other services were allowed to continue setting separate ceilings for women. Holm.

21. The Goldwater-Nichols Act was an attempt to reconcile interservice rivalry and stovepiping that had seriously hindered efforts during the Vietnam War, Iran hostage crisis, and Operation Urgent Fury in Grenada. The largest DOD reform since 1947, Goldwater-Nichols essentially overhauled the US military command structure to affect both peacetime and wartime. Changing the way we think about and fight war, Goldwater-Nichols had secondary and tertiary impacts on the further integration of women into the Air Force in the 1990s and beyond. Millett, *For the Common Defense*, 588.

22. The Navy was more closely aligned with the law, basing restrictions on missions rather than types of aircraft, meaning female naval aviators were gaining experience in types of aircraft that were closed to female Airmen. Additionally, and ironically, the USAF trained female pilots of other NATO nations to fly combat aircraft. Holm, 429.

23. Holm, 419.

24. Holm, 433.

25. Holm.

26. Holm.

27. Holm, 421.

28. Monahan and Neidel-Greenlee, *A Few Good Women*, 341.

29. The largest US military operation since Vietnam, the mission was to detain and capture Panamanian dictator Manuel Noriega to bring him back to the US for trial. Approximately 800 US Army and Air Force women took part in the operation. Monahan and Neidel-Greenlee, 336–37.

30. Monahan and Neidel-Greenlee, 337.

31. Monahan and Neidel-Greenlee, 336–42.

32. Though military intervention during the Reagan-Bush years had put American troops in combat throughout the world, there was a limited cost in military deaths. Between 1981 and 1993 there were 555 American troops killed in action in all operations as opposed to 1,200 accidental training deaths and approximately 300 suicide deaths each year for the same time frame. Millett, *For the Common Defense*, 607.

33. Holm, 397.

34. Holm, 421.

35. Operation Desert Shield (2 August 1990–17 January 1991) focused on the build-up of troops and defense of Saudi Arabia while Operation Desert Storm (17 January 1991–28 February 1991) was the combat phase.

36. Cantwell, *Citizen Airmen*, 364.

37. Holm, *Women in the Military*, 469. Though the majority of Air Force women deployed were active duty, the highest proportion of women were in the Reserve (13 percent of the total force and 21.3 percent of the Reserve officers).

38. Holm, 470.

39. Cantwell, *Citizen Airmen*, 364.

40. Cantwell, 366–69.

41. *Citizen Airman Magazine*, "History of the Air Force Reserve"

42. Holm, 470.

43. Monahan and Neidel-Greenlee, *A Few Good Women*, 357. The Iraqi capture of Army Specialist Melissa Rathbun-Nealy on 31 January 1991 helped the US military realize a "worst fear," as she became the first American enlisted woman to become a POW and the first US female military POW since World War II. No mention was made of Army Maj Rhonda Cornum's capture until after her release. Both quickly became key members of women's military history. Holm, *Women in the Military*, 469.

44. Robinson, interview.

45. Holm, *Women in the Military*, 442.

46. Journalists were reporting the two female POWs as the "first" female POWs, forgetting 85 female military nurses were captured and held by the Japanese for over 3 years in World War II. Monahan and Neidel-Greenlee, *A Few Good Women*, 357.

47. *People Magazine*, "Mom Goes to War."

48. By the 1990s, due to the AVF and policy changes allowing women to have a family and stay in the service, the Air Force was now composed of older individuals who likely had a family. Military policy shifted to reflect this reality, focusing on improving family services and quality of life. The extent to which the Air Force was now a "family force" became evident during the Gulf War when many active duty and Reserve members could not deploy without first arranging for appropriate childcare. Holm, 465.

49. Holm, *Women in the Military*, 474. Stating the case was committee member Heather Wilson, former Air Force officer and future Secretary of the Air Force, who was then working on the National Security Council.

50. Holm, 341.

51. Holm, 475–76.

52. Holm, 474.

53. Holm, 480.

54. Holm, 483.

55. Holm, 487.

56. Holm.

57. Holm, 490.

58. Holm, 491.

59. Holm, 492.

60. Holm, 494.

61. Holm, 503.

62. Monahan and Neidel-Greenlee, *A Few Good Women*, 360.

63. Monahan and Neidel-Greenlee.

64. Bergquist, "1st Air Force Female Pilot."

65. From 1986 to 1995 the total obligational authority of the budget declined 34 percent, total active-duty personnel strength 27 percent, total number of aircraft 20 percent, and base installations 24 percent. Boyne, *Beyond the Wild Blue*, 314.

66. Millett, *For the Common Defense*, 610.

67. Boyne, *Beyond the Wild Blue*, 316. Organizational changes began in 1991 with a dramatic effect on the reserve component. In February 1992 most major AF Reserve units were redesignated to better reflect the units' missions. Soon after, the Military Airlift Command, Strategic Air Command, and Tactical Air Command were inactivated, and the Air Combat Command and Air Mobility Command were activated in their place. One month later, the AF Logistics Command and Systems Command were consolidated into a single, new major command, the Air Force Materiel Command. The most significant organizational change was the implementation of the objective wing structure, as a means to reflect the changing geopolitical and economic realities of the decade. Ibid., 313–18.

68. Millett, *For the Common Defense*, 607.

69. Millett, 609.

Chapter 7

A New World

2000–2020

As of October 2020, over 72 years after the Air Force was established and women were first allowed into the armed services, 21.1 percent of the regular Air Force (69,772 total)[1] and 27.7 percent of the Air Force Reserve (approximately 19,000 total)[2] were composed of women. The percentage of women in both the regular and reserve components has been steadily ticking up over the last five years (see table 1). Across all ranks, the reserve component has maintained a consistently higher percentage of women than the regular component. Both regular and reserve components followed the same general trend, with the lowest percentage of women compared to men in the most senior ranks and the highest percentage of women in the lowest ranks.

Table 1. Women in Regular and Reserve Components of Air Force (2016), rounded to nearest 500

Regular component[a]	Total	No. Women	% Women
Regular enlisted	265,000	54,000	20.4
Regular officer	63,500	14,000	21.9
Regular total	328,500	68,000	20.7
Reserve component[b]	**Total**	**No. Women**	**% Women**
Reserve enlisted	55,000	14,500	26.4
Reserve officer	14,000	3,500	26.4
Reserve total[c]	69,000	18,000	26.4

Sources:

[a] "Total Force Military Demographics," 2016.

[b] "Total Force Military Demographics," 2016.

[c] Selected Reserve only (traditional reservist, active guard reservist, air reserve technician, individual mobilization augmentee); Total Selected Reserve Authorizations in 2019: 70,000; Total Reserve available (including all Individual Ready Reserve [IRR], retired and standby Reserve personnel) in 2019: 847,816.

After the end of the draft and the genesis of an all-volunteer military force in 1973, every service experienced a steady two-decade surge of women in the force. In 1973, women comprised 1.6 percent of all military personnel but by the end of 2019 the statistic was over 16 percent. The Air Force has consistently maintained the highest average percentage of women across all services, with 20 percent of its total force being female in 2019. Despite this growth, the female population across all services has mostly leveled off since the 1990s.[3] Retention of female Airmen, particularly officers, has become a high personnel priority over the last decade, with various aspects of the retention question undergoing active analysis at the time of this writing.

Prior to combat-related fields (aviation, missiles, special forces, etc.) being opened to women during the 1980s and 1990s, women's retention and promotion were not typically considered in force-management decisions. The last 25 years have seen a significant pivot in the manner and amount that the Air Force as well as the other services have adapted policies, created programs, and generally shifted their perspective to that of considering and supporting a woman's career in the military. The primary reason for this is the need to sustain the all-volunteer force.

AVF Sustainment

The door to the new millennium opened in peacetime. As the end of the Cold War forced America to reassess its military's structure and role in the world, a smaller Air Force focused on technological innovation emerged. After three decades of operating with an all-volunteer military, it was clear that while a professional, volunteer military force was more effective and efficient than its conscripted counterpart of the past, it also required more strategy (fiscal and otherwise) to maintain.

In the eyes of the American public, the Cold War and Gulf War proved that America could win wars with an all-volunteer force. Since 2000, particularly after the events of 9/11, the test and question for America's volunteer military became sustainability. The weight of continuous, worldwide military involvement since 2001, particularly in the Middle East, has required all the military services to create and enact both major and minor policy and cultural changes to support and maintain the AVF. They have little choice but to think in terms of families and minorities, generational patterns, and quality of life requirements to be able to recruit and retain individuals who are not only talented but also willing to serve. Supporting women's careers and leadership development has been a critical part of this process.

The evolving process of AVF sustainment has been a slow transformation from the belief that the military is, or should be, a traditional, masculine institution into one that is increasingly progressive and diverse. Military personnel diversity has moved from a congressional requirement to something that is viewed as advantageous to the force and the mission. However, the practical implementation and response to creating a diverse force has met some expected resistance along the way. Since 2000, the Air Force has led the way within the DOD in bridging the gap from theoretical diversity to practical implementation.

Diversity Initiatives

Since the Integration Act (Public Law 625) and Executive Order 9981 in 1948, the services have been on a slow march toward appreciating diversity as a core requirement and value of its mission, and therefore force, effectiveness. The Air Force has often led the DOD in taking initiatives to improve diversity and inclusiveness. The trend toward diversity in the military has mirrored a similar shift in the civilian sector, with the ultimate goal of maximizing quality of thought to gain competitive advantage. Since 2010, the trend toward organizational diversity has taken off in both the US government and popular culture. A key focus and beneficiary of these policy changes has been women in the military.

In August 2011 President Barack Obama signed Executive Order (EO) 13583, which established a coordinated, government-wide initiative to promote diversity and inclusion in the federal workforce.[4] The follow-on DOD *Diversity and Inclusion Strategic Plan, 2012–2017* outlined the implementation of EO 13583 and directed executive departments and agencies to develop and implement a more comprehensive, integrated, and strategic focus on diversity and inclusion as a key component of their human resource strategies for civilian and military personnel.[5] The plan included recommendations from the congressionally directed 2011 Military Leadership Diversity Commission (MLDC) report,[6] one of these being a requirement for the DOD to explore the gender gap in military retention.[7]

The *USAF Diversity Strategic Roadmap*, published in March 2013, states: "Diversity is a military necessity. Air Force decision-making and operational capabilities are enhanced by diversity among its Airmen, uniformed and civilian, helping make the Air Force more agile, innovative and effective."[8] The *Roadmap* was designed as an action plan to institutionalize diversity within the Air Force in order to attract, recruit, develop and retain a high-quality, talented force.[9] According to AFI 36-7001, *Diversity & Inclusion*, the concept of diversity in the Air Force includes but is not limited to: "personal life experiences, geographic background, socioeconomic background, cultural knowledge, educational background, work background, language abilities, physical abilities, philosophical/spiritual perspectives, age, race, ethnicity, and *gender*" (emphasis added).[10] One way the Air Force has changed processes to encourage more diversity in the ranks is to focus on recruitment in both the regular and reserve components. For example, in 2018 the Air Force changed the way it conceptualized and conducted recruiting. Under the leadership of Maj Gen Jeannie Leavitt, Air Force Recruiting Service commander, the recruiting process changed from a traditional stovepipe method into one that is a total force, centralized process.[11]

In March 2015, while speaking to attendees during the Center for New American Security "Women and Leadership in National Security" conference in Washington, DC, Secretary of the Air Force Deborah Lee James revealed nine initiatives to help build diverse teams across the Air Force. The plan introduced the Career Path Tool (later renamed MyVector), diversity and inclusion perspective training for development team boards, a promotion board memorandum of instruction, the Career Intermission Program (CIP), mandatory unconscious bias training, guidelines for how to identify high-performing enlisted Airmen for Officer Training School, a new postpregnancy deployment deferment, and the incorporation of panels in civilian hiring.[12]

In September 2016, 13 initiatives were added to the above list.[13] Released in April 2017, a second memorandum provided additional support to geographically separated military spouses, lengthened the early separation decision window for female Airmen who became pregnant, established diverse slates for key military development positions, promoted civilian participation in professional development programs, and directed better marketing for career fields that currently lack diversity.[14]

Secondary and Unconscious Bias

While the Air Force's recognition of, and dedication to, gender integration was at an all-time high between 2011 and 2019 and many "smoking guns" of institutional gender bias were eliminated, secondary (yet still impactful) policy biases continued to be identified within the organizational culture and personnel system. Some of these issues reflected larger cultural gender biases and mirrored similar issues within the civilian sector, such as the unpaid care burden still largely assumed by females.[15] However, certain Air Force policies remained in place that unintentionally had a secondary effect of inhibiting or even harming women's careers, such as the DOPMA-legislated promotion system and the Air Force Aviation Career Incentive Policy.[16]

To stay in touch with changing social norms and deal with underlying unconscious biases, the Air Force began to offer unconscious bias training, which was then mandated in the 2015 *Diversity & Inclusion* memo.[17] As of 2019, the Air Force required unconscious bias training to be provided immediately before promotion boards, development team meetings on school assignments, civilian hiring panels, and annual performance evaluations. In September 2020, Office of Management and Budget (OMB) director Russell Vought issued a memorandum ordering agencies to identify, and then look for ways to cancel or defund contracts or agency spending for training on critical race theory, white privilege, "or any other training or propaganda effort that teaches or suggests either . . . that the United States is an inherently racist or evil country or . . . that any race or ethnicity is inherently racist or evil." Vought also called such courses "un-American propaganda training sessions."[18] A follow up Air Force Judge Advocate document directed Air Force organizations to look at any existing or planned training, including diversity and unconscious bias training, to see if it meets the criteria barred by the OMB memo.[19]

Policy and Culture Changes

Over the last 20 years, Air Force women have taken command of air wings, led combat air campaigns, attained four-star rank, and taken command of a major unified combatant command.[20] Yet despite all these "firsts" for Air Force women since the late 1990s,[21] Air Force men still disproportionately hold the top ranks. In 2019, the House Armed Services Committee told military leaders to achieve more diversity in senior officer ranks, to include more women.[22] The Air Force women, both military and civilian, who did hold senior policy-making positions were critical to revising and creating new policies that helped support the recruitment and retention of women in the force.

Compared to the first 52 years women served in the Air Force, the span from 2000 to 2019 has seen an exponential change in both Air Force and Department of Defense policies concerning women. The Defense Advisory Committee on Women in the Services continued to be a primary player at the DOD level, helping push reform for sexual assault recognition and health care for female veterans, among many other topics. In response to DOD-mandated diversity initiatives, the Air Force created working groups and teams to uncover barriers to women's service as well as implement service-specific initiatives concerning women.

Defense Advisory Committee on Women in the Services

From 2000 to 2019 DACOWITS continued to be a positive force for change concerning women in the military. In 2002 the Office of the Secretary of Defense (OSD) allowed the DACOWITS charter to expire so as to issue a new charter.[23] This new charter reduced the number of committee members and modified the DACOWITS mission to include family members. Eight years later, in 2010, the charter was again updated, this time delineating military women as the sole focus. The number of women on the committee was also increased, allowing up to 35 women to be appointed. The current DACOWITS charter, filed 22 April 2018, states, "The Committee provides the Secretary of Defense and the Deputy Secretary of Defense, through the Under Secretary of Defense for Personnel and Readiness (USD(P&R)), independent advice and recommendations on matters and policies relating to recruitment and retention, employment, integration, well-being and treatment of highly qualified professional women in the Armed Forces of the United States."[24]

Since 1951, the committee has submitted over 1,000 recommendations to the Secretary of Defense for consideration. As of 2019, approximately 98 percent have been fully or partially adopted by the DOD.[25]

Air Force Barrier Analysis Working Group

Led by the Air Force Equal Opportunity Office, the Air Force Barrier Analysis Working Group (AFBAWG) was chartered to identify and, if appropriate, propose elimination of barriers to equal employment opportunity in the Air Force.[26] The working group was responsible for analyzing anomalies found in workplace policies, procedures, and practices with an eye toward identifying their root causes and, if those root causes were potential barriers, devising plans to eliminate them.[27] AFBAWG recommendations were made to senior leaders, major commands (MAJCOM), and other appropriate decision makers at all levels and also used to inform senior leadership of revisions to Air Force policies.

According to AFI 36-205, *Affirmative Employment and Special Emphasis Programs*, the AFBAWG is to be composed of representatives appointed by AF/A1(manpower, personnel, and services) in the equal opportunity, human resources, and other functional communities from the Headquarters Air Force, MAJCOM, and installation levels, while senior Air Force leaders volunteered to serve as team leads.[28] The AFBAWG is made up of five teams, one of which was the Women's Initiative Team.[29]

AFBAWG Women's Initiatives Team

The Women's Initiatives Team (WIT) was created to promote the advancement and retention of women in the Air Force, both military and civilian, through policy changes.[30] According to Maj Alea Nadeem, leader of the WIT (2017–present), the WIT "works to remove barriers for Airmen so they can continue to serve successfully and uses a common-sense approach to change outdated policies."[31] One member of the WIT was Lt Col Jammie Jamieson, Air Force Chief of Reserve Operations Integration and one of the first operationally qualified female F-22 Raptor pilot assigned to a combat-coded unit. As a parent of three, Jamieson stressed the importance of ongoing policy reform, stating she was "really proud to be part of a team [which has] done a lot of work this past year [2019] to tackle many policy barriers."[32] For example, in 2019 the WIT worked with numerous offices to publish a policy mandating the Air Force provide dedicated space for mothers who needed a place to pump breast milk. The team also worked to expand the availability of maternity uniforms and redesign female aircrew uniforms based on female measurements. The team also worked with the VA to create the AF-VA Women's Health Transition program.[33] The WIT continued pushing for policy reform into 2020 with successful bids to update policies regarding pregnancy discrimination, hair regulations, and medical benefits specific to women, among many other topics.

Sexual Assault Policies and Culture Change

Though both military women and men have dealt with sexual assault and sexual harassment in all eras, women were disproportionately more likely to have experienced one of these categories during their military service. In the late 1970s the DOD and the VA began to recognize sexual harassment and assault as a problem. However, the issue was not at the forefront of concern until after the scandal that occurred at the Navy's Tailhook Association Convention in 1991.[34] Since the 1990s, sexual assault and prevention offices, trainings, and systems have been created as stand-alone programs as well as integrated into larger Airmen resiliency programs. Mandatory annual training and "stand-down" resiliency days have been accompanied by an overall culture change regarding women and minorities.[35]

In 2003, the Air Force experienced its own sexual assault scandal at the USAFA.[36] According to a survey conducted by the DOD Inspector General in May 2003, nearly 12 percent of the women who graduated from the USAFA that year were victims of sexual assault or attempted sexual assault during their time at the USAFA. The vast majority never reported the incident to the authorities.[37] Leadership changes at the USAFA were closely followed with the creation of new sexual assault reporting procedures, including mandatory reporting, as part of an "Agenda for Change" program.

In February 2004, Secretary of Defense Donald H. Rumsfeld directed Dr. David S. C. Chu, undersecretary of defense for personnel and readiness, to review the DOD process for treatment and care of victims of sexual assault in the military services. In response, the DOD assembled the Care for Victims of Sexual Assault Task Force that, after a comprehensive review, released a series of recommendations in April 2004. One of those recommendations was to establish a single point of accountability for sexual assault policy within the DOD. This led to the creation of the Joint Task Force for Sexual Assault Prevention and Response, whose efforts were focused on developing a new, DOD-wide sexual assault policy which became permanent with the approval of DOD Directive 6495.01, *Sexual Assault Prevention and Response Policy*, in October 2005.[38] Additionally, the Task Force trained over 1,200 sexual assault response coordinators

(SARC), chaplains, lawyers, and law enforcement to create a cadre of Sexual Assault Prevention and Response (SAPR) first responders. That same year the Air Force created its SAPR program to prevent and respond to sexual assault within the ranks. The program addressed three major areas: definitions of sexual assault and consent, types of reporting, and assistance available to victims.

In 2009 the DOD Sexual Assault Prevention and Response Office (SAPRO) conducted a SAPR strategic planning effort to align priorities across DOD.[39] In response, the Air Force established a two-star level SAPR office in the Pentagon, trained Judge Advocate lawyers as special Victims' Legal Counsel, and created a policy requiring commanders to initiate administrative discharge processing for any Airman found to have committed a sexual assault offense.[40] After the release of the FY2012 *Annual Report on Sexual Assault in the Military*, Secretary of Defense Chuck Hagel directed implementation of the 2013 DOD SAPR Strategic Plan.[41] In conjunction, the secretary directed the DOD acting general counsel to amend Article 60 of the *Uniform Code of Military Justice* as well as any related proposed legislation and develop a method in coordination with the Joint Service Committee on Military Justice to incorporate the rights afforded to victims through the Crime Victims' Rights Act into military justice practice. The counsel was also required to evaluate the Air Force Special Victims Counsel pilot program, which included directives concerning enhanced commander accountability, increased focus on appropriate command climate, and improved response and victim treatment. In response, the Air Force launched an initiative to rid its ranks of material seen to objectify women. Pictures and calendars featuring physically objectified women were removed from Air Force workspaces and public areas to combat sexism and any perception of "rape culture."[42]

In 2015, Secretary James expanded SARC services to civilian members, including Air Reserve technicians who experienced sexual assault. The Air Force began employing full-time civilian SARCs who serve as the single point of contact to coordinate sexual assault victim care and facilitate communication and transparency regarding sexual assault response capabilities.[43] Similarly, the AFRC Sexual Assault Response Center provides SAPR support for all victims 24 hours per day, seven days a week.[44] Once requested, the VA maintains contact with victims as needed for continued support after a claim and resolution.[45]

Female Veteran Healthcare

In 1983, Congress established the Secretary of Veterans Affairs Advisory Groups on Women Veterans, and, over a decade later, in 1994 Congress passed legislation providing for a Center for Women Veterans within the department. As the number of women in the military had grown since the early 1980s, so too did the number of female veterans. The next major win for female veterans was the Caregivers and Veterans Omnibus Health Services Act of 2010. This act aimed at rectifying the disparity between male and female veteran care by bringing care and services provided to women veterans to the same level of quality as that of men.

Title II of the 2010 legislation sought to improve the VA's ability to meet the physical and mental health needs of female veterans. In 2002, the VA relaxed evidentiary standards for diagnosis and subsequent disability compensation for what is termed military sexual trauma (MST), a category that disproportionately affects women. In 2011 additional changes were made after the VA identified a gap in the percent of claims granted for posttraumatic stress disorder caused by MST compared to other causes, such as combat-related PTSD. For example, in fiscal year 2011, 59.5 percent of non–MST-related PTSD claims were granted compared to only 35.6 percent of MST-related PTSD claims, a nearly 24-point gap. Though disability compensation is not given for MST, service members can receive it if they have been diagnosed with PTSD as a result of the MST.[46] In 2011 the VA started providing special training for VA regional office personnel who process MST-related claims as well as specialized training to medical examiners that provide input on these cases. Additionally, more women's health providers were added to the staffs of veteran health clinics and primary care physicians were given refresher training on female-specific care, such as routine gynecological exams.

As women have been deployed, wounded, and killed in combat since 2001, the need to recognize and adapt to female-specific combat-related injuries became a primary focus of the VA.[47] In a 2010 address to a crowd gathered at the Women in Military Service for America Memorial at Arlington National Cemetery, VA Secretary Eric K. Shinseki noted, "We are late; the surge in women veterans has begun and will continue .... Time is not on our side."[48] After the 2010 Veterans Health Services act, an epidemiological study concerning the mental and physical health of women Vietnam-era veterans began. As of December 2019, seven studies have been published using the data collected, and continued data analysis is expected to shape future research, policy, and services concerning female veterans.[49]

In 2018 the VA Women's Health Services office partnered with the Air Force WIT to develop the AF-VA Women's Health Transition Training Program.[50] This program, which began implementing pilot training sessions at Air Force bases in July 2018, addresses the health needs of transitioning servicewomen.[51]

Mentorship and Networking

As has been seen through the history of women in the Air Force, female mentorship has proven to be a difficult subject. Though the Air Force has relied on mentorship to identify, cultivate, and promote talent, women were rarely mentored by other women due a fear of perceived gender favoritism as well as a simple dearth of women in the ranks. One attempted solution to this predicament, as well as a way to improve overall total force mentorship, was the formal, online mentor-matching program known as MyVECTOR.[52] Initially introduced as the Career Path Tool in the 2015 *Diversity & Inclusion Initiatives* memo, the program was designed to provide members seeking mentorship, or the chance to be a mentee, a means to do so. MyVECTOR offers a web-based mentoring plan as well as a dashboard that included a career plan, discussion board, and bullet tracker system.[53]

Outside of individual mentorship relationships, formal group mentorship options have become another option for female Airmen. One of the first was the Joint Women's Leadership Symposium (JWLS). Started in 1987, the JWLS is an annual DOD-wide, professional-development conference for women of all ranks and grades, including civilian employees. The goal is to assist each service's efforts to develop and retain a high-quality, talented, and diverse total force. As the decades have progressed, commands have started hosting their own JWLS to focus on more mission-specific networking and problem solving. At Air Force Materiel Command's (AFMC) first Women's Leadership Symposium,[54] held at Wright-Patterson AFB in November 2019, symposium lead Maj Julie Glover stated: "While the AF is working diligently to address a number of initiatives focused on the needs of female warfighters, to include uniform fit, childcare, maternity issues, and more, there is still a need to address those hard issues that often get overlooked in the workplace."[55]

In 2015 the DOD partnered with LeanIn.Org to launch lean-in circles throughout department and all military branches.[56] Circles consist of small peer groups of women who met monthly in a "safe space to share [their] struggles, give and get advice, and celebrate each other's wins."[57] As of 2019, most Air Force bases had women's groups that met regularly, as well as social media pages, groups, and platforms to pass along information, ask questions, answer questions, provide informal mentorship, create connections, and boost overall morale and connection among Air Force women.

Although the Air Force was more focused on diversity, inclusion, mentoring, and supporting the careers of female service members than at any other point in its history, women were still not serving in the numbers that might have been expected 20–30 years ago. The effect of the retention predicament was the familiar self-sustaining feedback loop women have been stuck in since their initial integration into the service. While women remain a minority in the force, their presence (and therefore needs and desires) will be insufficient to affect large-scale culture change. An example of policy with major secondary effects on the promotion and retention of women is the Defense Officer Personnel Management Act–legislated officer promotion system.[58] The resulting inflexible promotion track leads many to the assumption that military service and raising a family are diametrically opposed. Women understand what needs to be done to promote and succeed and if they feel they cannot "check the boxes," they will continue to separate or suboptimize their careers because family responsibilities, particularly having children, often require deviating from the prescribed promotion and career development track. It is interesting to note that most retention and recruitment studies and papers concerning women in the Air Force focus on officers. Despite all the changes to family policies over the last 50 years, the cultural stigma that one cannot have both a successful career and a fulfilling home life with children is still very much in place.

Career and Family Policies

In less than 50 years, the force has gone from seeing pregnancy and motherhood as entirely incompatible with military service to leading the way with policy reform to accommodate and support the realities and needs of women and families. In previous generations, particularly recruiting campaigns in the 1950s, the Air Force focused almost entirely on the recruitment of women with no hope or plan for retention. It was accepted and expected, by culture and reinforced by policy, that the Air Force was a pit stop on the path to marriage and children. As waivers became acceptable and policies changed to accommodate marriage and motherhood in a servicewoman's career, the focus shifted from recruitment to the retention of those women, particularly through childbearing years.[59] As the trend of both men and women seeking greater agency and flexibility in their careers and work-life balance has strengthened, American values and expectations concerning marriage, parenting, income, and career have also shifted. While family policies can either hurt or support both men and women, the current cultural reality is that women are the ones who most often alter their military career by separation or suboptimization in order to accommodate their families' needs. As a result, retaining women has become a more important factor—and revealing indicator—of proper force and talent management.

Since 2000, the Air Force Reserve has been increasingly leveraged as a way for women in the Air Force to balance motherhood and their career. Col Regina "Torch" Sabric, the USAFR's first female F-35 pilot, left active duty for the Reserve after the birth of her son because it offered more flexibility in how and where she served. In a 2018 interview she stated: "The Reserve provides an opportunity to serve either part time or full-time when it works for you and your family," she said. "It's unique because everyone is here by choice. About two-thirds of our Airmen serve part time, and they do a phenomenal job of balancing work—both military and civilian—and family, because they want to serve in some capacity."[60]

Pregnancy Discrimination

The historical relationship between pregnancy and military service is fraught with outdated policies that are reinforced by the cultural stigma attached to women as soon as their pregnancy is made public. While the Pregnancy Discrimination Act of 1978 made pregnancy discrimination illegal and the Department of Defense Directive (DODD) 1020.02E, *Diversity Management and Equal Opportunity in the DOD,* prohibits unlawful employment discrimination based on sex (to include pregnancy), these policies only apply to civilian employees. Current DOD nondiscrimination protections mirror categories protected under the Civil Rights Act (i.e., race, color, religion, sex, and national origin); however, pregnancy among military members is a glaring omission. Until 1975, pregnancy triggered an automatic discharge for military members. Though that is no longer the case, pregnancy remains a primary barrier to female recruitment, retention, and career advancement within the service. Within the last decade, this has started to change.

A major change for women in the Reserve came in 2017 when the Air Force changed its policy to allow pregnant reservists to continue serving on orders through the end of pregnancy. Previously, all active-duty operational support orders were automatically curtailed at 34 weeks of pregnancy. Following the policy change, Airmen who are pregnant or give birth while serving a continuous period of at least 12 months are eligible for up to 12 weeks of nonchargeable maternity leave during that order. Reservists not on 12-month continuous orders are not eligible for maternity leave but are no longer required to cut their orders short due to pregnancy.[61]

Female operators in particular face unique challenges balancing their chosen career path and pregnancy. A significant change occurred in September 2019 when remotely piloted aircrew, missile operations duty crews, and certain fully qualified pilots became authorized to perform their assigned duties during pregnancy without a medical waiver.[62] According to Lt Gen Mark Kelly, Air Force deputy chief of staff for operations, "Pregnancy is a planning factor that our Air Force policy makers and line commanders need to incorporate into daily business. As more women join the aviation workforce in the 21st century, we are taking proactive steps to ensure that our policies are revised now—to effectively execute the mission, retain our current workforce and attract the next generation of Air Force aviators."[63]

Another major change occurred in July 2020 when AFI 23-2670 was updated to allow pregnant and postpartum members to attend professional military education without an exception to policy (waiver). It is the member's choice to attend PME while pregnant or within the one-year postpartum deferment period, and if she does so she is exempt from the mandatory fitness assessment prior to attending.[64]

In July 2020 Defense Secretary Mark Esper put out a military-wide directive calling for an update to equal opportunity policy "to prohibit pregnancy-based discrimination."[65] The directive was part of a package of changes designed to root out "discrimination, prejudice and bias in all ranks."[66] Some of the changes were immediate, including a directive to end the use of photos in promotion boards. Others, such as orders to update hair regulations, were referred to the services or specific departments with a deadline to develop policy.[67] According to Cyrus Salazar, director of the Pentagon's Office for Diversity, Equity, and Inclusion, the Air Force had already approached his office with similar proposals in February 2020, but Esper's directive accelerated efforts to finalize the new policies.

Lt Col Jessica Ruttenber, a KC-135 Stratotanker pilot working (as of 2020) as a mobility planner at the Pentagon, has been instrumental in promoting policy change through her involvement on the WIT. She is the team's lead coordinator for pregnancy discrimination within the force. Her personal blog, hidden-barriers.org, serves as an open forum for women to discuss barriers to service and career advancement, particularly in relationship to motherhood. In 2020, one such post caught Rep. Debra Halland's (D-NM) attention.[68] In an interview, Halland remarked that even though there have been advances, "military women are still experiencing microaggressions and subtle forms of discrimination."[69] In 2020 Halland introduced the Equality for Military Mothers Amendment (EMMA) as an amendment to the fiscal 2021 National Defense Authorization Act (NDAA). The EMMA requires the defense secretary, along with the services, to develop a comprehensive plan 'that ensures Armed Forces members are not unduly affected due to pregnancy, childbirth, or medical condition arising from pregnancy or childbirth."[70]

Postpartum Support

One of the most far-reaching diversity and inclusion initiatives to benefit postpartum servicemembers was the updated postpartum deployment deferment policy. Effective 6 March 2015, deferment from deployment, short tour or dependent-restricted assignment, and temporary duty was extended to one-year post-birth experience, unless waived by the service member. For reservists, this included a 12-month deferment from involuntary recall to active duty. In June 2016, the Air Force updated the Air Force Instruction (AFI) 36-2110, *Assignments*, to officially implement the deployment deferment for women after having a baby from six to 12 months.[71] In July 2015, the AF announced it would also increase the postpartum deferment for female Airmen to accomplish their fitness assessments from six to 12 months, to align with the new deployment deferment policy. The change was updated in AFI 36-2905 on 27 August 2015.[72]

On the heels of postpartum deferment policies were rules to support female members with a more breastfeeding-friendly environment. By law, civilian and private sector employers were required to provide a clean, private place for women to pump milk while working.[73] AFI 44-102, *Medical Care Management*, dictated that supervisors should work with breastfeeding mothers to adjust work schedules to accommodate a 15–30-minute break every three to four hours to pump breast milk.[74] It emphasized that a suitable location for pumping must be provided. However, no policy determining the specifics of that location existed. Lactation rooms were required, but not enforced, and while many supervisors advocated for their Airmen to get a suitable location established, many also resorted to pumping in restrooms, closets, and empty offices. After directed efforts by the WIT, on 15 August 2019 the Air Force published a policy mandating units provide nursing mothers with access to a dedicated lactation room. The 2019 policy enabled commanders to support nursing mothers by outlining procedures and requirements for establishing a private, secure (lockable from the inside), and sanitary location for the purpose of breastfeeding or expressing breast milk or both. Air Force members who were breastfeeding or pumping remained eligible for field training, mobility exercises, and deployment. However, AFI 36-2110 supported deferment from deployment for six months postpartum. Additionally, Air Force commanders may consider supporting deferment of deployment for breastfeeding mothers for 12 months postpartum to "ensure the full medical benefits of breastfeeding."[75]

The most recent change in policy is the Mothers of Military Service (MOMS) Leave Act. Passed in the 2020 as part of the 2021 NDAA, the MOMS Leave Act ensures women who serve in the National Guard and Reserve are able to take maternity leave without it affecting their creditable military service.[76] The updated maternity leave policy passed in 2016 that allowed 12 weeks of fully paid maternity leave for primary care givers only applied to regular component members. Under the current system, women in the military's reserve components, particularly traditional reservists, can take time off after giving birth but are not paid and do not receive the points that count toward retirement for their missed drills and training weeks. Each member needs to earn 50 points per year in order for it to be counted as a "good year" and credited towards retirement. The bill provided compensation and credit for retired pay purposes during a 12-week maternity leave mirroring the regular component.[77]

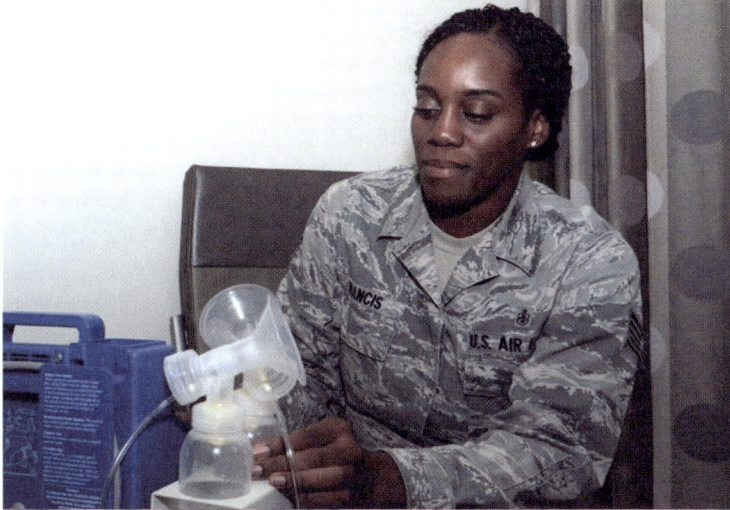

Fig. 20. SSgt Melishia Francis prepares her breast pump in a lactation room at Lackland Air Force Base's Wilford Hall Medical Hospital, 2018.

DOD Military Parental Leave Program

Until 2016, there was no authorized maternity leave for female service members, only convalescent medical leave for active duty service members to recover from childbirth.[78] On 28 January 2016, Secretary of Defense Ashton Carter announced that the DOD would be establishing new policies for maternity and parental leave as part of the department's "Force of the Future" initiative.[79] A major piece of the initiative was the addition of maternity leave to convalescent leave, giving new mothers a total of 12 weeks of leave after a "birth event." The Air Force enacted the policy on 5 February 2016. Later that year, section 521 of the 2017 NDAA authorized six weeks of leave for a primary caregiver in the case of birth or adoption of a child, which could be used in addition to the six weeks authorized for convalescent leave (totaling no more than 12 weeks). Secondary caregivers were also authorized to take up to 21 days of leave in connection with a birth or adoption.[80]

In June 2018, the Air Force announced a new policy for total force Airmen, to include birth mothers, fathers, same-sex couples, and adoptive and surrogate parents, in accordance with the Military Parental Leave Program (MPLP).[81] Effective immediately and retroactive to 23 December 2016, maternity convalescent leave is six weeks (42 days), primary caregiver leave is six weeks, and secondary caregiver leave is three weeks (21 days). Every birth mother received convalescent leave, with either primary or secondary caregiver leave taken in addition to the convalescent leave. Service members having a child by birth, adoption,[82] or surrogacy are responsible for determining caregiver status before the arrival of the child.[83] Commanders are not allowed to disapprove caregiver leave, and the policy protects Airmen from suffering any retaliation for taking the full leave, such as by receiving poor performance appraisals, missing out on advantageous assignments, or being passed over for PME.[84]

Single and Joint Spouse Parents

The allowance of accession and continued service for single parents and dual-military couples (termed "joint spouse") with dependents has evolved drastically over the last 20 years. The case of Rebecca Edmonds, a nurse who was kicked out of the service in 2011 when the Air Force found out she had commissioned while being unmarried and pregnant, was a high-visibility factor in prompting the service to re-examine its rules regarding single parents.[85] Previously, if a man or woman had full custody of a child and was not married they were not allowed to join the Air Force. However, if an unmarried woman became pregnant (or an unmarried man acquired full custody of a dependent under age 18) while serving, they were allowed to remain on active duty as long as their parenting responsibilities did not interfere with their service.

In 2013 the Air Force announced changes to its accession policies to make it easier for Airmen with families to enter the force. The new policy allowed Airmen with up to three children to enlist with a waiver and standardized pregnancy policies across the accessioning sources. "We discovered that the language in our pregnancy policy was too ambiguously written and could be interpreted in multiple ways," said Tina Strickland, chief of Air Force Accessions and Training Division. "We wanted to make sure the policy was being applied consistently across the Air Force. Reviewing the policy also drove us to examine our other rules for Airmen entering the Air Force with families."[86]

While the policy might have offered a way to work around previous accession policy restrictions, as of 2020 it is prohibited for individuals to transfer custody of dependents in order to enlist. Current accession regulations state:

> Married individuals with legal, physical custody of up to two children under the age of 18 and/or incapable of self-care may enlist provided you are otherwise qualified. For married individuals with three children, a waiver will be required to permit you to enlist. Single, divorced or separated parents or those in common law marriages with legal, physical custody of up to three children under the age of 18 and/or incapable of self-care may enlist provided you are otherwise qualified, but a waiver will be required to permit you to enlist. No waivers will be granted to those with four or more dependent children.[87]

Opening up accession to single and dual-military parents hinged on the enforcement of an up-to-date family care plan (AF Form 357). Updated and filed with a member's unit annually, the family care plan designates short- and long-term caregivers for dependents and is approved by a member's unit commander or first sergeant.[88] Though all total force members are responsible for creating and maintaining a formal family care plan once they have dependents, those who are single parents or married to another military member are required to do so or be subject to dismissal from the force if they do not comply.

Career Intermission Program

One of the first diversity and inclusion initiatives introduced in 2015 is the CIP, a DOD program for improving retention by providing a nontraditional option for work-life flexibility. Open to regular Air Force and career-status Active Guard and Reserve Airmen, men and women, officer and enlisted, the program allows individuals the opportunity for a one-time, temporary transition to the Individual Ready Reserve (IRR) to meet personal or professional needs. If accepted, the individual serves one to three years in the IRR and accrues an active-duty service commitment of two months for every one month on CIP. As of 2017, the most common reasons cited for application were education opportunities followed closely by family choices (wanting to grow the family or stay home with young children or both).[89] The CIP held its initial pilot program in 2014 with 32 Airmen, increasing to 40 Airmen in 2015 and 108 Airmen by 2017.[90]

Ultimately, the CIP enables the Air Force to retain the experience and training of participants, which would otherwise be lost due to short-term separation needs.

Female Operators

One of the most recognizable changes for women in the Air Force over the last 20 to 30 years has been the culture change surrounding women as operators.[91] Maj Gen Jeannie Leavitt claims many notable firsts—including being the first female fighter pilot in the Air Force—and has faced two major barriers through her career: policy and culture. Though the law allowing women to fly in combat changed in 1993, Leavitt remembers the work to overcome cultural barriers was even more difficult. Similarly, Heather "Lucky" Penney spoke about her experiences serving as a female fighter pilot in Iraq in the early 2000s.[92] At the time, her sister squadron was openly opposed to women pilots and refused to acknowledge her existence. When she sat at a table in the chow hall, the males already at the table would move. Much like Leavitt's dedication to being the best fighter pilot possible, Penney persisted by force of will and dedication to the mission. Penney stated: "You don't fly fighters, you are a fighter pilot, and you have to adhere to all of those cultural norms in order to belong."[93] Popular leadership literature during the late 1990s and early 2000s encouraged women to learn and adapt to the organization and hierarchy as they found it while avoiding drawing attention to themselves as women.[94] The potential negative implications of such attention, particularly in the operator world, were enhanced for those women who were also a racial minority.

Based on anecdotes and interviews, it is generally agreed that as of 2020, as long as a pilot can accomplish the mission, gender does not matter. Lt Col Christine Mau, 33rd Fighter Wing Operations Group, joked that the only difference between her and her fellow F-35 pilots is the size of her G-suit and facemask.[95] "Flying is a great equalizer," said Mau. "The plane doesn't know or care about your gender as a pilot, nor do the ground troops who need your support. You just have to perform. That's all anyone cares about when you're up there—that you can do your job, and that you do it exceptionally well."[96]

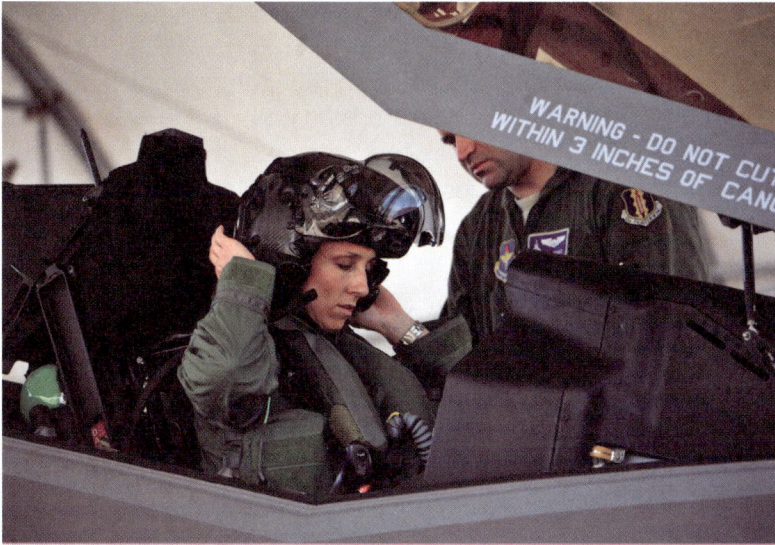

Fig. 21. Lt Col Christine Mau was the first female to fly the F-35. She was also the third woman assigned to the 492nd Fighter Squadron at Royal Air Force Lakenheath in the United Kingdom, where she flew the F-15E Strike Eagle in combat missions for Operations Southern Watch, Northern Watch, and Enduring Freedom.

While culture and policy have shifted, there are still ongoing concerns when it comes to female operator retention—specifically pilots. The USAF graduated its first 10 female pilots from Undergraduate Pilot Training on 2 September 1977. Just over 40 years later, only 5.8 percent of Air Force pilots were women. As of December 2019, 805 of 12,323 pilots, 347 of 3,265 navigators, and 233 of 1,306 air battle managers were female.[97] In her Air War College paper concerning Air Force female operator retention, Lt Col Anne-Marie Contreras stated: "I was the only female in my pilot training class in 1998 and the only female in my UPT-H class in 1999. Even now, in 2017, of the 237 students at Air War College, there are 29 women, only two of whom are operators—one pilot (me) and one Combat Systems Officer (CSO)." She asks: "With so many opportunities available in operations, where are all the women?"[98]

Uniform and Materiel Updates

Outside of policy and cultural changes, another response to the female operator question was to examine areas where within the operator community barriers to gender integration still existed, such as materiel and facilities. Air Force protective gear, such as body armor and flights suits, was developed, tested, and created anthropometrically for men's bodies. Therefore, most fit poorly on women, particularly in the waist and shoulders. According to Contreras, female flight suits existed but were "difficult to locate, take a long time to arrive once ordered, and feedback varies on the value versus the effort in finding them."[99] In recognition of this issues, the first ever "female fitment" took place in 2019 in which measurements from hundreds of female aviators were taken in an ongoing effort by the Uniform and Materiel Office to refine flight suits to better fit women.[100] "What has happened over the years is that a lot of our data and information we use to design these systems have traditionally been based on men," said Brig Gen Edward Vaughan, Air Force directorate of readiness and training. "The Chief of Staff of the United States Air Force is committed to seeing us make progress and better integrate humans into the machine environment mix."[101] Additionally, when an Air Force woman deployed to a combat zone and/or on expeditionary tasking with the Army, the issued "battle rattle" was not designed to fit female bodies and was therefore less safe.[102] With the integration of women into all military combat positions, the Army has added eight additional sizes of body armor to accommodate female body types, allowing the service to "fit the smallest two percent of its women for the first time."[103]

In the case of Air Force operators, what protects them most is their weapon system. The average age of an Air Force aircraft is 25 years and ICBM crew facilities are nearly 35 years old—constructed before women were serving in these weapons systems—and therefore did not include female-specific requirements.[104] Anthropometric data for most operators is based on eight cardinal measurements: standing height, sitting height, buttock-knee length, sitting knee height, arm span, sitting eye height, acromial height (standing height from the floor to tip of shoulder), and functional reach.[105] These eight measurements that define qualification for operator duties have evolved over time based on the medical community's response to the type of flying being accomplished.[106] Though the Air Force grants many anthropometric waivers, most women self-eliminate before even attempting to become a pilot due to the regulation alone.[107] According to Leavitt, height restrictions were a persistent hindrance for women trying to become pilots.[108] Once qualified as pilots, women still faced restriction from certain duties because of outdated anthropometric standards. For example, in 2015, the Air Force announced that pilots weighing less than 136 pounds would not be allowed to fly the F-35 due to unacceptable risk levels of neck injury during ejection at low-speed conditions.[109] With the small percentage of women in operations, the Air Force did not prioritize updating these requirements until November 2019 when a height standard review was announced, with the purpose of allowing more people, particularly women, in the Air Force the chance to become a pilot.[110]

Fig. 22. From left, Air Force A1Cs Tori Ann Bluhm, Anairis Ellis, and Ellyson Jimenez, 39th Security Forces Squadron (SFS) security response team members, pause together during a "guard mount" where SFS defenders don equipment before going out on shift at Incirlik Air Base, Turkey, 12 January 2021. Though women have been serving in the Security Forces career field since 1976, most clothing and gear previously issued was predominately male-body-type centered or unisex.

Hair Policy

A major policy change affecting all female Airmen was an update to the hair policy, the first since it was put in place in the late 1940s. As an outcome of the 101st Air Force Uniform Board in November 2020, women are now able to wear their hair in up to two braids or a single ponytail.[111] According to Major Nadeem, MSgt Johnathon "JB"

Lind and his wife, TSgt Jocelyn Lind, were critical to the multi-year policy update effort. The Linds started the Warrior Braids Project in which they interviewed hundreds of women, worked with various chains of command, and repeatedly pushed hair policy change proposals to the Air Force's Uniform Board, all of which were denied. In 2019 Warrior Braids joined with the WIT, and Nadeem contacted Lt Gen Richard Scobee, chief of the Air Force Reserve and commander of Air Force Reserve Command (AFRC), and CMSgt Timothy White, AFRC's command chief and senior enlisted advisor. Both supported the policy change and wrote a letter to the Air Force Uniform Board stating that the proposed changes would "mitigate safety, medical, and operational risks, while fostering a culture of inclusion within the Department of the Air Force."[112] Eventually the WIT got letters of support from seven of the nine major command commanders and more than 40 wing commanders, which were all funneled to the November uniform board.[113] (The new changes were approved in January 2021 and went into effect upon publication of the new standards in Air Force Instruction 36-2903.)

Combat Operations Since 2000

Since 11 September 2001, the women and men of the United States Air Force have performed major combat operations, sustained logistical operations over an extended period, and performed a wide range of missions under difficult and changing circumstances.[114] The wars contained within the umbrella of overseas contingency operations (OCO) are fundamentally different from the first Gulf War and other previous wars, in their heavy dependence on the Guard and Reserve branches, the pace of deployments, the duration of deployments, the number of redeployments, the short dwell time between deployments, the type of warfare, the types of injuries sustained, and the effects on service members, their families, and their communities.[115] Collectively, OCO between 2000 and 2020 constitute the longest sustained US military operation since the Vietnam War—and form the first extended conflict to depend on an all-volunteer military.

Fig. 23. Maj Christina "Thumper" Hopper. After the tragic events of 9/11, Hopper flew numerous combat air patrol missions in support of Operation Noble Eagle. In 2002–2003, she deployed to Kuwait supporting Operations Southern Watch and Iraqi Freedom. During those operations, Hopper flew more than 50 combat missions and became the first African-American female fighter pilot to fight in a major war.

In 2009, of all military personnel serving in Operation Enduring Freedom (OEF) and Operation Iraqi Freedom (OIF), 89 percent were men and 11 percent women. As a point of comparison, nearly all troops who served in Vietnam were men (only approximately 7,500 women served) compared with over 200,000 women who had served in OEF and OIF over a similar eight-year time span.[116] As of December 2019, 170 US servicewomen had been killed in OCO, by far the most servicewomen to die as a result of hostile action in any war. Of those killed, 18 were Air Force women. The first Air Force servicewoman to be killed in the line of duty supporting OEF was SSgt Anissa A. Shero. Shero, a loadmaster assigned to the 16th Special Operations Squadron, and two other Americans were killed when their MC-130H crashed shortly after takeoff south of Gardez, Afghanistan, on 12 June 2002.[117] The first female Airman to be killed in the line of duty supporting OIF was A1C Elizabeth Nicole "Liz" Jacobson. Assigned to the 17th Security Forces Squadron, Goodfellow AFB, Texas, Jacobson was killed on a convoy near Camp Bucca, Iraq, on 28 September 2005 when her vehicle was hit by an improvised explosive device.[118]

Fig. 24. The first all-female C-130 combat mission, 2005. From left to right, SSgt Josie E. Harshe, flight engineer; Capt Anita T. Mack, navigator; 1st Lt Siobhan Couturier, pilot; Capt Carol J. Mitchell, aircraft commander; and loadmasters TSgt Sigrid M. Carrero-Perez and SrA Ci Ci Alonzo pause in the cargo bay of their Lockheed C-130 Hercules for a group photo after their historic flight. The women were all permanently assigned to the 43rd Airlift Wing at Pope Air Force Base, North Carolina, and deployed to the 737th Expeditionary Airlift Squadron flying cargo and troops in and out of Iraq, Afghanistan, and the Horn of Africa.

Combat Exclusion Policy

In December 2015, Secretary of Defense Ashton Carter announced that, as of 1 January 2016, women could enter any career field and serve in any unit for which they met the standard.[119] This was a momentous decision and change from previous combat exclusion policies. Until this point the Direct Ground Combat Definition and Assignment Rule was still in effect.[120] Replacing the 1988 "risk rule" in 1994 as the primary policy concerning women in combat, the DGCDAR was not fully tested until operations in Iraq and Afghanistan started in 2001. The meaningless nature of a formal ban on women in combat quickly became evident in a post-9/11 world that consisted of a widespread combat environment across air, space, and cyberspace, but without front lines—and certainly without respect to gender partition.

A number of DOD programs (the Lioness program, Female Engagement Teams, and Cultural Support Teams) in which AF women participated required women to support ground combat and special forces teams.[121] In 2012, two lawsuits contesting limits on women serving in combat were filed, and in January 2013, upon the recommendation of the Joint Chiefs of Staff, Secretary of Defense Leon Panetta announced the lifting of the ban on women serving in all ground combat occupations and units. At that point the services had until May 2013 to draw up a plan for opening all units to women and until the end of 2015 to actually implement it.

Due to the nature of its mission, the Air Force has generally been further removed from direct combat and particularly the ground wars being fought in Iraq and Afghanistan. This distance has allowed more flexibility than the other services using women in "combat" prior to the exclusion being lifted. Compared to the other services, the Air Force has historically maintained the highest numbers of women but also had the fewest combat and infantry-type jobs and missions. Since the 1990s, the Air Force has allowed women to serve in nearly all combat-related roles. When DGCDAR was enacted in 1994, 99 percent of positions in the Air Force were open to women, with the last approximately 4,300 AF Special Warfare (AFSPECWAR) positions opened following the 2015 policy change. These previously closed career fields included two officer jobs—special tactics officer and combat rescue officer—and four enlisted jobs—combat controller, pararescue, special operations weather, and tactical air control.[122] As of November 2019 a total of 12 enlisted women had entered the AFSPECWAR pipeline, with two in training (one for combat controller and one for pararescue). Four women have attempted the special tactics officer or combat controller officer pipelines. In March 2020, the Air Force announced one special tactics officer candidate started the next phase of training, the first woman to advance that far within battlefield officer specialty training.[123]

While the debate over women in combat has shifted, the conversation is still ongoing. The Military Selective Service Act requires all male citizens between the ages of 18 and 26 to register for the draft. First enacted as the Selective Service Act of 1948, the act has been amended numerous times over the decades, including termination in 1975 and reestablishment in 1980.[124] Proposals to amend the act to permit registering and conscripting women have been attempted numerous times, starting with President Jimmy Carter in 1980, but so far the act has been upheld.[125] The National Commission on Military, National, and Public Service released its final report in March 2020 with the recommendation that the Selective Service System registration should be extended to include women between the ages of 18 and 26.[126]

The full inclusion of women into the most masculine of institutions has required a dance of external factors and internal influencers but is ultimately the result of every woman who has been willing to step into the arena along the way. External factors such as cultural values concerning the proper status and role of women in a society, current events (particularly war), and legislative and judicial decisions all shape the composition and focus of a nation's military, and in the case of this book, the Air Force. The question then becomes: what is next for women in the Air Force?

Notes

1. DOD, "2019 Demographics."
2. ARPC, "Air Force Reserve Snapshot: 3rd Quarter 2020."
3. Penney and Krieger, *Female Officer Retention*.
4. Office of the Press Secretary, Executive Order 13583.
5. DOD, *Diversity and Inclusion Strategic Plan 2012–2017*.
6. Established by the National Defense Authorization Act of 2009, the Military Leadership Diversity Commission was charged with conducting a comprehensive evaluation of diversity policy and practices in the military that shape the diversity of military leaders. In 2011, the MLDC reported its findings and 20 recommendations to the President and Congress in a final report titled *From Representation to Inclusion: Diversity Leadership for the 21st Century Military*.
7. US Public Law 110-417, "Duncan Hunter" and "From Representation to Inclusion."
8. The Air Force action plan to implement the 2011 Presidential Executive Order (EO) 13583, *Establishing a Coordinated Government-Wide Initiative to Promote Diversity and Inclusion in the Federal Workforce*; the *2011 Office of Personnel Management Government-Wide Diversity and Inclusion Strategic Plan*; the *2011 National Military Strategy*; the *Department of Defense Diversity and Inclusion Strategic Plan, 2012–2017*; Air Force Policy Directive (AFPD) 36-70, *Diversity*; and Air Force Instruction (AFI) 36-7001, *Diversity*.
9. Air Force Global Diversity Division, AF/A1DV, *USAF Diversity Strategic Roadmap*.
10. AFI 36-7001, *Diversity*. This AFI also governs the Air Force Diversity & Inclusion Action Group, which meets semiannually and includes

colonel/GS-15/senior NCO representatives from a variety of organizations, including the Air Force Reserve, to drive implementation and assessment planning for the Air Force Executive Diversity & Inclusion Council. The Air Force Reserve has its own chief diversity and inclusion officer who serves as a diversity advocate and adviser for senior leadership.

11. Leavitt, speech, 2020.

12. AFI 36-7001, *Air Force Diversity & Inclusion*.

13. AFGM, *2016 Diversity & Inclusion Initiatives*; and SAF Public Affairs, "AF Leaders Announce Latest."

14. SAF Public Affairs, "AF Leaders Announce Latest."

15. Ferrant et al. "Unpaid Care Work."

16. In 1974, Congress passed the Aviation Career Incentive Act creating aviation career incentive pay (ACIP) in an effort to solve pilot retention problems. Though commonly referred to as "flight pay," the two are different. ACIP was meant to provide incentive pay for cumulative aviation service throughout a career while flight pay incentivized active performance of flight duties. However, in practice and then regulation the fundamental difference between ACIP and flight pay was lost. AFI 36-2110, *Assignments,* adopted the gate month accumulation language for the ACIP entitlement. Based on the outdated nature of this regulation, a "pregnancy penalty" is created when female rated officers lose "gate months" while pregnant. Although each major weapon system is different, the average time out of the cockpit is approximately 12 months. Lt Col Anne-Marie Contreras explained that as a woman falls behind her peers in accruing gate months due to pregnancy, she must accept more flying assignments to catch up with her peers. The inescapable impact of this lost time is lost opportunity to go to a staff job or in-residence professional military education. Contreras, "Hemorrhaging Her," 2.

17. This is detailed in the 2016 Diversity and Inclusion Initiatives Implementation Guidance. The initiatives also required at least one diverse qualified candidate to be included in hiring processes.

18. Losey, "Air Force Moves to Cancel Contracts."

19. Losey.

20. Sisk, "Number of Female Generals."

21. Through the 1980s, women made up less than 2 percent of Air Force colonels, but as of February 2018, just over 50 years after the 2 percent restriction was removed in 1967, women accounted for 14.1 percent of Air Force colonels. As of February 2018, there were 63 female admirals and generals on active duty in the five services, compared to 30 in fiscal year 2000. Within the same 20-year window there has been a similar trend among Air Force senior enlisted women. According to a 2019 report from the Service Women's Action Network in 1988, less than 4 percent of those in the three senior enlisted pay grades (E7 to E9) were women. But as of February 2018, women constituted

20.3 percent of the E7 to E9 ranks. Service Action Women's Network, "Women in the Military."

22. Cox, "Congress Wants More Diversity."

23. The charter must be renewed every two years.

24. DACOWITS, "Charter."

25. DACOWITS, "Homepage."

26. The AFBAWG operates under a charter memo and is governed by AFI 36-205, *Affirmative Employment and Special Emphasis Programs,* as well as AFI 36-2706, *Equal Opportunity.*

27. Air Force Global Diversity Division, AF/A1DV, *USAF Diversity Strategic Roadmap.*

28. AFI 36-205, *Affirmative Employment and Special Emphasis Programs.*

29. In March 2021, the Department of the Air Force formally established two more teams within the AFBAWG: the Lesbian, Gay, Bisexual, Transgender and Queer/Questioning Initiative Team and the Indigenous Nations Equality Teams. This has brought the working group seven teams: Black/African American Employment Strategy Team, Disability Action Team, Hispanic Empowerment and Action Team, Indigenous Nations Equality Team, LGBTQ Initiative Team, Pacific Islander/Asian American Community Team, and Women's Initiatives Team. Secretary of the AF Public Affairs, "New Barrier Analysis Working Groups."

30. Nadeem, "Summary of Recent Accomplishments."

31. Joyner, "Behind the Braids."

32. SAF Public Affairs, "Air Force Reduces Barriers for Pregnant Aviators."

33. Nadeem, "Summary of Recent Accomplishments."

34. Vistica, *Fall from Glory.*

35. In addition to sexual assault prevention, the Air Force resiliency umbrella includes suicide prevention and interpersonal violence. In January 2010, the Air Force launched Bystander Intervention Training (BIT), a direct strategy to provide Airmen with knowledge to recognize potentially harmful situations and take action to mitigate possible harm to their fellow wingman. BIT was mandated for all military across the total force (active duty, ANG, and AFRC) and civilians who supervise military. On 5 December 2015, Col Ellen M. Moore of AFRC/A1 notified all AFRC wing and NAF commanders of the new Sexual Assault Prevention Strategy, which included "Green Dot" training. In January 2016 the Air Force launched a five-year strategy to decrease interpersonal violence through a partnership with Green Dot etc., a nonprofit organization committed to reducing violence measurably and systematically within any given community. The Green Dot strategy included prevention and intervention tools and training with the ultimate goal to change social norms related to sexual violence, dating violence, stalking, child abuse, elder abuse, and bullying. The Air Force adopted its total force

version of the program through a "train the trainer" concept, beginning with 1,500 command-designated Airmen acting as program implementers. The Air Force approved and funded GS-12 "primary prevention specialist for violence" positions at every base (including 10 Reserve positions) to manage prevention activities such as Green Dot. All Air Force members were required to complete mandatory, annual Green Dot training sessions. Kester, "AF Resiliency: Ten Year Lookback."

36. On 2 January 2003, an email was sent under the pseudonym Renee Trindle to various recipients, among them the secretary of the Air Force (SAF); the USAF chief of staff; Senator Wayne Allard; Senator Ben Nighthorse Campbell; other US congressmen; and media representatives. The email asserted there was a significant sexual assault problem at the Academy that had been ignored by USAFA leadership. The SAF immediately directed the general counsel of the Air Force (SAF/GC) to establish a high-level working group to review cadet complaints concerning the Academy's program of deterrence and response to sexual assault. The SAF also tasked the working group to review allegations of sexual assault reported from January 1993 through December 2002. The secretary subsequently directed the Air Force Inspector General to review individual Air Force Office of Special Investigations cases and to investigate cadet complaints concerning the alleged mishandling of sexual assault cases. Schemo, "Rate of Rape."

37. Schemo, "Rate of Rape."

38. US Department of Defense Sexual Assault Prevention and Response,. "Mission and History."

39. Secretary of Defense, memorandum. The National Defense Authorization Act for FY 2012 (PL 112-81) included a number of provisions to address sexual assault in the military.

40. "USAF Talking Points: Sexual Assault Prevention and Response." Additionally, the secretary of the Air Force directed stand-down training and a review of response coordinators and victim advocate qualifications and credentials by the Air Force Audit Agency.

41. "USAF Talking Points: Sexual Assault Prevention and Response."

42. According to the Marshall University Women and Gender Studies center, "rape culture" is defined as "an environment in which rape is prevalent and in which sexual violence against women is normalized and excused in the media and popular culture. Rape culture is perpetuated through the use of misogynistic language, the objectification of women's bodies, and the glamorization of sexual violence, thereby creating a society that disregards women's rights and safety." Examples of rape culture include blaming the victim, tolerance and/or trivializing of harassment and assault ("boys will be boys!"), sexually explicit jokes, degrading language or images, putting pressure on men to be dominant, and pressuring women to be submissive or not appear "cold." Marshall University, "Rape Culture."

43. The SARC also promoted events and other initiatives aimed at eliminating permissive behavior that tended to promote sexually aggressive behavior, as well as conducted mandatory training sessions. USAF Chief of Staff, "Sexual Assault Awareness and Prevention Month," email, 2015.

44. Active-duty members, Air Force Reserve and Air National Guard members, and their dependents 18 and older who are eligible for treatment in the military health system, and Air Force civilian (appropriated and non-appropriated) employees are eligible for SAPR support services. For Airmen on active duty for periods greater than 30 days, there is also the option of the Family Advocacy Program, which manages sexual assault allegations when the alleged offender is a partner (in context of a spousal relationship, same-sex domestic partnership, unmarried intimate partner relationship, or military dependents who are 17 years of age and younger). Airmen have the option of going to their installation SARC or if none are available then contacting the DOD Safe Helpline via website or phone number to be assigned a victim advocate. In August 2018, the Air Force rolled out the newest DOD program known as CATCH, Catch a Serial Offender, which allows victims to file a restricted report in a confidential DOD database. US Air Force. "Resilience."

45. "USAF Talking Points: Sexual Assault Prevention and Response."

46. Department of Veteran Affairs, "Military Sexual Trauma."

47. Major conflict in-theater casualties since 1947:

Conflict	Total	Total AF	AF Women
Korea	36,574	1,552	3
Vietnam	58,220	2,586	1
Persian Gulf	382	35	0
Overseas contingency operations (OCO)	60,260	1,031	18
Total (as of 21 April 2020)	155,436	5,204	22

Source: Report, "Defense Casualty Analysis System Conflict Casualties," 21 April 2020.

Expanded look at overseas contingency operations (OCO) casualties since 2001:

Operation	Total	USAF	USAFR	Total Women	AF Women
Iraqi Freedom (OIF)	36,412	419	22	110	3
Enduring Freedom (OEF)	22,498	540	24	51	9
New Dawn (OND)	372	5	0	1	0
Inherent Resolve (OIR)	318	16	3	7	2
Freedom's Sentinel (OFS)	660	51	0	4	4
Total (as of 21 April 2020)	60,260	1,031	49	173	18

Source: Rpt (U) Defense Casualty Analysis System (U) Conflict Casualties," 21 April 2020.

48. Rein, "VA Is Stepping Up Its Services for Female Veterans."

49. VA, "Health Outcomes of Women's Vietnam Service."

50. According to a 2019 WIT memo summarizing the team's recent accomplishments, the leading motivation behind these trainings was the negative trends in health outcomes for the female veteran population. Female military veterans have higher rates of suicide, homelessness, mental health, MST, and unemployment than their male counterparts. Additionally, women veterans face greater and different physical health-related challenges after military service compared to their male counterparts, including chronic pain, obesity, and musculoskeletal issues. Often, women veterans do not understand what women's health services are available to help them address their health-related challenges. Additionally, fewer women veterans seek services and support from VA and often do not connect with the VA until an average of 2.7 years postmilitary service or until mental/physical health issues have manifested. Nadeem, "Summary of Recent Accomplishments."

51. Nadeem.

52. MyVECTOR is governed by Air Force Handbook 36-2643.

53. Hendrix, "AF Launches MyVector."

54. The theme was "empower, encourage, and embrace," with a focus on women leadership and diversity in the workplace. Key speakers included Lt Gen Jacqueline Van Ovost, Headquarters Air Force director of staff, and Deborah Lee James, former secretary of the Air Force. Attendees had opportunities to interact with senior AFMC and Air Force leaders and also participated in collaborative breakout sessions on topics such as work and life balance, emotional intelligence, team development, and the art of self-promotion. Alia-Novobilski, "Women's Leadership Symposium Inspires Growth, Diversity."

55. Alia-Novobilski.

56. Leanln.Org is the nonprofit organization founded by Facebook's chief operating officer, Sheryl Sandberg, to empower all women to achieve their ambitions. Lean In, "Circles."

57. Lean In, "Circles."

58. The Defense Officer Personnel Management Act of 1980, which effectively consolidated the Officer Personnel Act (OPA) of 1947 and Officer Grade Limitation Act (OGLA) of 1954, for the first time standardized officer personnel management across all services. It established ceilings on the number of field grade officers and codified rules concerning promotion criteria, separation, and retirement. Ultimately the DOPMA created predictable career paths for officers as well as clear lines concerning whether an individual was allowed to stay in or was forced out. Promotion boards evaluated and compared officers in a single year group across dramatically different career occupations and missions, making quantifiable measures the only way to even begin to assess and rank officers. This process favored generic markers, such as below the zone, PME in-residence, stratifications, physical fitness

scores, and higher education over more specific, career field–related achievements and measures. This often meant that an officer must choose between promoting through the ranks (and thus being willing to navigate the wickets and check the boxes) or becoming a subject matter expert at their job. As a result, no matter how talented they are, those who cross-train or chose a path different from the one that results in checked boxes, to include women who choose to have children, are at a disadvantage and ultimately penalized under the "up-or-out" DOPMA system. While it can be assumed that most of the issues concerning female officer retention also apply to enlisted women, further study of this topic and group is certainly warranted. Penney and Krieger, *Female Officer Retention.*

59. As of 2019, the peak of female separation was between the four- to nine-year mark, which is approximately 25–35 years of age, prime marriage and childbearing years. Penney and Krieger, *Female Officer Retention.*

60. Magana, "Meet Air Force Reserve's First Female F-35 Pilot."

61. Headquarters Individual Reservist Readiness and Integration Organization, "AF Changes Policy."

62. SAF Public Affairs, "Air Force Reduces Barriers for Pregnant Aviators."

63. SAF Public Affairs.

64. Secretary of the Air Force Public Affairs, "Air Force Removes."

65. Seck, "DOD Set to Roll Out New Policy Targeting Pregnancy Discrimination."

66. Seck.

67. Seck.

68. Seck. The specific post is by Ruttenber, "How the Military Is Losing Its Top Talent Because of Pregnancy Discrimination and What We Can Do About It."

69. Seck.

70. Seck.

71. AFGM 2016-36-02, *Career Intermission Program (CIP);* and AFI 36-2110, *Assignments.*

72. Secretary of the Air Force Public Affairs, "Dwell Time."

73. Effective 23 March 2010, the Patient Protection and Affordable Care Act amended the Fair Labor Standards Act of 1938 (FLSA) to require employers to provide a nursing mother reasonable break time to express breast milk after the birth of her child. The amendment also required that employers provide a place for an employee to express breast milk. Fair Labor Standards Act, Section 7, "Break Time for Nursing Mothers Provision."

74. AFI 44-102, *Medical Care Management,* affirms "extensive medical research has documented that breastfeeding has significant health, nutritional, immunologic, developmental, emotional, social, and economic benefits to mother and baby" and that deferment from deployment for 12

months will give breastfeeding mothers the "full medical benefit of breast-feeding." AFI 44-102, *Medical Care Management.*

75. AFI 36-2110, *Assignments.*

76. Moran, "MOMS Leave Act Passes the Senate." Introduced by US Senators Jerry Moran (R-KS) and Tom Udall (D-NM), members of the Senate Appropriations Subcommittee on Defense.

77. MOMS Leave Act, S. 1721, 115th Cong. (2017).

78. Air Force policy (AFI 36-3003) authorized 42 days of convalescent leave after normal pregnancy and childbirth. The National Defense Authorization Act for Fiscal Year 2009 (PL 110-417) authorized up to 10 days of parental leave for service members whose spouses gave birth. Previous DOD policy (DODI 1327.06, Incorporating Change 2, effective 12 August 2013) defined maternity leave as "a convalescent period up to six weeks following pregnancy and childbirth" and also authorized parental leave, stating, "a married member on active duty whose spouse gives birth to a child shall receive 10 days of non-chargeable leave of absence to be used in connection with the birth of the child."

79. Fair Labor Standards Act, Section 7, "Break Time for Nursing Mothers Provision."

80. To be eligible for this leave, the individual must be a member of the active component or a member of a Reserve component performing active Guard and Reserve duty or subject to an active duty recall or mobilization order in excess of 12 months. Otherwise, the reservist must arrange annual tour and inactive duty for training schedules to accommodate for unpaid "maternity leave," that is, not getting on orders. Additionally, the bill does not establish this secondary caregiver leave, nor does it instruct the DOD to do so, meaning that this "secondary caregiver" parental leave is still at command discretion.

81. Air Force Guidance Memorandum 18-01 to AFI 36-3003, *Military Leave Program* (published 6 June 2018) addresses the changes to the Military Parental Leave Program (MPLP). Covered members are defined as active component service members, reserve component service members performing active Guard and Reserve duty or full-time National Guard duty for a period in excess of 12 months, and reserve component members subject to an active-duty recall or mobilization order in excess of 12 months. Air Force Guidance Memorandum 18-01.

82. Prior to this, adoptive parents were authorized 21 days of nonchargeable parental leave in conjunction with the adoption of a child. However, in cases where both parents were active duty, only one was permitted to take leave. SAF PA, "Air Force Implements New Parental Leave Policy."

83. SAF PA.

84. SAF PA.

85. Edmonds was nearly finished with her nursing degree and AFROTC program when she found out she was pregnant. She received her commission but did not disclose her pregnancy until she arrived at her first duty assignment. Soon after, the Air Force discharged her as an Airman Basic and billed her $92,000 for her scholarship on the grounds of a fraudulent commission. Johnston and Lah, "Single Mom Challenges Dismissal From Air Force."

86. Air Force Public Affairs, "Policy Changes Ease Enlisting with Families."

87. United States Air Force, "Meet Requirements."

88. DODI 1342.19 to AFI 36-2908, *Family Care Plans*, defines policy, assigns responsibilities, and prescribes procedures for the care of dependent family members of service members, including reserve component members, including the Ready Reserve. For taxation and benefit purposes, only one military member in a dual-military marriage can claim dependents (children or possibly elderly parents in their care). For example, one partner in a dual-military couple claims their two children, so she or he is assessed to have two dependents and receives benefits as such (housing, etc.). The other partner is assessed to have zero dependents.

89. DACOWITS, "RFI 3, 2019 Retention Survey."

90. Bailey, "Air Force Expands Career Intermission Program Opportunities."

91. "Operators" are typically defined as those in the following career fields: 11XX (pilots), 12XX (combat systems officers [CSO]), 13XX (space, nuclear and missile operations, and command and control [C2]), and 18XX (remotely piloted aircraft [RPA] pilots). The terms "operator" and "rated" are used synonymously. To become an operator, an officer must be commissioned (usually from ROTC, USAFA, or OTS), be medically qualified for the duty, be selected for training in that duty, and successfully complete that training. Contreras, "Hemorrhaging Her," 2.

92. Heather "Lucky" Penney, director of T-50A and US Air Force Training systems, Lockheed Martin, was one of the fighter pilots who, during the 9/11 attacks, received orders to ram her F-16 into United Flight 93 as it flew over Pennsylvania in order to stop it from reaching Washington, DC. Timmons, "Heather Penney Tried to Take Down Flight 93."

93. Smith, "Breaking the Gender Barrier."

94. Hegelson, "The Evolution of Women's Leadership."

95. Mau was the first female to fly the F-35 as well as the third woman assigned to the 492nd Fighter Squadron at RAF Lakenheath in the United Kingdom flying the F-15E Strike Eagle. It was there she flew combat missions for Operations Southern Watch, Northern Watch, and Enduring Freedom.

96. Mau, interview.

97. AFPC demographics 2019.

98. According to the 2016 Diversity and Inclusion Initiatives Implementation Guidance, the main career fields lacking representation from women

are RPA pilots, pilots, CSOs, special tactics officers, air battle managers, and space operators—all from the 11XX, 12XX, 13XX, and 18XX specialty codes.

99. Contreras, "Hemorrhaging Her." Women's uniform shortages and design flaws resulting in poor fit and/or function have been a long-standing issue, starting with uniform shortages in the early 1950s.

100. The Air Force female fitment program was established by Chief of Staff Gen David Goldfein to address the equipment performance issues experienced by women serving in roles that had job-specific gear requirements, such as security forces, pilots and air crews, firefighting, and explosives ordnance disposal. Air Force Life Cycle Management Center, "Air Force Female Fitment."

101. Bullock, "Flight Equipment Redesigned."

102. With women's shorter sitting height, narrower shoulders, breasts, and smaller frames, body armor was not suitable for all body types and may "compromise a woman's ability to lift her arm appropriately." Contreras, "Hemorrhaging Her," 12.

103. Contreras, "Hemorrhaging Her," 12.

104. Contreras. For example, although most women have received nothing but respect and privacy from their male crew members, a top issue for female operators was bathrooms. Aircraft bathrooms vary from full lavatories, such as that on a commercial airliners, to a "piddle pack" or plastic bottle. However, most restrooms female operators must use afford no privacy and are not maintained during flight. According to Contreras, women on the B-52 must maneuver backwards to use a urinal or use a FUD (female urination device) without a privacy screen. Women in helicopters use "tactical dehydration" as their method of choice—it is impossible to go to the bathroom in a nonpermissive environment or they use a FUD in a permissive environment. Upgrades to some of these weapon systems have included boosts in avionics, weapons, and flight components, but the bathrooms have not been a priority.

105. AFI 48-123, *Medical Examinations and Standards.*

106. In the early 1900s, medical standards were designed to keep aviators safe. As faster, higher, and more maneuverable technology became available in the 1930s, the medical community began to look at how to mitigate stressors in flight, such as the effects of cold, altitude, limited oxygen, and g-loading. The last major update to medical standards was made in conjunction with the arrival of the space age in the 1960s. Since then, medical standards have been updated marginally and incrementally. Contreras, "Hemorrhaging Her."

107. This includes not only total height but also proportional measurements, for example the length of knees to feet. All requirements are based on safety standards because each aircraft, each pilot, is different. The waiver process begins at each of the commissioning sources for pilot candidates.

According to Maj Gen Craig Wills, Nineteenth Air Force commander, approximately 95 percent of waivers for those above 5 feet, 2 inches have been approved. "Air Force Considers Expanding."

108. As of 2019, the height standard to become an Air Force pilot is a standing height of 5 feet, 4 inches to 6 feet, 5 inches and a sitting height of 34–40 inches. Approximately 43.5 percent of American women between the ages of 20 to 29 are 5 foot, 4 inches or shorter. "Air Force Considers Expanding."

109. Contreras, "Hemorrhaging Her."

110. "Air Force Considers Expanding."

111. Joyner, "Behind the Braids," 6. Additional restrictions on bulk and length apply.

112. Joyner, 8.

113. Joyner, 8–9.

114. On 11 September 2001, 19 militants associated with the extremist group al-Qaeda hijacked four airplanes and carried out suicide attacks against targets in the United States. Almost 3,000 people were killed during the 9/11 terrorist attacks, including ten active duty, Reserve, and retired servicewomen, which triggered major US initiatives to combat terrorism.

115. During a televised address to a joint session of Congress on 20 September 2001, President George W. Bush used the term "war on terror," stating: "Our war on terror begins with al-Qaeda, but it does not end there. It will not end until every terrorist group of global reach has been found, stopped, and defeated." "Address to a Joint Session," speech, 2001. In March 2009, the Defense Department officially changed the name of operations from Global War on Terror (GWOT) to Overseas Contingency Operation (OCO). Institute of Medicine, *Returning Home from Iraq and Afghanistan.*

116. Institute of Medicine.

117. Together We Served, "SSgt Anissa Ann Shero, Fallen."

118. Air Force Security Forces Association, "USAF Defenders Fallen Since 9-11."

119. Moore, "Women in Combat: 5-Year Status Update."

120. This 1994 policy directed that women were eligible to be assigned to all positions for which they qualified, except for units below brigade level whose primary mission was to engage the enemy in direct combat.

121. Moore, "Women in Combat: Five-Year Status Update."

122. Moore.

123. Pawlyk, "Airman Advances in Quest to Become First Female Special Tactics Officer."

124. Kamarck, "Women and the Selective Service."

125. Kamarck.

126. National Commission on Military, National, and Public Service, *Inspired to Serve.*

Chapter 8

Conclusions and Observations
2021 and Beyond

The glory of each generation is to make its own precedents.

—Belva Ann Lockwood

This final chapter takes the history of Air Force women and asks, so now what? Here I briefly offer my individual perspective based on three years of study, analysis, and thinking about the women in the Air Force, in addition to 10 years of being one. As with all perspectives, mine is shaped by my own biases, beliefs, and experiences, and the reality is that others in uniform likely hold very different views. That is a good thing. Diversity of thought and perception is part of being human and a critical value of America—one that this nation was founded on and that military members willingly serve to protect. It is also something that, when properly leveraged, is critical to winning future wars and maintaining an effective Air Force.

American women have always been part of the fight for national security and homeland defense. Certainly, their inclusion in the military and the extent of their involvement have developed rapidly over the last century. However, these changes have had nothing to do with a change in female capability or character. Women have always been just as brave, patriotic, smart, skilled, and willing to serve and fight as any man. It is our cultural perception of women and what they bring to the fight that has changed over time and is continuing to expand today.

Gender integration—into the military and American workforce at large—was one of the most hotly contested social issues of the twentieth century, demanding both men and women understand that femininity was not a bar to competence any more than masculinity was a guarantee of it. As of 2021, few could argue women were not fully included in the Air Force, at both a policy and practical level. But where the Air Force has the potential, and perhaps even responsibility, to go is full gender integration. Integration requires shifting foundational and fundamental perspectives related to the institution as a whole. It requires examining what the Air Force as an institution values in its Airmen and leaders, the way it sees itself as a military service, its place in the national defense strategy, and the problems it might face both right now and in the future.

Ultimately, the genuine integration of women—or any other minority—in the Air Force ultimately rests on perceived value. People will not show up, let alone speak up, if they do not feel their presence or opinion is genuinely heard and considered. Part of valuing female service members is having policies that support their career goals and ability to serve without undue stressors, both of which have been areas of focus over the last few years. But a deeper, more integrated way to value women is to change the culture around what it means to serve, lead, and be a good Airman.

Gender Integration: Why Does It Matter?

When it comes to thinking about the future of women in the Air Force, many variables arise for consideration. Some are tactical-level items that can be handled with action teams and policy changes. Others are big picture, strategic, harder-to-grasp issues that will take commitment and time to change but nevertheless will have a major impact on both the Air Force and the women serving in it.

But before we discuss problems and solutions, we must always first challenge our assumptions and ask the question: does it matter? At its core, the Air Force "is a utilitarian institution. Its bottom line is effective national defense, and the only viable metric is mission effectiveness. Anything that does not feed that core purpose is a luxury and un-affordable in the current fiscal, political, and strategic climate. This is true from hardware to personnel management, and it drives service emphasis on meritocratic personnel systems. Meritocracy is a deeply ingrained value and belief within the Air Force and broader DOD, and rightfully so; after all, our military requires superior performance to ensure our national security objectives."[1]

So then why should we focus energy and resources on caring about physical descriptors, such as biological gender, if the mission always comes first? Because the body we inhabit comes with a preordained value based on our cultural consciousness. One's body determines their experience of the world. Those experiences offer unique perceptions, skills, experiences, and ideas regarding perceived problems and solutions. Ultimately, mission effectiveness and diversity of thought are synergistic and becoming even more so as technology advances continue to shift the character of warfare.

In an era of great power competition with a level technological playing field and outmatched human resource pool, innovation is where future wars will be won.[2] On an official visit to the People's Liberation Army's National University of Defense Technology in Changsha, China, two colleagues from the Air Force Research Institute spoke with a group of senior Chinese officers about an edition of the *Air and Space Power Journal* (Chinese-language version). In the conversation, the officers noted "the People's Liberation Army Air Force could overcome American technology in a conflict, but—where they fell short in their eyes—was in ingenuity, independence, and creativity."[3] Innovation requires a culture that signals no one person, team, position, rank, or gender is the exclusive source of new ideas and solutions. Central to the Air Force's foundational identity and purpose, the service's long-term focus on innovation is perhaps the reason why women have generally been more integrated into the Air Force than any other service starting with the Army Air Force in World War II.

The military necessity for innovation goes hand in hand with the need for diversity. This imperative is echoed in the 2013 *Air Force Diversity Strategic Roadmap*: "Diversity is a military necessity . . . . [Diversity] opens the door to creative solutions to complex problems and provides our Air Force a competitive edge in air, space, and cyberspace. . . . Diversity is an imperative if the Air Force is to remain competitive in attracting, recruiting, and retaining America's best talent."[4]

In an increasingly competitive and dynamic global environment, encouraging diversity opens the discussion to different ideas, perceptions, and realizations concerning both problems and solutions. This is where the value of diversity—and for the purpose of this book, women—in the Air Force really lies: in expanding the toolbox to include the entire range of human experience, wisdom, talent, and capability. However, for diverse ideas and perceptions to be of value, they must be heard and understood. To get those innovative ideas and perceptions to the table in the first place, those who carry them must be valued for their outside-the-norm perception and line of thinking. Our current force management model is predicated on looking to past conflicts to prepare for future conflicts. The underlying bias here is believing that because our current systems have made us the greatest military and air force in the world since World War II, any change to the status quo is a fundamental threat to our military superiority.[5] At every major turn, the inclusion of women into fields previously prohibited, like aviation and combat, has felt like an existential threat to not only the culture but the effectiveness of the force. Unfortunately for those who are still unknowingly operating under these biases, the world is changing, as it tends to do. The rise of the great power competition and strategic level rivalries, artificial intelligence, and sociopolitical change on a global scale has affected the way we think about and fight wars. Innovation has become the name of the game over the last century, and the stakes feel higher now than ever.

Talent Management

A primary, if not the primary, weapon to combat current and future problems is talent management. By 2030, China will have four times the US population and 15 times the number of science, technology, engineering, and math graduates as the US.[6] Based on numbers alone, it would appear China has a significant advantage when it comes to leveraging human capital for the People's Liberation Army. However, as history often illustrates, military power cannot be measured in a simple one-for-one body count. Just as an aircraft, weapon, or sensor is only as good as the operator, a military is only as good as the way it is able to leverage its largest resource: people. While effectively managing the hundreds of thousands of individuals who compose the Air Force has never been a simple or straightforward feat, in an era of "do more with less" the importance of overcoming obstacles to recruiting, retaining, and managing a diversity of talent cannot be overstated.

A primary obstacle to effective talent management is that current personnel management policies are based on outdated cultural values. They were created by and for previous generations and are increasingly incompatible with those who serve today. The Air Force, as with all other services, must adapt to the larger American social climate in order to recruit and retain the best talent available. This is not a personal, moral, or even national defense issue; it is simply the reality of having a resource-constrained, all-volunteer force and a population where over two-thirds of adults are ineligible to serve.[7] No military service can afford to think of itself solely as an elite, masculine institution anymore. This type of self-image promotes homogenization of thought and perception and makes recruiting and retaining anyone who feels they do not fit this image very difficult. Broadly speaking, "we must reform our personnel practices into a talent management system that provides Airmen the flexibility they need to integrate their service-life balance across the span of their lives and career through greater agency and commander involvement."[8] Talent management has become the new name of the game. The Air Force will need to continue developing more "effective and holistic methodologies for defining, measuring, and identifying diverse talent" to cultivate the most effective force of the future.[9]

A major part of talent management—and indeed where most focus is placed—are the policies and systems in place that support service women on a daily basis. In the past, women have generally succeeded in integrating themselves into the force by keeping their heads down and continually proving themselves and their worth. They have found ways to work around existing policies that did not account for women's needs or simply accepted the reality of their career limitations. They have pumped breastmilk in storage closets, traded childcare with male coworkers' spouses, attempted to plan families around career opportunities, taken hormonal birth control in order to deploy, worn ill-fitting uniforms and protective gear, and dehydrated themselves so they would not have to use the restroom during a flight; these are just a few of the countless examples of ways women have made it work. The side effect of acceptance has been giving the perception to leadership that there are no problems or inequities, when in fact there are.

Since their inception, task forces and teams that support women's integration and advancement in the force, such as the WIT and AF-BAWG, have so far proven to be the most effective way to tackle those hidden problems through policy change. As we have seen through the history of women in the Air Force, diversity cannot be mandated—and when it is, it tends to be much less effective. Therefore, these groups have succeeded by focusing on identifying institutional barriers to female entry, retention, and advancement. So far, changes affecting women have primarily fallen into three categories: pregnancy and maternity issues, dress and appearance updates, and human systems integration.[10]

Historically, pregnancy and motherhood have been significant barriers to female retention and career advancement. In the 2018 Rand study "Addressing Barriers to Female Officer Retention in the Air Force," focus groups found that family and personal life were prevalent themes regarding a woman's decision to separate from the force.[11] Additionally, groups found that 83 percent of participants identified the importance of having female role models in senior leadership positions. Participants emphasized that they rarely see female leaders who are married with children. The resulting perception among younger female officers is that it is not possible for women to both have a family and become a senior leader in the Air Force. While the DOD has begun a policy review for the career enhancement of pregnant US service members,[12] a primary focus going forward needs to be destigmatizing pregnancy and motherhood in the military.

In her book, *Invisible Women*, Caroline Criado Perez opens with the point that "seeing men as the human default is fundamental to the structure of human society."[13] This male as universal bias is the foundation and the lens through which Western civilization has viewed the world and accordingly developed. The result of this bias is what Perez has termed the gender data gap: "From cars that are 71% less safe for women than men (because they've been designed using a 50th-percentile male dummy), to voice-recognition technology that is 70% less likely to accurately understand women than men (because many algorithms are trained on 70% male data sets), to medication that doesn't work when a woman is on her period (because women weren't included in the clinical trials), we are living in a world that has been designed for men because for the most part, we haven't been collecting data on women. This is the gender data gap."[14] Additionally, "one of the most important things to say about the gender gap data is that it is not generally malicious, or even deliberate. Quite the opposite, it is simply the product of a way of thinking that has been around for millennia and is, therefore, a kind of not thinking."[15]

While it is beyond the scope of this book to discuss all the ways human systems integration is currently being, or still needs to be, evaluated and updated with women in mind, key topics for the Air Force include:

- Job-specific height requirements (founded on outdated anthropometric data)
- Aircraft and flight equipment design, such as ejection seats, in-flight bladder relief, fixed wing helmets, and maternity flight suits
- Safety and protective equipment, such as body armor
- Facility adaptation
- Combat trauma care procedures
- Decision-making algorithms
- Maternity uniforms

Teleworking

As of 2020, we were still living the story of the COVID-19 pandemic. Starting in March 2020, the pandemic completely disrupted organizations, economies, societies, and families around the world, forcing us to abruptly alter how we live, work, communicate, and plan for the future. As we continue to move through this crisis, it is clear the long-term effects are still largely unknown. However, what was immediately clear with the abrupt shift to teleworking from home was the sudden dissolution of the divide between work and domestic life and responsibilities. Despite being an outdated, industrial-era practice, the boundary between worlds has persisted largely because that is the way it had long been done. As the primary caretakers, women have been disproportionately affected by the sudden requirement to work remotely while also taking care of children, elderly parents, or whoever else is in their care.[16] Women caring for, and even schooling, children while trying to keep up with Zoom meetings and regular job responsibilities has been a recipe for burnout. This challenge has been next to impossible for single parents, shift workers, or caretakers whose partners cannot or do not help with day-to-day childcare responsibilities.[17] Of course, men and fathers are also being pulled further into the realm of home and childrearing responsibility while attempting to telework. Air Force Chief of Staff Gen Charles Brown recognized the burden this has placed on parents, citing it as one of his main concerns during the pandemic.[18]

According to an article from September 2020, top Air Force leaders are fully embracing telework and factoring it into post–COVID-19 plans, seeing it as a way to save money for the service and increase productivity in some areas. Of course, not all jobs can be done remotely, such as aircrew or those worked on classified networks. When speaking about the reserve component, Air Force Reserve Chief Lt Gen Richard Scobee agreed: "We fully embrace this culture of teleworking. Even in the post-pandemic environment that we will find ourselves in eventually, a telework culture can remove barriers for us and the reserve component. It's really about making it easier for Airmen to serve. I want all our Airmen to find it easy to continue to serve, whether it's in a part-time or full-time capacity. Why would you go back to anything different?"[19]

Eventually support structures, such as school, daycares, and family members, will come back into play, but for now it has eroded a former cultural distinction between male and female domains.[20] Another cultural belief that we are witnessing erode is the association of men as the primary protectors, defenders, and leaders during a crisis.[21] Most health care and social service workers are women who are now suddenly perceived as heroines bravely willing to put their lives at risk. Of course, women have always done this, but this is the first time in recent history the public consciousness is truly witnessing it on a large scale and correlating the two.[22]

Policy is where the rubber meets the road—it is where the Air Force can display what it values and believes is required to have the best, most efficient and effective force possible. But policy changes and good intentions can only go so far. Discussions around gender integration often focus on developing policies to solve the recurring issues of recruiting and retaining women. These are incredibly necessary and appreciated, but policy changes are not the final solution. It is not enough to just get, keep, and promote women within the existing system—it is time for the system to update its values concerning women in the service.

Implicit Bias and Value

As we have seen over the course of the history of women in the Air Force, the inclusion and integration of minorities into the military is often a product of personnel needs rather than a moral or innovative imperative. Mandatory changes, particularly those that come from outside the force, that benefit women, people of color, or any other minority group can feel like a liberal agenda trying to "transform the military from a competitive meritocracy to an entitlement-oriented social justice organization."[23] This reaction is based on outdated cultural beliefs that place the experiences, perceptions, and understanding held by the masses as truer than those held by the few.[24] Though women compose 50 percent of the population, their less-than-50 percent representation in the force still qualifies them as "the few," immediately underestimating their value and therefore potential impact to the mission. This is not a conscious choice anyone makes—as beliefs and values are held at a deeper level than cognitive awareness—but instead illustrates implicit bias in action.

Bias is generally defined as attitudes, behaviors, and actions that are prejudiced in favor of (or against) one person or group compared to another. It is the physical manifestation of what we believe to be true. Though this is a cognitive reality we all engage in, biases are something we can become aware of and actively work to shift or even eliminate.[25] On the other hand, implicit bias is a judgment that occurs automatically, unintentionally, and is often at odds with what our minds believe to be true. It is the step before physical action existing in the seemingly murky realm of belief and value. Modern research on implicit bias suggests that people can—and do—act on deeply in-grained cognitive shortcuts such as stereotypes and prejudices without intending to do so. Programmed into us by our families, com-munities, and culture, implicit bias is essentially at the level of myth: it forms the foundation of our cultural narrative and reinforces the values we base our lives on, both individually and collectively. While psychologists in this field study "consumer products, self-esteem, food, alcohol, political values, and more, the most striking and well-known research has focused on implicit biases toward members of socially stigmatized groups, such as African-Americans, women, and the LGBTQ community."[26]

For example, imagine Steve, who intellectually believes that women and men are equally suited for service and careers in the military. De-spite his explicitly egalitarian belief, Steve might nevertheless behave in a number of biased but accepted ways (such as distrusting feedback from his female coworkers, describing a stern female leader as "bitchy," or choosing a man instead of a woman for a specific job opportunity where both candidates were equally qualified). Part of the reason for Steve's discriminatory behavior might be an implicit gender bias.

This is where the deeper roadblocks to gender integration truly lie: at the (often) unconscious level of belief and value. What we value is determined by what we believe, and what we believe is determined by our cultural, familial, and personal narratives, or myth. What our cultural myth tells us about the incompatibility of war and women is what we believe and therefore built into military institutions, whether or not our conscious minds agree. The good news is that myth can be updated, though it may take multiple generations to shift the collec-tive perspective. This is how social change typically works; the ac-tions of one generation becomes the common, accepted experience of the next. Recent cinematic trends that feature a female superhero-ine as the main character, such as *Wonder Woman* and *Captain Mar-vel*, are examples of how the myths concerning women and war can start to change. Along the same lines, in June 2019 the Air Force released a new commercial featuring all female pilots asking, "what will your origin story be?"[27]

These are important starts that will hopefully continue to be developed and expanded upon. When I started researching the history of women in the Air Force I was somewhat shocked to see that in entire volumes of Air Force history there would be, at most, one or two paragraphs referencing women. The word *woman* often did not even appear in the index. This is a perfect example of the unintentional story of absence. Women are rarely mentioned in standard Air Force history, but they also served, doing equally important things just as well as the men whose accomplishments fill unit heritage displays. While the Air Force and individual units can update their origin stories or creation myths to include women, ultimately there is still cognitive tension with the larger American mythos that does not correlate the idea of women in war outside a stand-alone, masculinized female superhero. A primary reason for this lies in deeply embedded cultural beliefs regarding gender and the proper structure of the world.

Military as a Masculine Institution

Our Western lens of the world stems from the ancient Greek worldview and philosophy—of which dualism is a primary characteristic.[28] The belief that situations, ideas, and people must either be this or that is deeply embedded into the way our civilization views the world, one another, and ourselves. To orient around this belief our brains create shortcuts: good is *this*, bad is *that*; right is *this*, wrong is *that*; masculine is *this*, feminine is *that*. Certain human qualities became prescriptions; assigned to either masculine and feminine and then conflated with biological gender, operating under the unwritten rule that nary the two shall meet. As such, in the Western psyche, war, violence, combat, and technology are perceived as exclusively masculine domains and qualities. Culturally, the military is one of the longest held and most traditionally masculine institutions there is—a man's world. The point here is not to argue the merits for or against this classification but to instead point it out as an operating assumption and therefore potential barrier to diversity and mission effectiveness.

By continuing to uphold the cultural belief that war and the military are masculine domains, we are perpetuating the "male as universal" view and institutionalizing it in the forms of policy, practices, and values. For example, when it comes to analyzing adversaries and war-gaming solutions, masculine-based thinking (linear, systems based, hierarchical) often perpetuates itself by viewing both the problem and solution through the same lens, potentially resulting in catastrophic blind spots. Overreliance and emphasis on technology, systems-based, and tactical-level solutions easily and imperceptibly turns into Maslow's law of the instrument—a cognitive bias that holds that when you have a hammer, everything looks like a nail.[29] As a military service, the Air Force must stay open and aware of ways it is self-limiting its innovation and effectiveness. If genuinely valued, different ways of thinking and perceiving can help cut through biases and assumptions we did not know we had.

Similarly, when it comes to recruiting and retaining a diverse force, institutionalized masculine perception ends up as a self-selection machine in which only those who think and see the world the same way are the ones who stay in the service and rise to the top. What we categorize and value as "military professionalism" is a codification of this homogenization. Conformity and compliance with protocol, uniforms, dress and appearance regulations, standardized operations, continuity processes, career development paths, promotion standards, and so on, are all external symbols of value. The institutional belief is that the better one conforms and complies with these measurements of professionalism, the smarter, more capable, and generally better the Airman is. While perhaps useful in certain circumstances, this belief also holds a high degree of tension opposing innovative thinking, creativity, independence, and diversity of thought. Likewise, the Air Force's historical bent toward viewing itself as an elite force with a core value of excellence can end up reiterating homogenization. This is not to say those are not well-intentioned values to uphold, but it is beneficial for leaders to question what they believe to be qualities of "excellence." Are they qualities typically thought of as male, white, or the otherwise ideal status quo?

This military as masculine bias continues down to the individual experience level. Though our conscious mind may tell us differently, our implicit biases (beliefs) still dictate who we perceive to be the best fit for a combat job (white, educated, physically fit man), the best family structure for supporting a career (1950s nuclear model with a full-time, domestic, non-career spouse), and appropriate career progression and promotion structure (DOPMA-legislated requirements in a certain time window that correspond with prime childbearing years and do not account for personal career goals). For example, many units and career fields retain the belief that those who show their face the most and stay in the office the longest are the best workers. We support that belief by valuing those who do so with awards, high rankings among peers, and leadership track opportunities. But this belief inherently negatively impacts parents, particularly mothers, as they are most often considered the default caregiver in most households. It is also a structure that is being challenged with pandemic-induced teleworking solutions.[30]

By watching their parents, schools, religion, media, and leaders in the community and world around them, children figure out at a young age which qualities are valued and rewarded in our masculine-oriented society: typically, assertiveness, ambition, action, and analytical orientation. Often these culturally approved "masculine" qualities can become overdeveloped to the exclusion of more "feminine" qualities, such as cooperation, empathy, and intuition.[31] This is why the presence of more women in the force does not always necessarily equate to the presence of more diverse strengths and skillsets. To reiterate, I am not speaking about biological gender here, nor implying that one is better than the other; simply that female inclusion policies and quotas are not enough, and in fact may encourage a scarcity mindset.[32] True integration, and the benefits of it, lie at the level of belief: that feminine perception and skills are equally critical to national defense and war fighting.

Though the character of warfare changes, the nature of war remains consistent.[33] At the heart of this consistency is humanness; war is a human attempt to sort out human problems—most of which defy technological and linear solutions. War is bigger than our cultural perceptions and classifications of it and therefore will always require appreciation and use of skills and strengths that cover the entire range of humanity. Empathy, emotional congruence (or intuition), creativity, collaboration, the ability to sit in nuance and complexity without action, the ability to nurture teams, projects, environments, and ideas: these skills are certainly not exclusive to women but are culturally associated as feminine.[34] Therefore, in a masculine-oriented culture their perceived importance and value have long been diminished. At the tactical and operational levels of war, the integration of masculine and feminine skills and strengths will most effectively handle the unavoidably human aspect of war. We must discard certain outdated aspects of our cultural conditioning around gender so we can embrace the full potential of human capability.

The military is a unique organization in that personnel practices should not be altered based on fairness or even moral obligation; mission effectiveness is the metric by which we must live and operate. As such, we must always stay open to the idea that we are blind to our blind spots, our assumptions (beliefs) might be faulty or outdated, military culture change is unavoidable, and war does not care about tradition, ego, or a combatant's gender.

Conclusion

Meeting the dynamic and complex challenges the nation faces both now and in the future will require innovative leaders who are able and willing to foster a culture of trust and respect for all, not just those who fit the current value system. Effective talent management and updated institutional values will encourage those with diverse skills, aptitudes, experiences, ideas, and perspectives to express them in pursuit of innovative solution sets. Women and gender integration are a big part of this.

For our nation to survive and thrive, we need to remember the inherent value of the feminine in what was previously considered masculine domains. History can offer us a place to start remembering the myths we need as we move into a new world: women as warriors and leaders. The first generation of female Airmen had to prove their worth despite their femininity by putting their heads down, accepting what was given, and pushing forward. The following generations had to overdevelop and overvalue masculine skills in order to be accepted. Standing on the shoulders of their predecessors, the newest generation of female Airmen is less likely to have to, or be willing to, do either of those things.

Examining the beliefs that undermine our individual and institutional values is a personal responsibility of both men and women. We are at a point in the gender integration story where the plotline is no longer that women must fight to be seen and included but instead where everyone must examine what they believe when it comes to the role and potential of women in the military. The goal of gender integration is not gender neutrality. It is to value the feminine and the masculine equally, realizing that every human embodies both aspects and skillsets. To stop wasting energy on outdated metrics of excellence and professionalism that promote homogeneity of thought, action, and perception. To encourage all Airmen to bring their strengths to the table in an environment where difference in opinion, personality, appearance, interests, and career goals is valued. This is the way to take diversity from a cognitive exercise to a realized strategic weapon.

Notes

1. An excellent resource for this topic and the source for this quote is a paper by Penney and Krieger titled *Female Officer Retention and the Millennial Imperative: Transforming Force Management into Talent Management*, 3.

2. First given a conceptual name in the 2017 National Security Strategy, the great power competition, or long-term strategic competition, is the modern phrase used to refer to conventional defense thinking and strategy, primarily against Russia and China. Boroff, "What Is Great Power Competition, Anyway?"

3. Lowther and Mitchell, "Professional Military Education."

4. "United States Air Force Diversity Roadmap," 4.

5. Penney and Krieger, *Female Officer Retention*, 3.

6. Poston, "3 Ways That the U.S. Population Will Change Over the Next Decade."

7. According to 2017 Pentagon data, 71 percent of young Americans between 17 and 24 are ineligible to serve in the United States military primarily because they do not meet educational or physical fitness requirements or they have a criminal history. Composing 50 percent of the US population, women qualify for military service at a higher rate than men but continue to be recruited and retained at much lower rates. Spoehr and Handy, "The Looming National Security Crisis."

8. Penney and Krieger, *Female Officer Retention*, 45.

9. Penney and Krieger, 22.

10. Human systems integration (HSI) is part of a total system approach to weapon systems development and DOD acquisition. HSI is the process of integrating humans in all their different roles (such as operator, maintainer, trainer, designer, etc.) with systems (such as hardware, software, and processes) to optimize the performance and safety of the whole in order to meet mission requirements. *Human Systems Integration Handbook*, 8.

11. Keller et al., *Addressing Barriers*.

12. Salazar, "Updates on DOD Directives and DOD Instructions."

13. Perez, *Invisible Women*, 1.

14. Perez, "We Need to Close the Gender Data Gap."

15. Perez, *Invisible Women*, 1.

16. Cummings, "Study Reveals Gender Inequality in Telecommuting."

17. Leitao-Marques and Regner. "Question for Written Answer…"

18. Maucione, "We're Not Going Back."

19. Maucione.

20. Helgesen, "The Evolution of Women's Leadership."

21. Helgesen.

22. Helgesen.

23. Penney and Krieger, *Female Officer Retention*, 3.

24. Surowiecki, The Wisdom of Crowds.

25. National Institutes of Health, "Implicit Bias."

26. National Institutes of Health.

27. USAF, "Origin Story."

28. Tarnas, *Passion of the Western Mind*, 2, 16–18.

29. Known as "the law of the hammer," "the golden hammer," or "Maslow's hammer," this bias was named in reference to psychologist Abraham Maslow's famous quote: "I suppose it is tempting, if the only tool you have is a hammer, to treat everything as if it were a nail." The Decision Lab. "Why Do We Use the Same Skills Everywhere?"

30. Helgesen, "The Evolution of Women's Leadership."

31. Vego, "Increasing Doctrinal Wisdom."

32. Helgesen, "The Evolution of Women's Leadership."

33. Vego, "Increasing Doctrinal Wisdom." As Professor Milan Vego of the Naval War College points out in his January 2009 *Joint Forces Quarterly* article, there is a difference between the nature and character of war. The nature of war refers to the "constant, universal, and inherent qualities that ultimately define war throughout the ages, such as violence, chance, luck, friction, and uncertainty." The character of war refers to "those transitory, circumstantial, and adaptive features that account for the different periods of warfare. They are primarily determined by sociopolitical and historical conditions in a certain era as well as technological advances." Vego, "Systems versus Classical Approach to Warfare," 46.

34. Vego, "Case Against Systemic Operational Design."

Appendix A

Women in the Air Force (WAF) Directors

Name	Tenure
Geraldine Pratt May	1948–51
Mary Jo Shelly	1951–54
Phyllis D. S. Gray	1954–57
Emma J. Riley	1957–61
Elizabeth N. Ray	1961–65
Jeanne M. Holm	1965–73
Billie M. Bobbitt	1973–75
Bianca D. Trimeloni	1975–76

Source: Air Force Historical Research Agency

Appendix B

Women's Armed Services Integration Act of 1948

Title III: Air Force

Chapter 449
June 12, 1948
Public Law 625

An Act

To establish the Women's Army Corps in the Regular Army, to authorize the enlistment and appointment of women in the Regular Air Force, Regular Navy and Marine Corps and in the Reserve components of the Army, Navy, Air Force, and Marine Corps, and for other purposes.

Be it enacted by the Senate and House of Representatives of the United States of America in Congress assembled, that this Act may be cited as the "Women's Armed Services Integration Act of 1948."

Title III
Air Force

SEC. 301. All laws or parts of laws which now or hereafter authorize enlistments, and appointments of commissioned and warrant officers in the Regular Air Force shall, subject to the provisions of this title, be construed to include authority to enlist and appoint women in the Regular Air Force.

SEC. 302. The authorized commissioned, warrant, and enlisted strengths of female persons in the Regular Air Force shall, from time to time, be determined by the Secretary of the Air Force, within the authorized commissioned, warrant, and enlisted strengths of the Regular Air Force, but shall not exceed 2 per centum of such authorized Regular Air Force strengths, respectively: *Provided,* That for a period of two years immediately following the date of this Act, the actual number of women in the Regular Air Force shall at no time exceed three hundred commissioned officers, forty warrant officers and four thousand enlisted women, and such number of commissioned female officers shall be appointed in increments of not to exceed 40 per centum, 20 per centum, 20 per centum, and 20 per centum at approximately equally spaced intervals of time during the said period of two years.

SEC. 303. (a) Commissioned female officers of the Regular Air Force shall be appointed by the President, by and with the advice and consent of the Senate, from female citizens of the United States who have attained the age of twenty-one years and who possess such qualifications as may be prescribed by the Secretary of the Air Force.

(b) Except as modified or otherwise provided in this title or by other express provisions of law, original appointments of female officers of the Regular Air Force shall be made in the manner now or hereafter prescribed by law for male persons in the Regular Air Force except as may be necessary to adapt said provisions to such female officers.

(c) Female officers shall be permanently commissioned in the Regular Air Force in grades from second lieutenant to lieutenant colonel, inclusive. The authorized number in permanent grade of lieutenant colonel shall be such as the Secretary of the Air Force shall from time to time prescribe but shall not exceed 10 per centum of the total authorized female commissioned strength.

(d) The provisions of section 509 of the Officer Personnel Act of 1947 shall not be applicable to promotion of female officers to the grade of lieutenant colonel. Female officers shall be appointed in the permanent grade of lieutenant colonel only when a vacancy exists in the number of lieutenant colonels authorized by the Secretary of the Air Force for female officers and only when selected and recommended for that grade by a selection board under regulations prescribed by the Secretary of the Air Force.

(e) As soon as practicable after completion of the appointments provided for in section 308 of this title, the name of each such female commissioned officer shall be entered on the Air Force promotion list in such position among officers of her grade as may be determined by a board of general officers appointed for this purpose by the Secretary of the Air Force and under such regulations as he may prescribe: *Provided,* That all such female officers shall be placed on the Air Force promotion list without change among themselves in their relative positions then held on the interim promotion list established under the provisions of section 309 of this title.

(f) Under regulations prescribed by the Secretary of the Air Force, any selection board convened to consider and recommend female officers of the Regular Air Force for promotion to any grade may contain female officers senior in permanent grade and temporary rank to any female officer being considered by such selection board for promotion.

(g) At any given time there may be one, but not more than one, female Air Force officer on duty serving in the temporary grade of colonel: *Provided,* That any female officer retired in the grade of colonel and recalled to active duty in such grade shall not be considered within this limitation. Appointment of a female Air Force officer on active duty to the temporary grade of colonel, if not sooner terminated, shall terminate on that date which is four years after the date of appointment to such temporary grade.

(h) Female officers of the Regular Air Force shall be eliminated from the active list and retired or separated, as the case may be, under the provisions of law now or hereafter applicable to male officers generally of the Air Force promotion list, and they shall receive retired pay or severance pay, whichever is applicable, computed as provided under such law: *Provided,* That any female officer in the permanent grade of lieutenant colonel may, in the discretion of the Secretary of the Air Force, be retained on the active list until that date which is thirty days after the date upon which thirty "years' service" is completed: *Provided further,* That any female officer in the permanent grade of lieutenant colonel, who is serving in the temporary grade of colonel, may, in the discretion of the Secretary of the Air Force, be retained on the active list while serving in such temporary grade: *Provided further,* That any female Regular Air Force officer who shall have served two and one-half years on active duty in the temporary grade of colonel may, upon retirement, at the discretion of the President, be retired in such higher temporary grade and with retired pay at the rate prescribed by law computed on the basis of the base and longevity pay which she would receive if serving on active duty in such grade, and if thereafter recalled to active duty shall be recalled in such grade: *Provided further,* That female officers in the permanent grade of major shall not be eliminated from the active list by reason of not having been selected for promotion to the permanent grade of lieutenant colonel: *Provided further,* That on and after June 30, 1953, each female officer in the permanent grade of major who is not retired or separated at an earlier date under other provisions of law shall be eliminated from the active list on that date which is thirty days after the date upon which she completes twenty-five "years' service" unless she is appointed in the permanent grade of lieutenant colonel in the Regular Air Force before that date: *And provided further,* That in its application to female officers of the Regular Air Force the term "years' service" as used in section 514 of the Officer Personnel Act of 1947, and as used in this paragraph, shall be defined as the period of service credited to a female officer on appointment into the Regular Air Force, increased by the period of her active commissioned service in the Regular Air Force subsequent to such appointment.

SEC. 304. Under such regulations as the Secretary of the Air Force may prescribe, female citizens of the United States may be appointed warrant officers in the Regular Air Force in each of the several warrant officer grades under the provisions of law now or hereafter applicable to the appointment of male persons in such warrant officer grades in the Regular Air Force.

SEC. 305. Original enlistments and reenlistments in the Regular Air Force from among female persons who possess such qualifications as the Secretary of the Air Force may prescribe may be accepted under applicable provisions of law which govern original enlistments and reenlistments in the Regular Air Force of male persons except as may be necessary to adapt said provisions to such female persons: *Provided,* That no woman shall be enlisted in the Regular Air Force who has not attained the age of eighteen: *And provided further,* That no woman under the age of twenty-one years shall be enlisted in the Regular Air Force without the written consent of her parents or guardians, if any.

SEC. 306. Except as otherwise specifically provided, all laws now or hereafter applicable to male commissioned officers, warrant officers, and enlisted men of the Regular Air Force; to former male commissioned officers, warrant officers, and enlisted men of the Regular Air Force; and to their dependents and beneficiaries, shall in like cases be applicable, respectively, to female commissioned officers, warrant officers, and enlisted women of the Regular Air Force, to former female commissioned officers, warrant officers, and enlisted women of the Regular Air Force, and to their dependents and beneficiaries except as may be necessary to adapt said provisions to such female persons: *Provided,* That the husbands of such female persons shall not be considered dependents unless they are in fact dependent on their wives for their chief support, and the children of such female persons shall not be considered dependent unless their father is dead or they are in fact dependent on their mother for their chief support.

SEC. 307. (a) The Secretary of the Air Force shall prescribe the military authority which female persons of the Air Force may exercise, and the kind of military duty to which they may be assigned: *Provided,* That they shall not be assigned to duty in aircraft while such aircraft are engaged in combat missions.

(b) The Secretary of the Air Force, under the circumstances and in accordance with regulations prescribed by the President, may terminate the commission, warrant, or enlistment of any female person in the Regular Air Force.

SEC. 308. (a) At any time not later than two years following the date of enactment of this title, the President is authorized to appoint female officers in the Regular Air Force, by and with the advice and consent of the Senate, in the grades of second lieutenant, first lieutenant, captain, and major, subject to the conditions and limitations hereinafter set forth. Persons appointed under the provisions of this section shall (1) be female citizens of the United States, at least twenty-one years of age, of good moral character, physically qualified for active military service, and have such other qualifications as may be prescribed by the Secretary of the Air Force; and (2) have served honorably in the active Federal service as commissioned officers in the armed forces of the United States, at some time between July 1, 1943, and the date of enactment of this Act.

(b) Each woman appointed as a commissioned officer in the Regular Air Force under the provisions of this section shall be credited, at the time of appointment, with service equivalent to the total period of active Federal service performed by her after attaining the age of twenty-one years as a commissioned officer in the armed forces of the United States from July 1, 1943, to the date of such appointment, or a period of service equal to the number of days, months, and years by which her age at the time of such appointment exceeds twenty-five years, whichever period is the greater: *Provided,* That in computing the total period of active Federal commissioned service of any such person who was honorably discharged or relieved from active service subsequent to May 12, 1945, there shall also be credited the period from the date of her discharge or relief from active service to the date of her appointment in the Regular Air Force under the provisions of this section.

(c) For the purpose of determining the grade in which each such person shall be originally appointed under the provisions of this section, a computation shall be made of the amount of service with which each such person would have been credited as of the date of enactment of this section under the provisions of subsection (b) of this section had she been appointed in the Regular Air Force under the provisions of this section on that date. The amount of service so computed for each such person is hereinafter referred to as the amount of such person's "enactment service." Persons with less than three years "enactment service" shall be appointed in the grade of second lieutenant; persons with three or more years "enactment service," but less than seven years "enactment service," shall be appointed in the grade of first lieutenant; persons with seven or more years "enactment service," but less than fourteen years "enactment service," shall be appointed in the grade of captain; and persons with fourteen or more years "enactment service," but less than twenty-one years "enactment service," shall be appointed in the grade of major.

(d) No woman with twenty-one or more years' "enactment service" shall be appointed as a commissioned officer in the Regular Air Force under the provisions of this section.

(e) For the purpose of determining eligibility for promotion, each person appointed as a commissioned officer of the Regular Air Force under the provisions of this section shall be credited, as of the time of such appointment, with continuous commissioned service on the active list of the Regular Air Force equal to the period of service credited to her under subsection (b) of this section.

SEC. 309. (a) Upon appointment of female officers in the Regular Air Force under the provisions of section 308 of this title, the names of all female commissioned officers of the Regular Air Force shall be carried on an interim Air Force promotion list for female officers and shall on each such officer's appointment be placed thereon next below the officer of her grade on such list having the same or next greater amount of service credit for promotion purposes.

(b) The Secretary of the Air Force following enactment of this Act shall reserve such portion of the vacancies existing on the Air Force promotion list as he may deem necessary in the grades of captain, major, and lieutenant colonel for promotion thereto of qualified female officers. There shall be no permanent grade promotion appointments of female officers of the Regular Air Force to the grades of captain, major, and lieutenant colonel until that date which is fifteen months after the date of enactment of this title; such promotions shall be made on such date or at the earliest practicable time thereafter: *Provided* That selection of such female officers for promotion shall be governed by regulations prescribed by the Secretary of the Air Force, which regulations, except where inconsistent with this section, shall be in general similar to the provisions prescribed for promotion of officers on the Air Force promotion list set out in section 518 of the Officer Personnel Act of 1947: *Provided further,* That in prescribing regulations for promotion of female officers to the grade of lieutenant colonel, the provisions of section 518 (b) thereof shall not be followed: *And provided further,* That the promotion of female officers here- under shall be made upon the interim promotion list described in this section.

SEC. 310. (a) Effective on the date of enactment of this title, the appointment and enlistment of women in the Officers' and Enlisted Section of the Air Force Reserve shall be authorized.

(b) Except as otherwise specifically provided, all laws now applicable to male commissioned officers and former commissioned officers of the Officers' Reserve Corps, to enlisted men and former enlisted men of the Enlisted Reserve Corps, and to their dependents and beneficiaries, shall be applicable, respectively, to female commissioned officers and former commissioned officers, to enlisted women and former enlisted women, of the Air Force Reserve, and to their dependents and beneficiaries, except as may be necessary to adapt said provisions to such female persons: *Provided,* That the husbands of such female persons shall not be considered dependents unless they are in fact dependent on their wives for their chief support, and the children of such female persons shall not be considered dependents unless their father is dead or they are in fact dependent on their mother for their chief support.

(c) Appointments of women to commissioned grade in the Air Force Reserve may be made by the President alone in grades from lieutenant colonel to second lieutenant, inclusive, from female citizens of the United States who have attained the age of twenty-one years and who possess such other qualifications as may be prescribed by the

Secretary of the Air Force: *Provided,* That any person who has served satisfactorily in the temporary grade of colonel in the Women's Army Corps established by Act of July 1, 1943 (57 Stat. 371), or in the temporary grade of colonel in the Regular Air Force, may, if otherwise qualified, be appointed in the grade of colonel in the Air Force Reserve.

(d) Enlistments of women in the Air Force Reserve may be accepted under the provisions of law now applicable to enlistments of male persons in the Enlisted Reserve Corps, under such regulations, in such grades or ratings, and for such periods of time as may be prescribed by the Secretary of the Air Force.

(e) The President may form any or all such female persons of the Air Force Reserve into such organizations and units as he may prescribe.

Approved June 12, 1948

Appendix C

Recommendations for Further Reading

Books

Jacqueline Cochran and Maryann Bucknum Brinley. *Jackie Cochran: The Autobiography of the Greatest Woman Pilot in Aviation History*. New York: Bantam Books, 1987.

Margaret Conrad Devilbiss. *Women and Military Service: A History, Analysis, and Overview of Key Issues*. Maxwell AFB, AL: Air University Press, 1990. https://www.airuniversity.af.edu/.

Nathan K. Finney and Tyrell O. Mayfield, eds. *Redefining the Modern Military: The Intersection of Profession and Ethics*. Annapolis, MD: Naval Institute Press, 2018.

Thomas X. Hammes. *The Sling and the Stone: On War in the 21st Century*. London: Zenith Press, 2004.

Jeanne Holm. *Women in the Military: An Unfinished Revolution*. New York: Presidio Press, 1992.

Evelyn M. Monahan and Rosemary Neidel-Greenlee. *A Few Good Women: America's Military Women from World War I to the Wars in Iraq and Afghanistan*. Norwell, MA: Anchor Press, 2011.

James E. Parco and David A. Levy. *Attitudes Aren't Free: Thinking Deeply about Diversity in the US Armed Forces*. Maxwell AFB, AL: Air University Press, 2010. https://www.airuniversity.af.edu/.

Maj Heather "Lucky" Penney and Maj Miriam "Blitz" Krieger. *Female Officer Retention and the Millennial Imperative: Transforming Force Management into Talent Management*. Washington, DC: Chief of Staff of the Air Force Special Project, 2016.

Service Women's Action Network (SWAN). *Women in the Military: Where They Stand*. 10th ed. Washington, DC: SWAN, 2019. https://www.servicewomen.org/.

Mary C. Smolenski, Donald G. Smith, and James Nanney. *A Fit, Fighting Force: The Air Force Nursing Services Chronology*. Washington, DC: Office of the Air Force Surgeon General, 2005. https://media.defense.gov/.

James E. Wise Jr. and Scott Baron. *Women at War: Iraq, Afghanistan, and Other Conflicts*. Annapolis, MD: Naval Institute Press, 2006.

Linda Witt, Judith Bellafaire, Britta Granrud, and Mary Jo Binker. "*A Defense Weapon Known to Be of Value*": *Servicewomen of the Korean War Era*. Lebanon, NH: University Press of New England, 2005.

Digital Collections

Defense Advisory Committee on Women in the Services (DACOWITS), Reports and Meeting Documents. https://dacowits .defense.gov/.

Library of Congress Veterans History Project, Oral History Collection. http://www.loc.gov/vets/.

Texas Woman's University, Women Airforce Service Pilots Official Archive. https://twu.edu.

University of North Carolina–Greensboro, Betty H. Carter Women Veterans Historical Project. http://libcdm1.uncg.edu/.

Women in Military Service for America, Exhibits and Oral History Collection. https://www.womensmemorial.org/.

Multimedia

Caitlin Hucik. "Their War Too: U.S. Women in the Military During WWII, Part I." National Archives, The Unwritten Record, 22 March 2018. https://unwritten-record.blogs.archives.gov/.

National Women's History Museum. "Women Airforce Service Pilots (WASPs) of WWII." Online Exhibit, 23 April 2019. https://www .womenshistory.org/.

Chronology

Date	Action
18 September 1947	The Air Force established as a separate service by the National Security Act of 1947.
14 April 1948	The Air Force Reserve formally established.
12 June 1948	The Women's Armed Services Integration Act (Public Law [PL] 80-625) is signed, allowing women to serve on a permanent basis in the regular and reserve component of all services as officers, warrant officers, and enlisted members.
16 June 1948	Geraldine Pratt May: first female Air Force colonel and director of the Women in the Air Force (WAF).
8 July 1948	Sgt Esther Blake, former Women's Army Corps: first woman to enlist in the Air Force.
1 September 1948	The WAF recruiting program begins with an interim ceiling of 4,300 WAF (300 officers, 4,000 enlisted) until June 1950.
July 1949	The first 16 women graduate from the new, gender-integrated Air Force Officer Candidate School (OCS).
1949	WAF basic training is separated from the Army and moved to Lackland Air Force Base, San Antonio, TX.
1949	An independent Air Force Medical Service is established with the Air Force Nurse Corps as an integral part.
June 1950 – June 1953	Korean War. WAF assigned to numerous support bases as air traffic controllers, radar operators, weather observers, and photo interpreters. Three Air Force women, all nurses, are KIA.
September 1950	The first WAF squadron of 48 women arrives in Tokyo in support of the Korean War.
1951	The first three black women commissioned as second lieutenants in the Air Force are Edwina Martin of Danville, VA; Fannie Jean Cotton of Jackson, MI; and Evelyn M. Brown of Shreveport, LA. All three graduated from OCS at Lackland AFB.
August 1951	At the suggestion of Assistant Secretary of Defense Anna Rosenberg, Secretary of Defense George Marshall establishes the Defense Department Advisory Committee on Women in the Services (DACOWITS) to provide guidance on policies related to women in the service. The first meeting is held 18 September.
1951	Executive Order 10240 authorizes the services to discharge any woman who becomes pregnant or becomes a parent through adoption or who has a minor child or stepchild in the home at least 30 days per year.
November 1951	The DOD launches a nationwide military women's component recruiting campaign to help offset draft calls for men. The Air Force sets the highest quotas of all the services, aiming for 4,000 officers and 44,000 enlisted by July 1952.

Date	Action
1954	Congress passes PL 83-349, the Officer Grade Limitation Act (OGLA) of 1954, placing ceilings on field grade officer ranks and centralizing the temporary promotion system.
1955	The Air Force Nurse Corps is opened to men.
June 1956	PL 845 permits appointment of women officers in the National Guard and Air National Guard.
1960	Grace Peterson: first female Air Force chief master sergeant.
1964–1973	US Air Force involved in Vietnam War. Approximately 600–800 WAF serve in Southeast Asia during official US involvement, with over half of them officers and the majority nurses.
June 1965	The WAF hits an all-time low, with 4,700 total personnel. Only 15 career fields and 151 Air Force specialty codes are available to women. Seventy percent of enlisted women and 75 percent of officers serve in administration positions; 23 percent work in medical facilities.
1966	The first 16 WAF nurses arrive for duty at the new 12th AF Hospital at Cam Ranh Bay, Vietnam.
June 1967	The first non-nursing WAF personnel, one officer and five enlisted, arrive for duty at the Headquarters in Saigon at the request of the Military Assistance Command.
November 1967	President Johnson signs PL 90-130, the first major policy change concerning women since 1948.
February 1968	In a controversial and precedent-setting decision, Air Force Chief of Staff Gen John McConnell lets women stay in theater following the coordinated Vietcong attack on US installations, known as the Tet Offensive, in January 1968.
1969	The Air Force opens ROTC to women after test programs at Ohio State, Drake, East Carolina, and Auburn Universities prove successful.
1969	The Joint Armed Forces Staff College starts admitting women.
2 March 1971	Following the case of Capt Susan Struck, an Air Force nurse in Vietnam, the Air Force permits women who become pregnant to remain on active duty or be discharged and return to duty within 12 months of discharge. Recruiting rules also change to allow the enlistment of women with children (the first service to do so).
17 March 1971	Jane Leslie Holley: first woman commissioned through AFROTC (Detachment 5, Auburn University).
16 July 1971	Jeanne Holm: promoted to brigadier general, the first woman to attain general officer rank in the Air Force.
1972	Frontiero v. Richardson Supreme Court decision finds dependent benefit differences between men and women unconstitutional.
October 1972	The first Air Force women train in marksmanship.

Date	Action
January 1973	The draft ends with the expiration of the Selective Service Act, and the all-volunteer force begins. This is a major turning point for military personnel policies, particularly the inclusion and use of women.
1974	Women's enlistment and promotion requirements are made equal to men; married women and mothers are now allowed to enlist.
1974	Air Force Reserve nurses participate in NASA tests to establish physical and psychological standards for female astronauts.
4 April 1975 **1975**	Capt Mary T. Klinker: first and only Air Force woman to die in Vietnam (during Operation Babylift). Air Force Chief of Staff David C. Jones establishes a test program that allows women to enter pilot and navigator training.
28 June 1976	PL 94-106 opens service academies to women.
26 September 1976	Ten women, alongside their 35 male classmates, begin UPT at Williams AFB, AZ. They graduate in September 1977.
10 March 1977	The first female navigator candidates report to Mather AFB, CA, to begin undergraduate navigator training. They graduate in October 1977.
1978	As required by PL 95-79 Sec. 303, the Department of Defense provides a definition of *combat* to Congress.
1978	Congress passes PL 95-202, granting veteran's status to the Women Air Force Service Pilots (WASP) who served during WWII.
1980	Congress passes the Defense Officer Manpower Personnel Management Act (DOPMA), requiring the Army, Navy, and Marine Corps to match the Air Force single personnel system process.
1980	The first Congressional hearings on sexual harassment in the military are held by the subcommittee on Military Personnel of the House Committee on Armed Services.
May 1980	The first Air Force Academy class of women graduates with 97 women receiving commissions in the regular Air Force.
1981	The Supreme Court decision in Rostker *v.* Goldberg upholds the constitutionality of a male-only draft.
1983	Air Force women deploy to support air transport missions to Grenada during Operation Urgent Fury. Female pilots, navigators, and enlisted crew members are aboard the aircraft.
1983	Congress passes PL 98-160, establishing the Secretary of Veterans Affairs Advisory Committee on Women Veterans.
August 1983	Air Force Col Frances Mossman: the first woman in any reserve component to achieve the rank of brigadier general.

Date	*Action*
25 March 1985	The Secretary of the Air Force changes the combat exclusion policy for women. Women can now serve as forward air controllers, pilots and crew of various models of the C-130 Hercules, and work in munitions storage facilities.
April 1986	Air Force women serve as pilots, copilots, and boom operators in KC-135 and KC-10 tanker crews that refueled FB-111s on the way to their targets as part of Operation El Dorado Canyon.
1986	The AF opens 1,645 positions aboard aircraft that were previously closed to women, including the latest RC-135 reconnaissance aircraft, EC-130 electronic warfare or radar jamming aircraft, the U-2 and the RS-71 strategic reconnaissance aircraft.
1988	The "risk rule" is announced, introducing a standard DOD interpretation of combat exclusion laws, and effectively opens 30,000 noncombat positions across the services, with over 2,700 of those being Air Force positions, to women.
1 January 1988	SAC changes Minuteman and Peacekeeper ICBM crew assignment policy to permit mixed gender crews in missile launch facilities.
1989	The Military Child Care Act passes, making high-quality childcare available to military members.
14 December 1989	MAC allows women to serve as crew members on C-130 and C-141 airdrop missions. This marks the official entry of women into combat crew roles.
December 1989	Air Force women fly and serve as crew members on cargo aircraft and tankers in support of Operation Just Cause in Panama.
August 1990—April 1991	Gulf War: 40,782 military women deploy to the area; 15 are killed and two taken as prisoners of war. The Gulf War brings military women to the forefront of public consciousness.
5 December 1991	Pres. George H. W. Bush signs the National Defense Authorization Act (NDAA) for FY 1991–93; women can now serve aboard combat aircraft engaged in combat missions.
13 January 1993	Air Force Maj Susan Helms: first US military woman in space as part of the space shuttle *Endeavor* crew.
28 April 1993	Secretary of Defense Les Aspin directs all services to open combat aviation to women, including enlisted aircrew. Women are now eligible to fly any aircraft in the Air Force inventory.
6 August 1993	Sheila Widnall: sworn in as Secretary of the Air Force, becoming the first female armed services secretary.
1994	Congress rescinds the risk rule, replacing it with the Direct Ground Combat Definition and Assignment Rule (DGCDAR).

Date	Action
1994	PL 103-446 requires the establishment of the Center for Women Veterans within the Department of Veterans Affairs.
April 1994	Lt Jeannie (Flynn) Leavitt: completes training in the F-15E Strike Eagle, officially becoming the first female AF fighter pilot.
1995	Capt Martha McSally, A-10 Thunderbolt II pilot: first female Air Force pilot to fly in combat while enforcing the no-fly zone over southern Iraq in support of Operation Southern Watch.
1995	The DOD Task Force on Discrimination and Sexual Harassment convenes.
1996	Col Betty L. Mullis (USAFR): first woman to command a USAF flying wing when she assumes command of the 940th Air Refueling Wing at McClellan AFB, CA.
1998	In response to the incidents at Aberdeen Proving Ground, MD, Congress orders its own commission—the Congressional Commission on Military Training and Gender-Related Issues—to review gender issues in the military.
11 September 2001	Nineteen militants associated with the extremist group al-Qaeda hijack four airplanes and carry out suicide attacks against targets in the United States. Almost 3,000 people are killed in these attacks, including 10 active duty, reserve, and retired servicewomen, which triggered major US initiatives to combat terrorism.
	ANG Lt Heather Penney, F-16C pilot and the first woman to serve in her unit (121 Fighter Squadron, Andrews AFB, MD), was one of two pilots ordered to intercept and take down the remaining hijacked airliner in Pennsylvania.
7 October 2001	Operation Enduring Freedom (OEF) begins. Military women deploy to the Afghan theater as part of Combined Forces Command Afghanistan.
12 June 2002	Staff Sgt Anissa A. Shero: first Air Force servicewoman to be killed in the line of duty supporting OEF.
January 2003	USAFA sexual assault scandal emerges.
2003	The Air Force Academy removes its sign stating, "Bring Me Men." In 2004 they replace it with a sign stating "Integrity First. Service Before Self. Excellence in All We Do," which is the Air Force's statement of core values.
2003	Congressional hearings are held after charges of sexual assaults perpetrated by US servicemen against US servicewomen serving in Iraq are made public. A Joint Task Force on Sexual Assault Prevention and Response is established as the single point of accountability on sexual assault policy matters within the DOD.
March 2003– December 2011	Operation Iraqi Freedom (OIF).

Date	Action
2005	PL-109-163 (FY 2006 NDAA) sec. 541 mandates that before opening or closing any military career designator to women the Secretary of Defense must first submit advanced notice to Congress.
28 September 2005	A1C Elizabeth Nicole "Liz" Jacobson: first female Airman to be killed in the line of duty supporting OIF.
December 2006	The number of American servicewomen killed in Iraq and Afghanistan reaches 70, more than the total from the Korean War, the Vietnam War, and Operation Desert Storm combined.
2010	The Caregivers and Veterans Omnibus Heath Service Act passes. Title II of the legislation aims to improve the Department of Veteran's Affairs' ability to meet the physical and mental health needs of female veterans.
March 2011	Air Force Maj Gen Margaret Woodward: first American woman to lead a combat air campaign. She directs the airstrikes over Libya for 11 days, until NATO takes over.
June 2012	Janet Wolfenbarger: first female four-star general in the Air Force.
June 2012	Col Jeannie Leavitt: first woman to command an Air Force combat Fighter Wing (4FW, Seymour Johnson AFB, NC).
2012	The AF launches an initiative to rid its ranks of material seen to objectify women. Pictures and calendars featuring pin-up women are banned from Air Force workspaces and public areas.
2012	The collocation clause of the 1994 DGCDAR is abolished.
2012	The AF investigates sexual assault charges by 54 women against at least 35 instructors at Air Force Basic Training and at follow-on Technical Training Schools at Joint Base San Antonio-Lackland.
2014	Gen Lori J. Robinson: new commanding general of the Pacific Air Forces in Hawaii, first US female four-star commander of combat forces.
December 2015	Secretary of Defense Ash Carter announces that, as of 1 January 2016, women can enter any career and service in any unit for which they meet the standards.
January 2016	The Secretary of Defense announces that all maternity leave is extended from six to 12 weeks.
May 2016	The Senate confirms General Robinson as head of US Northern Command, making her the first woman to command a major unified combatant command.
July 2016	Lt Gen Maryanne Miller: first woman to be promoted to three-star general and Chief/Commander of the Air Force Reserve. Miller is the Air Force Reserve's first female lieutenant general and the first female Chief of the Air Force Reserve.

Date	Action
August 2017	The Air Force's first female enlisted pilot completes undergraduate remotely piloted aircraft training.
June 2019	"Female fitment" event at Joint Base Langley-Eustis, VA, obtains measurements from hundreds of female aviators in an ongoing effort by the Uniform and Materiel Office to refine flight suits to better fit women. The Female Fitment Program continues into 2020 with events at bases across the country.
September 2019	Remotely piloted aircrew, missile operations duty crews, and certain fully qualified pilots now authorized to perform their assigned duties during pregnancy without a medical waiver.
January 2020	Air Force Chief of Staff Gen. David Goldfein approves updated lyrics to the official Air Force Song, written in 1938, to be gender neutral.
19 June 2020	Chief Master Sergeant JoAnne S. Bass: selected as the the 19th CMSgt of the Air Force, becoming the first woman in history to serve as the highest ranking noncommissioned member of a US military service.
December 2020	Some of the first security forces women begin receiving updated body armor specifically designed for women.

Bibliography

Air Force Historical Research Agency (AFHRA) Archives

AF Personnel Policy Board. "Commissioned Women Personnel in the Services." Results from AF Personnel Policy Board Study, 1 January 1951.

Cochran, Jacqueline, Special Consultant to the Chief of Staff for the Chief of Staff. WAF Program. Memorandum, 6 December 1950.

Cross, Martha. "WAF Administration and Control." Staff Study Report, WAF Deputy Director, 6 April 1956.

Director of WAF, Deputy Chief of Staff for Personnel (DCS/P). Historical Summary: 1 Jul 1950–31 Dec 1950. 1 March 1951.

Director of WAF, DCS/P. Annual Report of the WAF Program for 1956. 12 February 1957.

————. Historical Summary: 1 Jan 1951–30 Jun 1951. 18 June 1951.

————. Historical Summary: 1 Mar 1955–1 Dec 1955. 1 March 1956.

————. Historical Summary: 1 Jan 1957–1 Jun 1957. July 1957.

————. Historical Summary: 1 Jan 1958–1 Jun 1958. July 1958.

————. Historical Summary: 1 Jul 1958–31 Dec 1958. February 1959.

————. Historical Summary: 1 Jan 1959–1 Jun 1959. July 1959.

————. Historical Summary: 1 Jul 1959–31 Dec 1959. February 1960.

————. Historical Summary: 1 Jul 1960–31 Dec 1960. February 1961.

————. Historical Summary: 1 Jan 1961–1 Jun 1961. July 1961.

————. Historical Summary: 1 Jul 1961–31 Dec 1961. February 1962.

————. Historical Summary: 1 Jan 1962–1 Jun 1962. July 1962.

————. Historical Summary: 1 Jul 1962–31 Dec 1962. February 1963.

————. Historical Summary: 1 Jan 1963–1 Jun 1963. July 1963.

————. Historical Summary: 1 Jul 1963–31 Dec 1963. February 1964.

————. Historical Summary: 1 Jan 1964–30 Jun 1964. September 1964.

————. Historical Summary: 1 Jul 1964–31 Dec 1964. February 1965.

————. Historical Summary: 1 Jul 1965–31 Dec 1965. March 8, 1966.

————. Historical Summary: 1 Jan 1956–1 Jun 1957. September 1957.

Greene, Maj Gen G. B., assistant deputy chief of staff for personnel. Memorandum. Subject: Eligibility of WAF Officers for Senior Service Schools, 1965.

Holm, Maj Gen (Ret.) Jeanne. "Highlights of 100% Survey." February 1955.

————. "Transcribed remarks made by Col Jeanne Holm, WAF Director, at the 1st Meeting of the ADHOC Committee on Utilization of Women in the Air Force." Air Force Historical Research Agency Archives, 25 July 1967.

————. "Transcribed remarks made by Col Jeanne Holm, WAF Director, at the Arnold Air Society, University of South Carolina." Air Force Historical Research Agency Archives, 15 November 1967.

————. "Transcribed remarks made by Col Jeanne Holm, WAF Director, at the Luncheon of the Theta Sigma Phi Fraternity, Southern Illinois University." Air Force Historical Research Agency Archives, 11 November 1967.

————. "Transcribed remarks made by Col Jeanne Holm, WAF Director, at the Professional Management Course, Maxwell AFB." Air Force Historical Research Agency Archives, 14 March 1966.

Ray, Col Elizabeth. "The WAF Commander—Key to the Airman Program." WAF Director's Conference 11–12 September 1963, 1963.

————. "Transcribed remarks made by Col Elizabeth Ray, WAF Director, at WAF Director's Conference." Air Force Historical Research Agency Archives, 12 September 1963.

————. "We Can Develop Our Future Leaders." WAF Director's Conference 11–12 September 1963, 1963.

————. Non-Commissioned Officer Training. Memorandum, 15 September 1965.

————. Participation of WAF Personnel in Olympic Games. Memorandum, 16 June 1964.

————. Statement Concerning Women of the Air Force. Memorandum, 23 January 1962.

Riley, Emma Jane, Col, WAF director. Memorandum, Subject: Women in the Air Force, 1959.

————. Memorandum. Subject: Responsibility of WAF Commander, 16 August 1959.

"Transcribed Notes from WAF Staff Directors Meeting." 19–20 March 1959.

Ulrich, Elvena. WAF Officer Procurement Conference Agenda, 16–18 January 1957. 23 January 1957.

Vandenberg, Gen Hoyt, to Acting Deputy Chief of Staff, Personnel. Memorandum. 25 October 1950.

WAF Director's Conference 11–12 September 1963. "WAF Officer Strength FY 60-FY 65." Table, 1 September 1963.

Wilson, Jean, Lt Col, deputy director Women in the Air Force. Memorandum. Subject: Designation of Bachelor Officers' Quarters. 11 March 1964.

Young, Lee, Lt Col, executive director of plans and programs, Deputy Chief of Staff/Personnel. Memorandum. Subject: Officers' Quarters. 19 May 1964.

Interviews

Adams, Gail. Interview by Therese Strohmer, 30 October 2008. Transcript. Women Veterans Historical Project, University of North Carolina–Greensboro. http://libcdm1.uncg.edu/.

Galloway, Kimberly. Interview by Therese Strohmer, 20 December 2008. Transcript. Women Veterans Historical Project, University of North Carolina–Greensboro. http://libcdm1.uncg.edu/.

Hoefly, Brig Gen (Ret.) Ethel. Transcribed Interview with Brig Gen Ethel Hoefly. Air Force Historical Research Agency. 13 May 1983.

Hunter, Yardley Nelson. Interview by Therese Strohmer, 24 October 2010. Transcript. Women Veterans Historical Project. University of North Carolina Greensboro. http://libcdm1.uncg.edu/.

March, Cherise Miller. Interview by Kimber Heinz, 8 August 2016. Transcript. Women Veterans Historical Project. University of North–Carolina Greensboro. http://libcdm1.uncg.edu/.

Masek, CMSgt (Ret.) Sharon. "Transcribed Interview with CMSgt Sharon Masek (Gaskill)." March 1988.

Riley, Emma Jane, and Geraldine P. May. "Transcribed Interview with Col Emma Jane Riley and Col Geraldine P. May." Maxwell AFB, AL: Air Force Historical Research Agency Archives, May 1989.

Robinson, Therese. Interview by Herman Trojanowski, 30 November 2008. Transcript. Women Veterans Historical Project, University of North Carolina–Greensboro. http://libcdm1.uncg.edu/.

Sykes, Cathy Illman. Interview by Hermann Trojanowski, 25 January 2006. Transcript. Women Veterans Historical Project. University of North Carolina–Greensboro. http://libcdm1.uncg.edu/.

Veterans History Project. "Interview with Maj Gen Jeanne Holm (Ret)." Library of Congress, 23 January 2003. https://memory.loc.gov/.

Wicks, Patricia. Interview by Marissa Kester. 16 March 2019.

Books, Periodicals, and Other Publications

AFI 36-7001, *Diversity & Inclusion*. 19 February 2019. https://www.af.mil/.

Air Force Global Diversity Division, AF/A1DV, *USAF Diversity Strategic Roadmap*, 12 March 2013. https://www.af.mil/.

Air Force Guidance Memorandum. *2016 Diversity & Inclusion Initiatives Implementation Guidance*. 19 January 2017.

Air Force Inspector General Summary Report to SECAF, Air Force Inspector General Summary Report Concerning the Handling of Sexual Assault Cases at the United States Air Force Academy, 14 September 2004. https://media.defense.gov/.

Air Force Instruction (AFI) 36-205. *Affirmative Employment Program (AEP), Special Emphasis Programs (SEPS) and Reasonable Accommodation Policy*. 1 December 2016. https://www.af.mil/.

Air Force Instruction (AFI) 36-2110. *Assignments*, June 2016.

Air Force Instruction (AFI) 36-2905. *Air Force Physical Fitness Program*. August 2015. https://static.e-publishing.af.mil/.

Air Force Personnel Command. "Active-Duty Demographics." Accessed September 2019. https://www.afpc.af.mil/.

Air Force Public Affairs. "Policy Changes Ease Enlisting with Families." 31 July 2013. https://www.af.mil/.

Air Force Reserve Command. "AFR Snapshot." April 2019. https://www.afrc.af.mil/.

Air Force Security Forces Association. "USAF Defenders Fallen Since 9-11." 2020. http://www.afsaonline.com/.

Air Training Command (ATC) Manual 35-2. *A Handbook for Air Force Women*. 1957.

Alia-Novobilski, Marisa. "Women's Leadership Symposium Inspires Growth, Diversity." Air Force Materiel Command Public Affairs, 18 November 2019. https://www.af.mil/.

An Act to Amend Titles 10, 32, and 87, United States Code, to Remove Restrictions on the Careers of Female Officers in the Army, Navy, Air Force, and Marine Corps, and for Other Purposes. Public Law 90-130, 81 Stat. 90th Cong., 1st sess., 8 November 1967. https://www.govinfo.gov/.

Army Air Forces War Department. Establishment of Office of Special Assistant for Women Pilots. Memorandum, 21 June 1943.

Asch, Beth, Trey Miller, and Alessandro Malchiodi. *A New Look at Gender and Minority Differences in Officer Career Progression in the Military*. Technical Report TR-1159-OSD. Santa Monica, CA: RAND Corporation, 2012. https://www.rand.org/.

Bailey, Kat. "Air Force Expands Career Intermission Program Opportunities." Air Force Personnel Center Public Affairs, 23 May 2016. https://www.afpc.af.mil/.

Ball, Gregory. "2003-Operation Iraqi Freedom." USAFR History Office, 13 June 2013. https://www.afhistory.af.mil/.

Blau, Francine D., and Lawrence M. Kahn. "The Gender Pay Gap." The National Bureau of Economic Research, 2001. https://www.nber.org/.

Boyne, Walter J. *Beyond the Wild Blue: A History of the U.S. Air Force 1947–1997*. New York: St. Martin's Press, 1997.

Bullock, Marcus M. "Flight Equipment Redesigned to Better Fit Female Aviators." US Air Force, 5 June 2019. https://www.af.mil/.

Bush, George W. Address to a Joint Session of Congress and the American People. US Capitol, Washington, DC, 20 September 2001. https://georgewbush-whitehouse.archives.gov/.

Callan M. A. "Military Draft or Volunteer Plan: Which for Women?" *Los Angeles Times*, 9 August 1961.

———. "Jacqueline Cochran Top Woman Flier." *Los Angeles Times*, 5 December 1954.

Cantwell, Gerald T. *Citizen Airman: A History of the Air Force Reserve, 1946–1994*. Washington, DC: Air Force History and Museums Program, 1997.

Carl, Ann B. *A WASP Among Eagles: A Woman Military Test Pilot in World War II*. Washington, DC: Smithsonian Books, 1999.

Carney, Stephen. *Allied Participation in Operation Iraqi Freedom*, CMH Pub 59–3–1. Washington, DC: Center of Military History, 2011. https://history.army.mil/.

Carter, Ash, secretary of defense. To Secretaries of the Military Departments, Acting Undersecretary of Defense for Personnel And Readiness, Chiefs of the Military Services, Commander, US Special Operations Command. Memorandum. Subject: Implementation Guidance for the Full Integration of Women in the Armed Forces. 3 December 2015. https://dod.defense.gov/.

Cartier, Brenda. "Brenda Cartier: A New Vision for Leadership in the Military." Filmed February 2019 in New York. TED video, 11:13. https://www.ted.com/talks/.

Cashel, W. F. "The Perception of the USAF Company Grade Officer Role by Women Officer Trainees." PhD diss., Ohio State University, 1975.

Chicago Daily Tribune. "A Woman Has Her Way with the Air Force." 17 August 1950.

Chicago Defender. "Set Air Force Female ROTC." 30 June 1970.

Chicago Defender (National Edition). "Sister Airmen Training in Texas." 15 January 1949.

Cochran, Jacqueline, Director of Women Pilots. "American Women Pilots." 14 September 1942. https://www.eisenhowerlibrary.gov/.

Cochran, Jacqueline, and Maryann Bucknum Brinley. *Jackie Cochran: The Autobiography of the Greatest Woman Pilot in Aviation History.* New York: Bantam Books, 1987.

Collins, Gail. *When Everything Changed: The Amazing Journey of American Women from 1960 to the Present.* New York: Little, Brown and Co., 2009.

Contreras, Anne-Marie. "Hemorrhaging Her . . . A Capability Gap Analysis on Why the Air Force Can't Retain Female Operators." Master's thesis, Air War College, 2017.

Cox, Matthew. "Congress Wants More Diversity in the Ranks of Military Generals." Military.com, 11 December 2019. https://www.military.com/.

Crumm, R. K. "Of Hoes and Heroes: An Ethnographic Study of Gender Identity Among Women in the Air Force." PhD diss., University of Iowa, 2005.

Defense Advisory Committee on Women in the Services (DACOWITS). "Charter—Defense Advisory Committee on Women in the Services." Accessed 22 April 2018. https://dacowits.defense.gov.

———. "Homepage," accessed 2 April 2021. https://dacowits.defense.gov/.

Defense Casualty Analysis System. "Conflict Casualties." Accessed 21 April 2020. https://dcas.dmdc.osd.mil/.

———. "Worldwide US Active Duty Military Deaths 1980–1999, Females by Service—Air Force," 2020. https://dcas.dmdc.osd.mil/.

Department of Defense. "Operation Inherent Resolve." Accessed 20 April 2021. https://dod.defense.gov/.

———. *Diversity and Inclusion Strategic Plan 2012–2017.* 2012. https://diversity.defense.gov/.

Department of Defense Instruction 1342.19/Air Force Instruction 36-2908. *Family Care Plans.* 24 January 2019. https://static.e-publishing.af.mil/.

Department of the Air Force. "USAF Talking Points: Sexual Assault Prevention and Response," 19 July 2013. (Current guidance available: https://www.resilience.af.mil/; accessed 16 June 2021.)

Department of Veteran Affairs. "Military Sexual Trauma (MST)." 27 January 2021. https://www.va.gov/.

Deputy Director, WAF. "Change of WAF Airman Utilization." Transcribed remarks at USAF Recruiting Conference. Air Force Historical Research Agency Archives, August 1961.

Devilbiss, Margaret Conrad. *Women and Military Service: A History, Analysis, and Overview of Key Issues.* Maxwell AFB, AL: Air University Press, 1990. https://www.airuniversity.af.edu/.

Directive Type Memorandum (DTM) 16-002. *DOD-Wide Changes to Maternity Leave,* 5 February 2016. https://dacowits.defense.gov/.

DiSilverio, Laura A. H. "Winning the Retention Wars: The USAF, Women Officers, and the Need for Transformation." Fairchild Paper. Maxwell AFB, AL: Air University Press, August 2003.

Douglas, Deborah G. *United States Women in Aviation 1940–1985.* Washington, DC: Smithsonian Institution Press, 1990. https://doi.org/10.5479/si.01977245.7.1.

Duncan Hunter National Defense Authorization Act for Fiscal Year 2009. Public Law 110-417, Stat 4476 Sec 596. 110th Cong., 2nd sess., 14 October 2008. https://www.congress.gov/.

Dunivin, Karen O. "Adapting to a Man's World: United States Air Force Female Officers." Defense & Security Analysis Journal 7, no.1(1991):97–103.https://doi.org/10.1080/07430179108405487.

Dye, S. K. "Female Top-Three Enlisted Ranks in the US Air Force Reserves: The Perceived Impact of Conflict Management Strategies on Careers, A Qualitative Study." PhD diss., Purdue University, 2008.

Fedrigo, John A. Air Force Guidance Memorandum (AFGM) 2019-36-02. *AFGM Establishing Requirement of Lactation Rooms for Nursing Mothers.* 15 August 2019. https://www.airforcemag.com/.

Finney, Nathan K., and Tyrell O. Mayfield, eds. *Redefining the Modern Military: The Intersection of Profession and Ethics.* Annapolis, MD: Naval Institute Press, 2018.

Gates, Susan, Gail Zellman, and Jos Moini, with Marika Suttorp. *Examining Child Care Need Among Military Families.* RAND Technical Report. Santa Monica, CA: RAND National Defense Research Institute. 2006. https://www.rand.org/.

Gomez, R. A. "Daedalus' Daughters: The Army Air Forces and its Women Pilots." PhD diss., George Washington University, 2003.

Gonzalez, Jennifer. "Aspiring Air Force Pilots: Don't Let Height Standards Get in the Way." AETC News, 5 November 2019. https://www.aetc.af.mil/.

Grant, Rebecca. "The Quiet Pioneers." *Air Force Magazine*, 1 December 2002. https://www.airforcemag.com/.

Gross, Mary E., and Stacie E. Taylor. "Flight Suit Sizes for Women." Human Effectiveness Directorate Crew System Interface Division, United States Air Force Research Laboratory, Wright Patterson AFB, OH, January 2000.

Haring, Ellen. "Women in Combat: Adaptation and Change in the US Military." Women in International Security (WIIS), February 2014. https://wiisglobal.org/.

Harrison, Brig Gen Bertram, deputy director personnel procurement and training, deputy chief of staff for personnel. Memorandum. Subject: Integration of WAF Procurement with Officer Training School Program, 26 June 1959.

Headquarters US Air Force. *Operation Anaconda: An Air Power Perspective*. Washington, DC: Office of Air Force Lessons Learned, February 2005. https://apps.dtic.mil/.

———. "RFI 3: 2019 Retention Survey." DACOWITS (website), 3 December 2019. https://dacowits.defense.gov/.

Holm, Maj Gen (Ret.) Jeanne. *Women in the Military: An Unfinished Revolution*. New York: Presidio Press, 1992.

Holm, Maj Gen (Ret.) Jeanne, and Brig Gen Sarah P. Wells (Ret.). "Air Force Women in the Vietnam War." Vietnam Women's Memorial Foundation. Accessed 3 May 2021. http://www.vietnamwomensmemorial.org/.

Hopka, Rich. "SSgt Anissa Ann Shero, Fallen." Together We Served. Accessed 1 June 2019. https://airforce.togetherweserved.com/.

Hosek, Susan D., Peter Tiemeyer, M. Rebecca Kilburn, Debra A. Strong, Selika Ducksworth, and Reginald Ray. *Minority and Gender Differences in Officer Career Progression*. RAND Report MR-1184-OSD. Santa Monica, CA: RAND, 2001. https://doi.org/10.7249/MR1184.

Humphrey, Kelly. "Niceville Woman Has Fond Memories of F-4." *Northwest Florida Daily News*, 21 December 2016.

Institute of Medicine. *Returning Home from Iraq and Afghanistan: Preliminary Assessment of Readjustment Needs of Veterans, Service Members, and Their Families*. Washington, DC: National Academies Press, 2010. https://doi.org/10.17226/12812.

James, Deborah Lee, secretary of the Air Force. To all Airmen. Memorandum. Subject: Air Force Diversity & Inclusion, 4 March 2015. https://www.af.mil/.

———. To all commanders. Memorandum. Subject: 2016 Diversity & Inclusion Initiatives, 30 September 2016. https://www.af.mil/.

Kamarck, Kristy. "Military Maternity and Parental Leave Policies." Congressional Research Service (CRS) Report IN10436, 3 February 2016. https://digital.library.unt.edu/.

Keller, Kirsten M., Kimberly Curry Hall, Miriam Matthews, Leslie Adrienne Payne, Lisa Saum-Manning, Douglas Yeung, David Schulker, Stefan Zavislan, and Nelson Lim. *Addressing Barriers to Female Officer Retention in the Air Force*. Research Report RR-2073-AF. Santa Monica, California: RAND Corporation, 2018. https://www.rand.org/.

King, Erika Lee. "Retaining Women in the Military: Historical Perspectives on Policies and Current Work and Family Factors." PhD diss., University of Texas at Austin, August 2016.

Lambeth, Benjamin. "Air Power Against Terror: America's Conduct of Operation Enduring Freedom." RAND, 12 December 2015.

Lepore, Jill. *These Truths: A History of the United States*. New York: W. W. Norton & Company, 2018.

Little, Cynthia. "A Look at Women Cadets after Four Years." USAF Academy, 1980.

Lockwood, Martha. "Women's Legacy Parallels Air Force History." Air Force News Service, 18 September 2014.

Los Angeles Times. "Women of the Air Force Reserve to Be Called." 2 August 1950.

Losey, Stephen. "Air Force Considers Expanding Pilot Height Requirements as It Seeks More Female Aviators." *Air Force Times*, 15 November 2019. https://www.airforcetimes.com/.

Lowther, Adam, and Brooke Mitchell. "Professional Military Education Needs More Creativity, Not More History." War on the Rocks, 28 May 2020. Accessed 5 February 2021. https://warontherocks.com/.

Magana, Bryan. "Meet Air Force Reserve's First Female F-35 Pilot." 419th Fighter Wing Public Affairs, 6 September 2018.

Manning, Lory. *Women in the Military: Where They Stand*, 8th ed. Washington, DC: Women's Research & Education Institute, 2013. http://www.wrei.org/.

———. "Women's Roles in the Military." C-SPAN, 19 May 2012. https://www.c-span.org/.

Mau, Christine. "Life as a Female Fighter Pilot." Smithsonian National Air and Space Museum, 3 October 2016.

Maucione, Scott. "'We're not going back,' Air Force leadership says telework is here to stay." Federal News Network, 16 September 2021. Accessed February 5, 2021. https://federalnewsnetwork.com/.

McConnell, Brig Gen J. P., Deputy Special Assistant for Reserve Forces, Memorandum, 9 May 1950.

McFarland, Stephen L. *A Concise History of the U.S. Air Force.* Air Force History and Museums Program, 1997.

Medical Care Management. *Air Force Instruction 44-102*, March 2015.

Military Leadership Diversity Commission, *From Representation to Inclusion: Diversity Leadership for the 21st Century Military*, 2011.

Military Personnel: Administration of Women in the Air Force. Air Force Regulation, 35-20.

Millett, Allan R., Peter Maslowski, and William B. Feis. *For the Common Defense: A Military History of the United States from 1607–2012.* New York: Free Press, 2012.

Mitchell, L. E. "The Value of Special Projects for Group Development." WAF Director's Office, 1 January 1957.

Mitchell, Vance O. Air Force Officers: Personnel Policy Development 1947–1974. Air Force History and Museums Program, 1996.

Moore, Emma. "Women in Combat: Five-Year Status Update." Center for a New American Security, 31 March 2020. https://www.cnas.org/.

Mosley, Lt Gen Michael. USCENTAF Assessment and Analysis Division. Operation Iraqi Freedom—by the Numbers. April 2003.

Nadeem, Maj Alea, Air Force Barrier Analysis Working Group (AFBAWG) Women's Initiative Team (WIT) Team. Summary of Recent Accomplishments. Memorandum, 2019.

National Commission on Military, National, and Public Service. *Inspired to Serve: The Final Report of the National Commission on Military, National, and Public Service.* March 2020. https://www.inspire2serve.gov/.

National Women's Hall of Fame. "Jeanne Holm." Accessed 16 June 2021. https://www.womenofthehall.org/.

NATO-OTAN. Resolute Support Mission (RSM): Key Facts and Figures. June 2019.

Nelson, J. "Judge Bars Discharge of Unwed AF Mother." *Los Angeles Times*, 7 August 1971.

New York Times. "Commissions for Women." 1 December 1948.

———. "First Women Reservists Here to Get Air Force Posts." 20 March 1949.

New York Times. "No. 1 Woman Flier." 13 July 1941.

———. "Swearing in WAS and WAF Recruits Here Yesterday." 28 September 1948.

———. "The Armed Forces Find Woman Has a Place." 26 December 1948.

———. "The Supreme Court: Excerpts from the Hearing on the Ginsburg Nomination." 22 July 1993.

———. "Women Officers Needed." 11 July 1951.

Office of Deputy Assistant Secretary of Defense for Military Community and Family Policy. "2016 Demographics Report." Department of Defense, 2016. https://download.militaryonesource.mil/.

Office of the White House Press Secretary. "Transcribed Remarks Made by the President to DACOWITS." 28 April 1964.

Parco, James E., and David A. Levy. *Attitudes Aren't Free: Thinking Deeply about Diversity in the US Armed Forces*. Alabama: Air University Press, 2010.

Pawlyk, Oriana. "Two More Women Attempt Air Force Special Warfare Training Courses." *Military Times*, 1 November 2019.

Penney, Heather, and Miriam Krieger. CSAF Special Project. *Female Officer Retention and the Millennial Imperative: Transforming Force Management into Talent Management*. 2016.

Pennsylvania State University. "Jeanne Holm." A Few Good Women Collection. 11 November 1998.

Perez, Caroline Criado. *Invisible Women: Data Bias in a World Designed for Men*. New York: Abrams Press, 2019.

———. "We Need to Close the Gender Data Gap by Including Women in Our Algorithms." *Time Magazine*, 2020. Accessed 5 February 2021. https://time.com/.

Personnel, Civilian Women Airforce Service Pilots. Army Air Force Regulation 40-8, Apr 1944.

Rein, Lisa. "VA Is Stepping Up Its Services for Female Veterans." *Washington Post*, 29 July 2010.

Reserve Officer Personnel Act of 1954. Public Law 773, 3 September 1954. https://www.govinfo.gov/.

Rickmann, Sarah Bryn. So, Who Are the WASP Anyway? Texas Woman's University, 2011. https://www.womenofwwii.com/.

Ripley, Josephine. "GI Garb Chic on Bay State WAF Girls." *Christian Science Monitor*, 25 October 1948.

Rostker, Bernard. *I Want You!: The Evolution of the All-Volunteer Force*. RAND Report MG-265-RC. Santa Monica, CA: RAND, 2006. https://www.rand.org/.

Schemo, Diana Jean. "Rate of Rape at Academy is Put at 12% in Survey." *New York Times*, 29 August 2003.

Secretary of Defense. To Secretaries of the Military Departments, Chairman of the Joint Chiefs of Staff, Undersecretary of Defense for Personnel and Readiness, Chiefs of the Military Services, Chief of the National Guard Bureau, General Counsel of the Department of Defense. Memorandum. Subject: Sexual Assault Prevention and Response, 6 May 2013. https://www.sapr.mil/.

Secretary of the Air Force (SAF) Public Affairs. "AF Leaders Announce Latest Diversity, Inclusion Initiatives," 30 September 2016. https://www.af.mil/.

———. "Air Force Implements New Parental Leave Policy, Secondary Caregivers Given 21 Days." 8 June 2018. https://www.af.mil/.

———. "Air Force Reduces Barriers for Pregnant Aviators," 23 September 2019. https://www.af.mil/.

———. "Air Force Removes Administrative Burden, Allows Pregnant, Postpartum Women to Attend PME." 29 July 2020. https://www.af.mil/.

Service Women's Action Network (SWAN). *Women in the Military: Where They Stand*, 10th ed. 2019. https://www.servicewomen.org/.

Silva, Maj Stephanie. "Postpartum Policies for Military Mothers: Their Impact on Retention of Female Air Force Officers." Research Report. Maxwell AFB, AL: Air Command and Staff College, 2016. https://apps.dtic.mil/.

Sisk, Richard. "Number of Female Generals, Admirals Has Doubled Since 2000, Report Finds." *Military Times*, 17 April 2019. https://www.military.com/.

Smith, Antoinette. "Breaking the Gender Barrier." SAF Public Affairs, 19 September 2017. https://www.af.mil/.

Smith, R. L. "Jacqueline Cochran: An American Aviator in Peace and War." PhD diss., University of Kentucky, 1999.

Stanford Encyclopedia of Philosophy. "Implicit Bias." Accessed 31 July 2019. https://plato.stanford.edu/.

Streeter, Suzanne M. "The Air Force and Diversity: The Awkward Embrace." *Air & Space Power Journal* 28, no. 3 (May–June 2014): 104–32. https://www.airuniversity.af.edu/.

Swick, Andrew, and Emma Moore. "The (Mostly) Good News on Women in Combat." Center for a New American Security, 19 April 2018. https://www.cnas.org/.

The Women's Memorial. "Highlights in the History of Military Women." 2017. Accessed June 2019 (archive discontinued).

Thirman, Penny Sue. "Female Colonel Advocates Draft." Associated Press, 1974.

Timmons, Greg. "On 9/11, Heather Penney Tried to Bring Down Flight 93 in a Kamikaze Mission." *Seminole Source*, 10 September 2020. https://theseminolesource.com/.

Trobaugh, Elizabeth M. "Women, Regardless: Understanding Gender Bias in U.S. Military Integration." *Joint Force Quarterly* 88 (1st Quarter 2018): 46–53. https://ndupress.ndu.edu/.

United States Office of Personnel Management (OPM). *Handbook on Leave and Workplace Flexibilities for Childbirth, Adoption, and Foster Care.* Washington, DC: OPM, April 2015.

US Air Force and Space Force Recruiting. "U.S. Air Force: Origin Story." 28 June 2019. Video, 0:15. https://www.youtube.com/.

US Department of Veterans Affairs, Public Health Epidemiology, Health Outcomes of Women's Vietnam Service, January 2020. https://www.publichealth.va.gov/.

US War Department. "Jacqueline Cochran Named Director of Women's Flying Training in Army." Bureau of Public Relations, 14 September 1942.

USAF Chief of Staff. "Sexual Assault Awareness and Prevention Month." Email to all members, 2 April 2015.

USAF Fact Sheet. Officer Training Program (OTS) and USAF Commissions for College Graduates. 1959.

Van, Mary R. T. "Previewing Air Force's Program for Training its Feminine Contingent." *Washington Post*, 15 September 1948.

Wackerfuss, Andrew T. "Women's Army Auxiliary Corps." Air Force Historical Support Division, 2011. https://www.afhistory.af.mil/.

WAF Director Office to Deputy Chief of Staff, Personnel. Memorandum. Subject: Report of WAF Program, 1 August 1954–15 February 1955. March 1955.

WAF Director's Conference 11–12 September 1963. "Level of Education of WAF Officers." Table, 30 June 1963.

Washington Post. "Aviatrix Donates Air Reserve Pay to Fund Drive." 12 August 1963.

———. "Colonel May Heads Women of Air Forces." 17 June 1948.

———. "Officer Grades Offered Women in Air Force." 11 July 1951.

———. "Services Say Women Are as Welcome as Men, IF…," 31 July 1950.

———. "Women's Services Calling 80,000." 19 August 1951.

Weinraub, Bernard. "Air Force to Assign Women as Noncombat Pilots." *New York Times*, 11 March 1979.

Wise, James E., and Scott Baron. *Women at War: Iraq, Afghanistan, and Other Conflicts*. Annapolis, MD: Naval Institute Press, 2006.

Witt, Linda, Judith Bellafaire, Britta Granrud, and Mary-Jo Binker. *"A Defense Weapon Known to Be of Value:" Servicewomen of the Korean War Era*. Lebanon, NH: University Press of New England, 2005.

Wolfe, Thomas. "Gender Integration in the USAF Fighter Community: 25 Years of Progress and Persistent Challenges." Master's thesis, Air War College, 25 April 2017. https://apps.dtic.mil/.

Woman's Collection, WASP History. "The Leaders." Texas Woman's University, 2019. https://twu.edu/.

Women's Armed Services Integration Act of 1948. Public Law 625. 80th Cong., 2nd sess. 12 June 1948.

Zehner, Gregory, and Jeffrey Hudson. *Body Size Accommodation in USAF Aircraft*. USAF Research Laboratory Report AFRL-HE-WP-TR-2002-0118. Wright-Patterson AFB, OH: Human Effectiveness Directorate, Crew System Interface Division, January 2002. https://apps.dtic.mil/.

Index

Afghanistan, 141–43

Air Evacuation, 67

Air Force Academy, 44, 80, 81, 93n41, 95n55, 147n36

Air Force Nurse Corps, 27, 67

Air Force Reserve Officer Training Corps (AFROTC), 42, 43, 80

Air Transport Auxiliary (ATA), 5, 6

Air WACs, 7, 15n46, 20, 22, 30, 47. *See also* Women's Army Auxiliary Corps (WAAC)

all–volunteer force, 69, 73–75, 117–18, 140, 158, 185

appearance, 26, 38–41, 159, 165, 168

Arnold, Henry H. 5, 8–10, 17

assignment, 7, 25, 45, 63, 77, 88, 108–10, 131, 142

attrition, 31, 44, 49, 52, 77, 79, 81, 98, 99

basic training, 21, 46, 47, 82

body armor, 138, 160

call up, 104, 105

casualties, 17, 28, 67, 68, 148

Cochran, Jacqueline, 4–6, 8–10, 17, 22, 24–26, 49

combat pilot, 109

Congress, 2, 7, 18, 21, 22, 29, 63, 69, 73, 76, 77, 84, 97, 99, 101, 108, 126

Defense Advisory Committee on Women in the Services (DACOW-ITS), 29, 30, 38, 41, 62, 63, 65, 73, 89, 97, 102, 107, 108, 122

Defense Officer Personnel Management Act (DOPMA), 98, 128

Department of Veterans Affairs (VA), 69, 123–27

dependents, 19, 42, 51, 64, 77, 78, 134, 135

Direct Ground Combat Definition and Assignment Rule (DGCDAR), 110, 142, 143

draft, 17, 29, 55, 61, 65, 74, 86, 117, 143

enlisted, 2, 7, 13, 18, 22, 24, 26–31, 40, 42, 44, 46–52, 54, 61, 62, 65, 66, 68, 75, 79, 82, 86, 88, 89, 97, 98, 105, 110, 112, 117, 120, 135, 140, 143

Executive Order (EO) 9981, 18, 23, 119

Executive Order (EO) 10240, 78

family policies, 76, 128, 129

Frontiero, Sharron, 77

Gates commission, 74

general, 5, 7–10, 20, 25–27, 32, 37, 38, 48, 52, 63, 64, 73, 79, 84, 97, 99, 105, 109, 110, 117, 124, 125

Gray, Phyllis, 42

Hobby, Oveta Culp, 7, 12

Holm, Jeanne, 21, 37, 44, 62–65, 67, 73, 76–79, 82, 83, 89, 98, 99

housing, 22, 29, 53, 54, 65, 82

Integration Act, 18–20, 22, 24, 28, 32, 41, 50, 52, 61, 63, 85, 101, 103, 119

Iraq, 109, 110, 136, 141–43

Korean War, 22, 27, 28, 30–32, 37, 38, 48, 52, 61, 64, 75

Leavitt, Jeannie (Flynn), 110, 120, 136, 138

Love, Nancy Harkness, 5, 6, 8, 9, 10, 14n20, 14n34

manpower shortages, 5, 7, 9, 18, 47, 64, 74

marriage policies, 31, 39, 51, 52, 59n78, 77, 79, 82, 129, 135, 152n88

May, Geraldine Pratt, 6, 7, 9, 20, 21, 24–26, 30, 46–48, 53, 76, 77, 79, 80, 89, 107, 124, 132, 135, 143, 163, 165, 166

McPeak, Merrill, 108, 110, 111

McSally, Martha, 106, 110

media, 103, 128, 166

missile, 82, 85, 106, 111, 130

mobilization, 17, 24, 105, 117

navigator, 82, 84, 85, 101, 142

Officer Candidate School (OCS), 39, 41, 42, 80
Officer Training School (OTC), 21, 42, 80, 120
officer, 6, 7, 9, 21, 23, 24, 28, 37–39, 41–47, 49, 54, 63–66, 76, 79, 80, 87, 97–99, 112, 117, 120, 122, 128, 135, 137, 143, 159
Olds, Robert, 5, 14n20
overseas, 3, 7, 28, 45, 54, 66, 67, 69, 140, 148

Persian Gulf War, 103, 104
pilot training, 4, 9, 82–84, 99, 127, 137
pilot, 4–6, 8, 9, 11, 12, 25, 82–85, 99, 101, 106–108, 110, 123, 125, 127, 129, 131, 135–39, 141, 142
pregnancy, 50, 78, 79, 82, 99, 124, 128–131, 134, 159, 160
promotion, 19, 21, 44, 45, 47, 63, 64, 80, 84, 98, 118, 120, 121, 128, 131, 165
Public Law 625, 119
Public Law 90–130, 61, 63

Ray, Elizabeth, 54
recruiting, 5, 22, 23, 26, 28–32, 37–39, 41, 42, 45, 49, 54, 55, 65, 74, 75, 79, 81, 98, 99, 101, 120, 128, 157, 158, 162, 165
Reserve, 2, 5–7, 17, 18, 22–24, 27, 28, 42, 44, 64, 74, 78, 80, 88, 99, 103, 105, 117, 120, 123, 125, 129, 130, 132, 135, 140, 161
rights, 61, 73, 74, 88, 89, 107, 125, 129
Riley, Emma J., 40, 42, 49–51
risk rule, 86, 101–3, 110, 142
Rogers, Edith Nourse, 7, 83
Roosevelt, 4, 5, 8
Rosenberg, Anna, 29

segregation, 4, 23

Selective Service Act, 143
sexual assault, 122, 124, 125
sexual harassment, 90, 99, 124, 147n42
Shelly, Mary Jo, 30, 31, 45
single parents, 134, 135, 161
smear campaign, 32
Smith, Margaret Chase, 18, 90
Supreme Court, 76–78

Tet Offensive, 66

uniforms, 2, 3, 22, 25, 29, 49, 53, 123, 159, 160, 165

Vietnam War, 13, 64, 73, 74, 76, 99, 140

WAF director, 21, 24, 26, 30, 37, 40–42, 45, 46, 49, 50, 53, 54, 62, 67, 75, 76, 80, 82
woman pause, 97, 98
Women's Airforce Service (WAF), 4, 24, 26, 28, 35n48, 39, 44, 48, 50, 51, 63, 66, 67
Women Airforce Service Pilots (WASP), 4, 6, 10–12, 24
Women's Army Auxiliary Corps (WAAC), 7, 10, 23, 47. *See also* Air WACs
Women's Army Corps (WAC), 6, 7, 10–12, 18, 22–24, 46, 47, 62, 87
Women's Auxiliary Ferrying Squadron (WAFS), 6, 8–9, 19n34, 22
Women's Flying Training Detachment (WFTD), 8–9, 22
women's rights, 61, 73, 74, 88, 89, 93n34, 107, 112n4, 129, 147n42
World War I, 2–4
World War II (WWII), 4, 7, 11, 13, 17–20, 22, 23, 27, 28, 30–32, 47, 48, 53, 69, 76, 82, 89, 102, 104, 105, 157